PEN

Small Island

Philip Parker is a historian specializing in ancient and medieval political and military systems. He studied history at Trinity Hall, Cambridge and is the author of works including *The Empire Stops Here: A Journey Around the Frontiers of the Roman World* and *The Northmen's Fury: A History of the Viking World*.

With a background in international affairs, including as a member of the Diplomatic Service, Philip has a keen interest in maps from his time as a publisher of historical atlases. He lives in London with his partner and daughter.

1

Small Island

12 Maps That Explain the History of Britain

PHILIP PARKER

PENGUIN BOOKS

PENGUIN BOOKS

UK | USA | Canada | Ireland | Australia
India | New Zealand | South Africa

Penguin Books is part of the Penguin Random House group of companies
whose addresses can be found at global.penguinrandomhouse.com.

First published by Penguin Michael Joseph 2022
Published in Penguin Books 2023

002

Copyright © Philip Parker, 2022
Maps designed by Jeff Edwards

The moral right of the author has been asserted

Set in 10.88/13.05pt Garamond MT Std
Typeset by Jouve (UK), Milton Keynes
Printed and bound in Great Britain by Clays Ltd, Elcograf S.p.A.

The authorized representative in the EEA is Penguin Random House Ireland,
Morrison Chambers, 32 Nassau Street, Dublin D02 YH68

A CIP catalogue record for this book is available from the British Library

HARDBACK ISBN: 978–0–241–36827–5

www.greenpenguin.co.uk

To Livia, who will see what shape Britain turns out to be

Contents

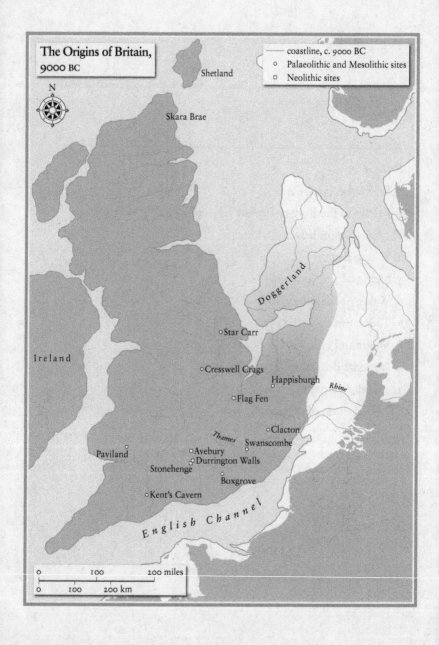

The Origins of Britain,
9000 BC

N

—— coastline, c. 9000 BC
○ Palaeolithic and Mesolithic sites
□ Neolithic sites

Shetland

Skara Brae

Doggerland

Ireland

Star Carr

Cresswell Crags

Happisburgh

Rhine

Flag Fen

Clacton

Thames

Swanscombe

Avebury

Durrington Walls

Paviland

Stonehenge

Boxgrove

Kent's Cavern

English Channel

0   100   200 miles
0   100   200 km

Prologue

Britain is facing a unique moment of national crisis. Or so many commentators would have us believe.

This book is an attempt to explain why neither the moment, the crisis, nor indeed the 'Britain' of today are unique. We have been here many times before, legs dangling awkwardly over the precipice of the future, fingertips desperately clinging to the certainties of the past. Each time the Britain (or earlier, the England or the Wessex) that conservatives or incumbents have fought to preserve, and incomers or radicals have struggled to overturn, has been a different one. To help illustrate this I have picked eleven moments in the evolution of Britain and British identity, and one attempt to predict a possible future, both to show how we have arrived at our current state and to suggest that challenge and change are inevitable companions to a nation's growth.

Change, indeed, is the heartbeat of history, a reminder that we – as individuals, groups, countries or ideologies – are not moribund, safely trussed up in a library with the other tombstones of long-dead peoples and vanished beliefs. In the seventh and sixth centuries BC, the pre-Socratic Greek philosophers, the first to see the world as a subject for critical thought rather than the plaything of the gods, expended much effort on trying to discover the prime force that made up and moulded the Universe. Thales of Miletus, the pioneer, came up with water, his successor Anaximenes plumped for air, Empedocles hedged his bets with earth, air, fire and water, while Anaximander tried to side-step the issue with a vague 'boundless' substance. Heraclitus of Ephesus – who was rather unkindly nicknamed the 'obscure' for his riddling demeanour – came up with the best solution of all. For him, change was the constant, the one thing that could be relied on. As he memorably summarized his view of history and the world: 'You cannot step into the same river twice.'

The image of history as a river, and time as a stream which carried us helplessly forwards, is not a novel one. Yet it is a particular conceit of our own times to insist that we can dam this river, stop history and even wade backwards a decade or two to some imagined moment when national myths nurtured an idyll of self-contented ease. History has an awkward habit of breaking through. The fall of the Berlin Wall in 1989 was supposed to mark an end, as the triumph of liberal democracy in Europe left governments free of the age-old fear of war. That optimism was misplaced: within a decade the Balkans were once more ablaze, and twenty years later Ukraine.

We live in an age of anxiety, where the simpler the message, the more potent seems its force, the greater the throng who gather around its standard. Yet history is a complex and unsettling place, full of confusing counter-currents and rip-tides, which is why, perhaps, so many reject any but a stylized version of the past.

History has varied uses: as salve for national pride, inspiration for martial endeavour or simple treasure-trove of stories. But above all, it is our ancestor's greatest gift to us, a means to discern through the medium of their travails and triumphs how we arrived at where and who we are. We cannot know the future and we can scarcely grasp the present. History, then, is our single touchstone in deciding how to act, which social movements to embrace and which political utopias to reject.

The current question of whether Britain should be a primarily maritime (or global) power, with its face to the Atlantic, or a land power, fully engaged with our European neighbours, was just as real to our Elizabethan ancestors, who wondered whether a future as carrion crows picking on the entrails of Spanish America was preferable to the more mundane and muddy slog of sending battalions to defend their Protestant co-religionists in the Netherlands. Tied to this is how far out Britain's defensive bulwark should lie. One increasingly favoured view is that Britain ends at the Channel and the White Cliffs of Dover, and that this is the most advantageous point from which to repel invaders, both political and economic. Yet in the fourteenth century, Bordeaux was the frontline, in the sixteenth and seventeenth centuries the Netherlands were England's rampart, in the eighteenth century British armies fought along the Rhine and Chesapeake, and in the late twentieth century the Falkland Islands, deep in the South Atlantic, lay inside the perimeter that Britain found essential to preserve. In none of these cases did Britain's rulers choose to begin the defence of our interests in our own front yard, and we might do well today to heed their example.

It is Britain's borders which lie at the heart of this book. The twelve maps which precede each of its chapters portray its frontiers (or those of one of its ancestor states) at a particular point in time. Many of these are startling. In 878 the borders of Alfred the Great's Wessex (which would one day become England and then Britain) were confined to a small patch of marshland in Somerset. This, in a sense, was Britain. Four centuries later, and the country straddled the English Channel, embracing much of what we now know as France, and 600 years further on, its boundaries were to be found in the Caribbean, the Arabian Sea, the Indian Ocean and the Malacca Strait. These, too, were Britain. Any current nostalgia for a return to a Britain of the past must take account of the many Britains there have been, and of the likelihood that there are yet more Britains to come, all different, but all linked to those of the past.

How these borders came to be (and where they might now be leading us) is but the most obvious physical manifestation of the story. Much as the land which has made up the nation has shifted over time, so has its people, sometimes violently, with the great Anglo-Saxon and Viking invasions, occasionally on a large scale, with the recent migration from former British colonies and the European Union, but always at least with a steady demographic tide. Likewise, the notion that our nation and in particular its borders have a historical solidity – a bedrock on which British culture and traditions have always stood fast – soon proves to be an illusion, a cartographic and political sleight of hand. It is telling that Britain, unlike most nation-states, has no national day to celebrate its birth and no independence day to mark its emergence from foreign control: 14 October for the Battle of Hastings in 1066 or 1 May for the Act of Union with Scotland in 1707 have very little resonance in the public imagination and are certainly not the occasion for large-scale celebrations as 4 July in the United States or 14 July in France. We may celebrate our antiquity as a nation, but we are very unclear about how, or even when, it came into being.

That we have ended up with the Britain that we now have is something of a historical accident. For nearly four centuries, Britain was a Roman colony, whose capital was not in London (or Brussels), but in Rome, in which a foreign language (Latin) was that of government. It gained its name (Angle-Land – the land of the Angles) from a sixth-century invasion from Europe which overthrew the 'native' Britons, who had just recently chased out their Roman overlords. And for five centuries after 1066, when Duke William of Normandy routed the descendants of those Angles (who by then regarded themselves as authentically English), 'England' straddled the Channel. Its kings engaged in a series of wars with their French counterparts for control of northern France, accompanied by an especially vicious side struggle between the two monarchies over Bordeaux and its lucrative wine trade. Once England's first European venture was over, almost as compensation, it began to absorb its neighbours in the British Isles, first bringing Wales into its administrative structure under Henry VIII, subsuming Scotland via the union of the Scottish and English Crowns in 1603 and then incorporating Ireland by a process of violent conquest, migration and economic domination. It was only then that 'Britain' as a political entity was finally born.

There are many possible Britains that never came into being. At quite a few moments in this process, an alternative future seemed possible (had Elizabeth I borne an heir, then Scotland and England might not have been united in 1603 under the rule of her Scottish cousin, or had Alfred the Great's children and grandchildren not proved quite such energetic campaigners, the north and east of England may have remained under Viking rule and Danish become the lingua franca of a north English state based on York). Similarly, the exact point at which the border between Scotland and England would be fixed was in doubt for many centuries (Scottish kings pushed their control down as far as Newcastle and Carlisle in the Middle Ages, while Anglo-Saxon rulers held sway at times as far north as Edinburgh). It is even possible that Scotland, Ireland or Wales might never have come into the British orbit, or that the nucleus of the British state might have been formed in one of those countries, rather than in England.

And now, in the twenty-first century, we stand at another fork in the road. Fifty years in the future, the choice we have made, and its consequences, will be clearer, whether Britain opted for a clean break with Europe and a fragmented future quite possibly shorn of Scotland and Northern Ireland, or an awkward patchwork compromise with the European Union. Changing borders and reshaped notions of the land, identity and people that make up our nation may have forged a quite different Britain to that of today. If so, it will simply mark another waypoint on Britain's long journey of formation, expansion, contraction and reinvention. If we can recognize this and, like Heraclitus, embrace change as a constant force, then history will be a potent source of lessons, guides and maps to navigate our future. If not, as mere nostalgia, it may drown us.

But before considering the question of how Britain might now evolve, it is necessary to look deep into its past. When (and where) did Britain begin?

Celtic Britain, 100 BC

PARISI main tribal groups,
early 1st century AD

hill fort zones
□ hill forts
● oppida
area of Arras culture

N

CALEDONII

VOTADINI

SELGOVAE

NOVANTAE

CARVETII

BRIGANTES

PARISI

DECEANGLI

ORDOVICES

CORNOVII

CORITANI

ICENI

DOBUNNI

CATUVELLAUNI

TRINOVANTES

Grim's Ditch ●

Camulodunon ●

DEMETAE

SILURES

Bagendon ●

Verlamion ●

Beacon Hill □

Silchester ●

ATREBATES

CANTIACI

DUROTRIGES

Hod Hill □

□ Danebury

Hengistbury ●

Chichester ●

DUMNONII

Maiden Castle □

0   100 miles

0   100 kms

1. Britain before Britain

Before 9000 BC, anyone who wanted to come to Britain (or merely happened upon it by accident), simply had to walk. Sea-levels were much lower, with most of the world's surface water bound up in glaciers and frozen waste-lands, and Britain was joined to continental Europe by a land corridor. When temperatures began to rise after the end of the last Ice Age, meltwater flooded into a channel off south-west Scotland and separated Britain from Ireland. The English Channel first appeared around 8000 BC, but a wide, low plain still connected eastern Britain to Europe, occupying much of what is now the North Sea (and named by archaeologists as Doggerland, after the shallows of the present-day Dogger Bank which lie within it). The final land-link to Europe was only broken by a further massive flood around 6100 BC.

Britain really was now an island, and for the next 8,100 years the question of what this meant would never go away. Ignoring the outside world was not an option once complex societies began to evolve. The elites needed (or at least craved) goods which could only be obtained elsewhere, and getting hold of them meant trade. Right from the start this pulled Britain in two ways. Would its commerce be focused to the west, across Atlantic sea-ways to Ireland and Spain, or south and east towards France and Germany?

Trade and decisions about where to direct it would also be shaped by geography. Divided by a spine of hills which bisects the country from the Chilterns to the Highlands of Scotland, Britain falls naturally into a number of zones. A western region, including much of Scotland (including the islands), Wales and Cornwall, looks to the Atlantic sea-lanes. Mineral-rich (in tin and gold), its inhabitants were natural traders, but the highland barriers which shielded them from outside influence (and invaders) also promoted a tendency to

7

political fragmentation. The south-east, the area closest to continental Europe, had less to trade, but benefited from the accessibility of the lowlands and the relative ease of travel across the narrow Strait of Dover. These advantages would shape its inhabitants into voracious consumers of goods from elsewhere, sucking in people, merchandise and innovations and pulled this more politically cohesive zone into a millennia-long dance of engagement with Europe. Between these two poles lies a transitional region in the Midlands and parts of the north, which developed its own traditions but was most often sucked into the orbit of political authority emanating from the south. Many of the tensions and grievances which later became embedded in the political and constitutional make-up of Britain have their deep roots in these prehistoric divisions.

But before there could be merchants or monarchs, there needed to be people.

The first settlers of Britain arrived around 950,000 years ago, their touch on the empty landscape barely detectible, save in a scattering of flint tools at Happisburgh in Norfolk, and a set of forty-nine footprints found on the beach there, including the poignant imprint of several children's feet. These pioneers were not even human, and they soon died out, as the temperatures plunged at the onset of a new Ice Age, driving almost all life from Britain's frozen landscape. It was a story that would be repeated several times; each time Britain was colonized from Europe, the glaciers advanced southwards, pushing out or killing the settlers. The hunters who lived at Boxgrove in Sussex around 500,000 BC (members of *Homo heidelbergensis*, another human-like species), enjoying the rich pickings of a warm land, full of prey such as deer and rhinoceros, were driven out by the Anglian glaciation, which scoured great valleys in the landscape around 470,000 BC. It was a particularly severe Ice Age, wrapping Britain in an icy shroud as far south as Oxfordshire and Essex, and diverting the course of the River Thames, which had previously flowed into the Wash in Lincolnshire. The land was reshaped by these massive climatic fluctuations, but people found them unbearable.

Modern humans may finally have appeared in Britain for the first time around 40,000 years ago, bringing with them slightly more advanced tools and scrapers, but they, too, were defeated by the ice and retreated to warmer climes to the south. For the next 30,000 years small bands made tentative probes into Britain, but the cold was too intense to remain for long. Among them were a group archaeologists call the Gravettians, reindeer and bison hunters who roamed north in search of prey. The skeleton of one of them, discovered in 1823 by Dean William Buckland, gave rise to one of British archaeology's more curious misunderstandings. A devout Christian, the Dean's religious convictions forbade him to contemplate that any remains could possibly pre-date the Biblical Flood. They must instead be those of a woman of Roman origin. It turned out, once modern techniques of analysis became available, that the 'Red Lady of Paviland' (so named for the cave on the Gower Peninsula where the skeleton was found and the red ochre with which it was daubed) was in fact that of a young man in his early twenties, who had died around 34,000 years ago. Buckland's error is a pointed reminder that viewing the past through the prism of current prejudices is a particular hazard when reconstructing our nation's evolution.

None of the settlers between Happisburgh Man and the Red Lady were our ancestors. Only around 12,000 years ago did humans manage to convert tenuous toeholds into permanent occupation of the land. Startling evidence of their passing was found in 1997, when DNA extracted from the tooth pulp of a 10,000-year-old skeleton found at Cheddar Gorge in Somerset was matched to that of a local history teacher. He, at least, can trace his 'British' ancestry over ten millennia.

The descendants of 'Cheddar Man' gradually filtered across Britain. It was a wild landscape, predominantly wooded, with birch and pine forests edged out by oak, elm, ash and beech as temperatures rose. In this Mesolithic period (a 'middle' time between the dawn of humanity and the appearance of agriculture), small bands clustered around areas where large mammals came to water, establishing seasonal camps at places such as the reed-fringed shores of a long-vanished lake at Flixton in Yorkshire's Vale of Pickering. At one of them, Starr Carr (which dates from around 10,500 years ago), they built timber platforms made of willow and aspen and constructed wooden huts. For the first time there was such a thing as 'home', and humanity began to establish a relationship with the land that resembled territorial occupation more than transient exploitation. They started to modify it, too, setting fires selectively around Lake Flixton. This encouraged the growth of young shoots, enticing woodland animals to the area and providing rich targets for waiting hunters.

A far more radical change to Britain's landscape occurred when knowledge of agriculture arrived around 6,000 years ago. It took only four centuries or so for the new way of life, revolving around the cultivation of crops such as wheat and barley, and the raising of sheep, pigs and goats, to extend to virtually the whole British Isles. In its wake, life became more settled. Agriculture is a harsh master, demanding constant attention to fields and livestock to ensure a supply of food over the coming year.

Now that they were tied to a particular landscape, Neolithic peoples began to transform it by building monumental structures, starting with long barrows and cairns around 3800 BC and reaching a spectacular climax with the construction of the inner stone circle at Stonehenge about 2500 BC. The level of resources required to build these structures was immense, but it is impossible now to understand exactly why our distant ancestors bothered to do so. The monuments clearly have some ritual purpose, commonly being oriented in the direction of sunset or sunrise at key times of the year; they may have represented symbolic points of transition into another world. They would certainly have played a role in promoting cohesion amongst communities that were becoming larger than bands of several families.

The impact of humans on the land grew more profound. Ancestral woodland was felled to make way for cultivation, and field systems were laid out, often divided up by ditches. Plough marks found at South Street Long Barrow in Wiltshire suggest the presence of fields as early as 3600 BC, and the sectioning-off of the landscape spread to encompass much of the English highlands and lowlands by the middle of the Bronze Age in 1500 BC. The outlines of some of these early fields have survived, such as those lined by ancient hedges near West Penwith in Cornwall. While England's external borders have swelled and contracted to the rhythm of history, in places its internal boundaries have remained unchanged from the very beginning.

Field systems fringed settlements which were becoming larger. The fixed resources of agricultural communities provided enticing targets for raiders, and defensive structures appeared for the first time. Ring forts, surrounded by ditches and palisades (such as at Mucking North Ring in Essex), must have required the devotion of significant effort on the part of the communities to construct, suggesting a high level of social organization and a will to defend the community's riches from outsiders.

Society was becoming more complex, and with complexity came conflict. Britain had nothing like the vast temple sites of pharaonic Egypt or the city-states of Greece, but its land was rich enough to support a clutch of tribal mini-chiefdoms. At their head was a warrior elite, who by 1000 BC had taken command of the resources they were supposed to defend, feasting heroically and leaving a variety of bronze cauldrons and meat-hooks for archaeologists to dig up. When required they also fought. Bronze shields, spearheads and sword bosses have been found in Britain and Ireland (although nothing like the magnificent bronze cuirasses discovered in Greece), many of them deposited in rivers, bogs and lakes. Some of them had been deliberately broken up, as though the weapons had been ritually 'killed' to deprive them of power.

The Celts

Names are a powerful thing. Our early ancestors toiled, built, feasted and fought, but for the first 400 generations from the permanent settlement of Britain they are entirely anonymous. It is no surprise that the first group whose presence in British history has lodged itself in the collective consciousness is the first whom we can name: the Celts. Rather than a move from prehistory to history, it is as if Britain moves into an age of names, in which the island (as Prytania), its inhabitants and its rulers seem more real for being labelled.

The term 'Keltoi' was first used by Greek writers such as Herodotus in the fifth century BC. Born in Halicarnassus in what is now the west coast of Turkey, Herodotus was the first proper historian with an interest in the human – as opposed to the divine – origins of events. As well as being a firm believer in conducting his own research by visiting as many of the places he wrote about as possible, Herodotus also had something of a magpie mind, collecting ethnological and historical oddments from all over Europe. He delighted in exotic fables, such as the story of the inhabitants of a region beyond Scythia whose men were said to have feet like goats, or the Neuri, who allegedly turned themselves into wolves once a year (although he covered himself in the more outlandish cases by casting doubt on the veracity of his own sources).

Herodotus is a little vague about the original homeland of the Celts, locating them at the mouth of the Ister (or River Danube), but also saying that they dwelt 'beyond the Pillars of Hercules' (i.e. in southern Spain beyond Gibraltar, at the opposite end of Europe). Of the two, an Iberian origin for the Celts perhaps makes more sense because of the strong trade links which developed between the western Atlantic seaboard and the west of Britain, notably through the export of tin (whose principal use in the ancient world was its alloying with copper to make bronze). From Spain, the original Celts could have plugged into a series of long-distance trade networks which encompassed the western Mediterranean, with its sprinkling of Greek and Phoenician colonies, and even further east to the riches of Lebanon and Egypt and the Greek homeland itself.

Rumours spread of tin-rich islands far to the north-west. It was in search of this precious commodity that the Greek explorer Pytheas came all the way from Massilia (modern Marseilles) around 320 BC. His account of a 'congealed sea' on the way north from Britain to the mysterious island of Thule and of six months of darkness after the winter solstice seemed so fantastic as to provoke disbelief, but they are precisely the details which indicate that as well as the British Isles he probably had reached Iceland, or at least Scandinavia. Pytheas also seems to have travelled widely in Britain and described the British penchant for fighting with war-chariots. He also chronicled that 'because they have no pure sunlight' – a lament subsequent visitors would echo – they were forced to thresh grain indoors.

Diodorus Siculus, who wrote in the first century BC, was the first to use the term 'Britain', which he renders as 'Pretannike'. He speaks of miners extracting tin from seams and then working it into smaller pieces 'the size of knuckle bones'. They probably crushed the ore by pounding to remove lighter impurities and then smelted it in furnaces to drain off the pure tin (which melts at 232°C). They carried the resulting ingots to an offshore island called Ictis, which may have been either St Michael's Mount or Mount Batten in Plymouth Sound. There, foreign merchants came to buy the metal and transport it across the Channel. Our very first glimpse of Britain from the outside shows it as a merchant nation, dependent on trade with Europe. In that sense, little has changed.

Although it was tin that first drew Britain to outsiders' attention, the beginning of the Celtic era in Britain coincides with the start of the Iron Age. The period around 800 BC was one of great change – a shift which in general privileged the emergence of aristocratic warrior elites (iron is a much harder metal, creating superior weapons and so making warfare a potentially much more profitable enterprise for those organized or aggressive enough to wage it). It was possible with better weaponry to forge larger chiefdoms and to defend them effectively against outsiders. While in 800 BC there is nothing identifiable as an incipient British state, a process of consolidation was slowly taking place, so that seven centuries later a patchwork of tribal kingdoms had appeared, including the Atrebates in Sussex and the Silures in south Wales, with the Catuvellauni (north of London) showing signs of dominating the whole southeast of England and creating an Iron Age British superpower.

The interaction between Britain and the Continent was instead largely in the form of trade. Much of this was carried out in ports such as Hengistbury Head, a peninsula jutting out into the English Channel near Bournemouth, a geographical feature which must have provided traders with a reassuring sense of security from surprise attacks. Through it flowed a wealth of goods, including pottery from Armorica (Brittany), Cornish tin, shale armlets from the Isle of Purbeck, south of Poole, and wine from the Mediterranean, carried in the pottery amphorae which have been found in large numbers at Hengistbury. A darker side of the exchanges was slavery; Britain later became renowned as a source of high-quality slaves, and a set of first-century BC neck-irons found at Llyn Cerrig Bach in Anglesey with room for five captives to be shackled is sinister testimony of the human cost of Iron Age trade.

As a result of the traffic through ports such as Hengistbury, British elites now had access to desirable goods from Europe – swords, alcohol, jewellery, even figs. Showing them off doubtless enhanced the owner's status, but it is not a sign of a foreign influx into Britain, any more than the availability of French cheese or Japanese cars in the twenty-first century is a sure indication of large-scale French or Japanese migration.

Even without invasions from abroad, there was plenty of insecurity to deal with at home. Between 600 and 400 BC, the trade routes dried up. These troubled times saw the building of hill-forts, a new form of defensive site, in a wide zone that stretched from the south-east along the south coast as far as Somerset and then up through the Welsh Marches into north Wales. Typically, they were defended by a single earthwork rampart with a more complicated system of tunnels or off-set approaches to the gateways. This meant that would-be attackers could not simply attack head-on but were forced to navigate a labyrinth of entrance traps, all the while vulnerable to the missiles being rained down upon their heads.

The largest hill-forts, such as Danebury in Hampshire, give the impression of veritable fortified villages, with houses and granaries inside the walls to house and feed local people at times of threat.

The stakes were clearly growing bigger – now that much of the land had been divided up, the easiest way to gain additional resources was to attack neighbouring groups, and this meant, in turn, more elaborate defensible centres in case they attacked back.

Trade in time recovered, and the Celtic kingdoms of Britain continued to grow in power and wealth. They produced striking pieces of art, such as the bronze shield-facing decorated with animal patterns, including a boar, which was dredged up from the River Witham in Lincolnshire, and ornate shield-bosses adorned with birds found in the Thames at Wandsworth. While the political organization of Britain more or less mirrored that on the other side of the English Channel, there was equilibrium: tin and slaves for wine and fancy brooches seemed a fair exchange that suited both Britons and their Gaulish cousins.

The Romans Are Coming

All this changed with the appearance of an aggressive and acquisitive power from the Mediterranean bringing alien notions of law, constitutional organization and an army shaped more by training drills than mead-fuelled bragging. The Romans had arrived in Gaul, and at their head one of history's most ambitious, ruthless and successful generals, Julius Caesar.

Caesar invaded and conquered northern Gaul between 58 and 50 BC, hugely exceeding his brief as governor of Transalpine Gaul (a Roman enclave in the south). His establishment of a Roman province caused significant disruption to the political balance in Britain and to long-established trading connections. By 56 BC he had destroyed the Veneti, a tribe based in Armorica (modern Brittany), who had been the chief operators of the tin trade with southern Britain and whose possession of a significant navy made them a threat to the Romans. Their kidnapping of several Roman officers gave a pretext, if one was needed, for a swift campaign which ended with most of the tribe being sold into slavery.

For the first time, the Britons faced an organized (and expansionist) power on the southern shores of the Channel and one which was happy to use its control of the trade routes to ensure rulers in southern Britain did not meddle in Gaul. At the same time, and although the conquest of Gaul had brought Caesar great prestige, he craved even greater military successes to keep up with other ambitious generals such as Pompey. He also needed an insurance policy to help him retain his appointment in Gaul and avoid being recalled to Rome, where he would be vulnerable to his political rivals. An expedition to Britain offered him the perfect opportunity. Britain was about to experience its first historically attested invasion, not a violent influx of agriculturalists, or a tribal host of ancestral Celts, but the full force of the ancient world's most effective fighting machine: the Roman legion. It was to prove a surprisingly close-run fight.

Military man though he was, Caesar was no hothead, and he tried to inform himself as best he could about conditions in Britain. In his *Gallic Wars*, the account he wrote of his campaigns in France and Britain (which, naturally, sheds the best possible light on his actions), he complains that he tried to gather information from merchants but found that they were ignorant about Britain 'except the sea coast and those parts which are opposite to Gaul' and so could not provide him with a full picture of the opposition he might face. Caesar then turned from intelligence gathering to a fully fledged diplomatic offensive, despatching a Gaulish ally, Commius, chief of the Atrebates – a tribe whose identical name to a group in Sussex might indicate some kinship – to canvass support and to try to negotiate an unopposed landing. The mission was a miserable failure, and Commius was arrested and thrown in chains. Armed with very patchy intelligence and with few reliable local allies, Caesar's first entry into Britain, in summer 55 BC, was nearly a disaster. It was a relatively modest affair, involving two legions (around 10,000 men) and a small force of cavalry. Local tribesmen were waiting for him on the cliffs near Deal, and, though Caesar managed to land and beat them back, a storm badly damaged most of the transport ships, and the Romans were forced to retreat hastily back to Gaul.

Undaunted, Caesar returned the next year with a much larger force of five legions and around 2,000 auxiliary cavalry. He had made some progress diplomatically, enlisting the support of Mandubracius, son of the king of the Trinovantes (whose main centres were in the region of modern Essex). He would need this, as he now faced a larger coalition of British tribes, led by Cassivellaunus (whose power-base lay north of the Thames). This time, Caesar managed to strike deeper into Kent and, despite fierce British opposition, forced a crossing of the Thames and attacked Cassivellaunus' capital (which was situated somewhere near St Albans). He was impressed by the Britons' fighting abilities and tactics, many of which, such as the use of the war-chariot, were unfamiliar to the Romans. They would swoop down on Roman detachments, dismount to fight and then make their getaway, while the heavily armoured legionaries struggled to catch them (or if they did pursue, risked being cut apart in the wooded territory into which they were lured). As a result, the Romans were slowed down by the need to keep their own cavalry in tight support of the infantry columns. Caesar was also struck by their appearance, remarking that: 'All the Britons dye themselves with woad, which occasions a blue colour, and thereby have a more terrible appearance in fight. They wear their hair long, and have every part of their body shaved except their head and upper lip.' Fierce and honourable opponents they might be, but disciplined Roman legionaries they certainly were not.

An attack in the rear by several Kentish tribes and the progression of the season (making the weather in the Channel more hazardous – many of the Roman transport ships had already been damaged by another storm) persuaded Caesar that the prudent course was to declare victory and leave. After securing the restoration of Mandubracius as ruler of the Trinovantes – so acquiring a useful political ally – and agreeing the handing-over of hostages and an annual tribute to be paid to Rome, he returned to Gaul.

Although Caesar managed to talk up the results of his two invasions of Britain – largely for the benefit of the Senate back in Rome – they did not result in any immediate political transformation. It was instead his occupation of Gaul that helped accelerate changes which were already underway in Britain. For the first time a single power was in control of the entire Channel coast opposite England, and its gravitational pull shifted trade towards the more direct overland routes to Italy and away from the traditional Atlantic sea-lanes which had carried British tin for centuries. Rulers with access to the wealth that flowed from trade with the Romans became comparatively more powerful. Modern complaints that the south-east gets 'more than its fair share' of the nation's resources might have found some sympathy in the British Iron Age.

As a demonstration of their new-found authority and by means of aping the sophistication of their new southern neighbours, British kings began to issue coins. It is a further sign that 'ownership' of the land had progressed one stage further and that territorial units with shifting, but very real, spheres of control would now vie for control of Britain.

Now that there was an outside power to which those in Britain who came off worse in power struggles could appeal to, they promptly began to do so, beginning two millennia of foreign intervention, exiled princelings, marriage alliances, territorial occupation and complaints of 'European influence'. In AD 7 Tincommius and another British chieftain, Dubnovellaunus, fled to Rome to throw themselves on the mercy of the emperor Augustus. The Greek historian Strabo notes that British kings had 'obtained the friendship of Caesar Augustus by embassies and courtesies and have set up offerings in the Capitol'. It did them little good, as Tincommius was not restored, and Augustus connived in the granting of the throne to his brother Eppillus.

In the south of England, the elites enjoyed a lifestyle which was very similar to their counterparts under Roman rule in Gaul; they ate off the same type of plates and enjoyed wine served in similar sorts of vessels. The developed hill-forts of preceding centuries were displaced by even larger settlements, known as *oppida*, which bear some of the hallmarks of proto-towns, with elaborate defences, many structures within their walls and populations of several thousand people. Among the largest were Camulodunon (on the site of modern Colchester), the tribal centre and royal capital of the Trino-vantes, and Verlamion (St Albans), the chief settlement of the Catuvellauni tribe. Independent, and yet enjoying many of the benefits of life in the Roman province, Britain seemed to have the best of both worlds.

Britain had a name, but there was still no sense that there was a British people, or that the island of Britain was a unit that belonged together under one ruler. The later construction of a 'Celtic' identity by antiquarians and historians was a retrospective one intended to fill this gap. Medieval chroniclers such as Geoffrey of Monmouth, who told the tale of 'Brutus', an alleged descendent of refugees from the Trojan war who eventually settled in Britain (and whose name bore a convenient resemblance to his new home) were trying to give an ancient seal to Britain's unity, which in truth it lacked.

Britain's identity was not to coalesce out of the tribal groups which made up its Celtic kingdoms. None of them can claim any direct political links with what followed or to have formed the nucleus of what would become Britain. Although their heritage casts a long shadow and would re-emerge in the fifth century and again in the formation of separate national identities in Wales, Scotland and Ireland during the Middle Ages, the idea that there was such a thing as 'Britain' that was not a mere geographical description fell, paradoxically, to outsiders, to the Romans.

Roman Britain, AD 128

N

PARISI tribal groups

Roman frontier c. AD40

area occupied by Romans by AD83, evacuated by AD108

Roman Britain AD108

■ wall forts

□ legionary fortresses

● major towns

□ Inchtuthil

Tay

Croy Hill
Bar Hill

Antonine Wall

DAMNONII   VOTADINI

SELGOVAE

Vercovicium (Housesteads)   Bremenium
Fanococidi   Segedunum
NOVANTAE   Hadrian's Wall
Camboglanna   Corstopitum (Corbridge)
Banna (Birdoswald)   Vindolanda

BRIGANTES

Eboracum □   PARISI

Anglesey   □ Deva

Trent   CORIELTAUVI

Viroconium

ORDOVICES   ICENI
            CORNOVII

DEMETAE   Camulodunum
        Glevum   CATUVELLAUNI
SILURES DOBUNNI   Verulamium ●
Isca □   Thames TRINOVANTES
                  Londinium ●
            ATREBATES   Durovernum ●   Medway
                        CANTII
        BELGAE   Rutupiae
                    REGNI
    DUROTRIGES
DUMNONII

0 ─────────────── 100 miles
0 ─────────────── 100 kms

2 Britain in the Roman Empire

The Romans made Britain. What was previously a loose gathering of tribal states or (from the point of view of the rest of Europe) simply an unfathomable blank at the end of the world, became a defined political entity, complete with governors, garrisons, buildings and a border. After the Romans left, the island's rulers spent a millennium trying to recreate the premature unity Rome had brought. The monuments the Romans built, like the fort-studded stone-and-turf colossus of Hadrian's Wall, left a physical imprint on the landscape. Curiously, though, their most tangible legacy was not the most lasting. The experience of being conquered was transformative.

For over 350 years, Britain was a military colony of a foreign power. Those centuries as an unimportant backwater on the fringes of the Roman empire brought peace, economic prosperity and a political unity that had been inconceivable before. Although the inhabitants of Britain had migrated from Europe and traded with it for millennia, being subject to a power that exercised control over much of the European continent, with an emperor who held sway from Devon to Damascus, and from Carlisle to Carthage, was a revolutionary experience.

Much as Rome invented Britain, its vast extent also gave birth to the idea of Europe and the notion that those who had once been ruled by it formed part of a perpetual community of interest. It was under the Romans that the question of how Britain, at the edge of Europe, should relate to its core first became an issue (and a pressing one). As an occupied land, Britain was ruled by Roman governors and procurators (financial officials), but with economic prosperity assured and tribal warfare abolished, the Britons received a fair exchange for their loss of independence.

Three hundred and sixty-seven years passed between the landfall of Emperor Claudius' legions in eastern Kent in AD 43 and the departure of his distant successor Constantine III with the remnants of the Roman garrison, almost the same time-span that separates the present day from the English Civil War, or the signing of the Magna Carta from the defeat of the Spanish Armada. It is tempting to see the period as obscured by an imperial purple haze in which, after the initial conquest period – and Britain was a tough nut to crack, taking forty years and a number of false starts to accomplish – nothing really happened. In reality, it was a period of profound change and not a little political excitement, particularly in the later Roman period, when the province became something of a nursery for rebellious generals and usurpers.

Full-blooded Roman imperial ideology was an aggressive beast, the perfect counterpart to its ruthlessly effective legions in justifying and implementing a policy of continual expansion. Virgil, the propagandist-poet of Rome's very first emperor, Augustus, had Jupiter declare, 'I set upon the Romans bounds neither of space nor of time,' and that they are destined 'to impose the ways of peace . . . and to crush those proud men who will not submit'. This arrogant self-confidence was hardly a recipe for peace with the neighbours, and allowed the Romans to subdue first the Italian peninsula and then to burst its banks and spill over into Gaul, Spain and the Balkans. From there, the empire seemed set to continue its expansion unabated, its bounds determined only by what its legions could conquer.

Britain's geographical isolation, though, made it a special case. The island, Roman authors agreed, was fabulously remote. Virgil referred to 'the Britons, completely cut off from the whole world' and anyone writing about Britain found it hard to resist mentioning that it lay beyond the bounds of the 'Ocean' supposed to mark world's end. Crossing over this forbidding barrier, as Julius Caesar had done, was a dangerous enterprise and not one to be undertaken lightly.

Britain was not only hazardous, fashionable opinion at Rome concurred, but unprofitable. The first-century AD Roman geographer Strabo takes a surprisingly pragmatic approach, judging that 'the expenses of situating an army' in Britain would be calamitous, especially as the Celts currently had to pay the heavy customs duties levied on goods carried into and out of the empire. 'The duties would have to be decreased if tribute were imposed,' he warns, in a note that could as well have been written by a Victorian administrator (or even a twenty-first-century governor of the Bank of England). Two thousand years ago, the Romans were already debating whether it was wise to have the British inside their version of a European customs union and judging that the financial balance would be in Britain's favour.

Strabo's portrait of Britain is in general unappealing (at least for a member of the Roman urban elite). He writes that the 'forests are their cities' and that the weather is truly appalling: 'the air is rainy rather than snowy, and when it is clear it is foggy for long periods, so that the entire day the sun may be seen for only three or four hours around midday'. Its exports were hardly glamorous stuff, either: hunting dogs, cattle and, probably of most interest to the Romans, slaves and the iron and grain they needed to equip and feed the army. In return, the Britons imported ivory, amber and glass beads – low-grade trinkets to please barbarous tastes, which Strabo sniffily dismisses as 'minor objects'. A century later the historian Florus acidly commented that the only reason that Britain was kept on in the empire, despite its poverty, was the glory and titles that the emperor derived from its conquest.

It was all hardly a resounding vote of confidence in Britannia. Apart from the loss of customs dues, the cost of garrisoning the island would be prodigious. At the height of the Roman occupation, there were roughly 50,000 troops stationed in Britain (including three of the empire's entire complement of twenty-eight legions), who munched their way through 45 tons of grain every day (as well as consuming copious quantities of pork, the Roman soldiers' favourite meat, and quaffing over a third of a million litres of wine each week). So why exactly did the Romans bother to cross the Channel and conquer the island and why, given the massive expense, did they bother to stay?

The answer was glory – the same thirst for military success which had brought Caesar into Gaul and then across the English Channel. Victory enhanced the reputation – and power – of a ruler and never more so if he was lacking in obvious martial qualities himself. Claudius, who ascended the imperial throne in AD 41, was badly in need of an infusion of glory. The adoptive grandson of Augustus, he had been sidelined from the succession at an early age. With a severe limp caused by a childhood illness, a rasping voice further marred by a lisp, a tendency to laugh uncontrollably and an inability to deliver the public speeches so vital for a young Roman aristocrat on the make (he had to give them sitting down and tended to wander off the point into long historical digressions), Claudius was a figure of derision at court. By way of compensation, he hid himself in the library, writing a history of the Etruscans in twenty books, eight on Rome's long-time foes, the Carthaginians, and advocating for the introduction of three new letters into the Roman alphabet.

Claudius' physical appearance and reputation as a scholar with no political ambitions or ability shielded him from the murderous attentions of his nephew Caligula, who had become emperor in AD 37 and who disposed of both favourites and opponents at a quite alarming rate. When a faction of the praetorians, the imperial guard, lost patience with their master's patent mental instability and arranged Caligula's assassination in AD 41, they were faced with a problem. The Senate threatened to dispense with the imperial office altogether and restore the old republic. No emperor meant no imperial guard, which meant no lucrative salaries, bribes or bonuses for the praetorians. In desperation they hunted down Claudius in the imperial palace and promptly elevated him to the throne.

Far from being a pliable nonentity who would quietly do their bidding, Claudius turned out to be very independent-minded. For the moment, though, he still badly needed the support of the army to consolidate his hold on power. What better way to do this than to achieve what the great Julius Caesar could not, by extending the empire into Britain? A century had passed since the first Roman incursions into Britain, and no serious attempt had been made to follow up with a more substantive campaign. The Roman state had been consumed by the civil wars that broke out after the assassination of Caesar in 44 BC and which rumbled on for nearly fifteen years, the trials of establishing the imperial system, revolts in the Alps and Balkans and a succession of campaigns in Germany.

There was never quite enough attention available to return to the matter of Britain, but that finally changed in AD 40, when the mercurial Caligula was induced to launch an invasion by Adminius, an exiled British prince of the Catuvellauni. Possibly the head of a pro-Roman faction, he had lost out in a power struggle to his brothers and was forced to flee to Rome, where he threw himself on the mercy of Caligula. The emperor was so taken with his new British subject that he decided to launch an expedition to subdue the rest. Diverting the army from the Rhine, where he was on campaign, he marched with several legions to the Channel coast in preparation for the conquest of Britain. The troops were reluctant to take ship, and in the end Caligula merely ordered the puzzled soldiers to collect sea-shells as a sign they had overcome the limitless Ocean beyond which the island lay. He had the huge pile of shells sent back to Rome as 'tribute', which most likely merely confirmed the Senate and praetorian guard's concerns about his instability. The whole show may have been a sign of Caligula's madness, his warped sense of humour or worry that the task was simply too daunting.

When Claudius replaced Caligula, he needed his own pretext for an attack on Britain. Dissension among the British tribal kingdoms presented a golden opportunity. Cunobelinus, the ruler of the Catuvellauni – immortalized by Shakespeare as Cymbeline – played a central role. Although Shakespeare has him dismiss the strength of the invading Romans with the bold declaration that 'We fear not what can from Italy annoy us' and then anachronistically defeat them before declaring a harmonious peace in which 'Roman and a British ensign wave friendly together', in truth he was already dead by AD 40.

Caratacus and Togodumnus, Cunobelinus' sons, inherited their father's penchant for expansion, pushing beyond the Thames and

Kent into Sussex, where they forced the pro-Roman Verica, king of the Atrebates, into exile. There, he threw himself on the mercy of Claudius, pleading for imperial help to restore him to his throne. Verica's expulsion was a severe affront to Roman honour and made worse by the Britons' demands that he be returned to them.

It was too good an opportunity to miss. In summer 43, Claudius ordered Aulus Plautius, governor of Pannonia (a province including much of modern Hungary and Austria), to assemble an attack force of four legions (the II Augusta, IX Hispana, XIV Gemina and XX Valeria Victrix), which, together with large numbers of auxiliaries – non-citizen soldiers from more recently conquered provinces – brought the expedition's numbers up to around 40,000.

Its sheer size showed that Claudius was serious. The legionaries were the ancient world's most formidable fighting force – each legion comprised around 5,000 men, largely infantry, but with a supporting element of cavalry, whose drill and discipline enabled them to manoeuvre in battle in a way their more enthusiastic but ill-trained opponents could not. Facing a Roman legion meant submitting to volleys of large stones and other missiles by ballistas – a type of early catapult-like artillery – then a rain of javelins, before an infantry charge and close-order fighting. The legionaries' *gladius*, a short sword, was perfectly designed for a quick cut and thrust into an opponents' vital organs. Any who fled the onslaught were mopped up by the legionary cavalry or by units of auxiliaries (who served twenty-five years in the army, hoping to survive long enough to gain the coveted prize of Roman citizenship on their retirement). And the legions did not only fight, they built – each soldier carried a shovel and entrenching tools to construct a marching camp each night, complete with earth embankments, making night-ambushes on the Romans almost impossible.

Despite the huge force, and the Roman superiority in tactics, logistics and equipment, the enterprise was fraught with risk. On hearing that they were being sent to Britain, the army almost mutinied and was only persuaded to embark when the emperor sent his personal envoy Narcissus, an imperial freedman (or former slave) to convince them. Plautius – unlike Caesar – was fortunate to have his landing unopposed by the Britons, who in a bid to avoid an open battle had decided to muster their forces further inland from the Roman beachhead, which probably lay at Richborough in Kent.

Caratacus and Togodumnus led the resistance to the Romans. Their efforts to beat back the invaders were hampered by the defection of several tribes, including the Dobunni, who saw the Romans as a convenient means to curtail the Catuvellauni's encroachment on their territory. The Britons did best when harassing the Roman advance in wooded or hilly territory, picking off stragglers. Their warriors were generally armed only with a long sword and had little armour (unlike the Romans with their bands of metal plate). Only the elite had helmets or shields. In pitched battle against the Romans their only hope was that a massed charge would break the Roman line or their chariot force would outmanoeuvre any Roman force unsupported by cavalry. The Britons finally made a stand along the Medway, but failed to slow the Roman advance; a party of specially trained German auxiliaries swam across the river and dispersed Caratacus' chariots, allowing the legions to follow up and defeat the main Catuvellaunian force. Before long, Caratacus and Togodumnus pulled back behind the Thames and retreated towards their stronghold at Camulodunum (Colchester).

Now that the campaign was nearing its triumphant climax, Claudius crossed over into Britain to bask in its reflected glory. He brought with him a large number of senators, possibly to stifle any disloyal plotting they may have got up to in his absence, elements of the VIII Legion, a section of the praetorian guard and several elephants – though they were not quite the first to be seen in Britain since the Ice Ages, as Julius Caesar had brought a single war elephant with him. This whole unwieldy, and rather impressive, entourage caught up with the main advancing forces just in time to witness the final storming of Camulodunum. Then, having spent just sixteen days in the latest addition to the Roman empire, and satisfied that he was now in the same world-conquering category as Alexander the Great, the emperor returned home to enjoy the triumph, or victory procession, which a grateful Senate felt obliged to bestow upon him.

Triumphal processions were magnificent affairs, with thousands of dignitaries and commoners lining the route, and generally featuring captured foreign rulers laden with chains. By tradition a slave would accompany the triumphant general, whispering every so often in his ear to remind him he was not a god, but still a mere mortal. Claudius milked his triumph for all it was worth. It was said that 'To witness the sight he allowed not only the governors of the provinces to come to Rome, but even some of the exiles; and among the tokens of his victory he set a naval crown on the gable of the Palace beside the civic crown, as a sign that he had crossed and, as it were, subdued the Ocean.' In full military dress, his head crowned with a laurel wreath – a traditional token of victory – he soaked up the adoration of the crowds. He even found a place for his wife, Messalina, who rode behind in a covered carriage. Although as a gesture of humility Claudius made the final few steps up to the Capitoline Temple on his knees, he was quick to accept the victorious title 'Britannicus' bestowed on him by the Senate and ordered the erection of a victory arch in which he lauded his own achievement as the first to make conquests beyond the edge of Ocean and for his winning the submission of eleven British kings to imperial rule.

With the Catuvellauni cowed, it seemed as though the rest of Britain would fall rapidly under Roman control. Things did not go as smoothly as hoped. The reality was a stop-start conquest which proceeded in several stages, as the Romans were gradually drawn out of the lowlands into the highlands and peripheries, where long-term resistance was to prove most bitter. By AD 47, Ostorius Scapula, who had been appointed as Plautius' successor, had established a line of control between the Severn and the Trent. A network of forts and a new road system along the frontier, based on the Fosse Way, together with large legionary bases at Lincoln and Gloucester, briefly held an equilibrium between the shocked Britons and the triumphant invaders.

The Romans may have intended to pause there, but there were

always unconquered tribes along the periphery of their advance and so they were continually drawn into further campaigns to deal with their resistance. Caratacus, who had escaped the defeat around Colchester and found acceptance among the Welsh tribes as a leader, managed to suck the Romans into a series of drawn-out campaigns there against the Ordovices of the north and the Silures in the south. In the end he was captured and handed over by a fellow Briton, Queen Cartimandua of the Brigantes, who felt the independence of her own kingdom (centred on Yorkshire) would be better preserved by currying favour with the Romans. The British resistance hero was carted off to Rome, where he was paraded in a triumph three years later, though he avoided his intended fate of being strangled after the parade by an impassioned and eloquent plea to Claudius. 'If you want to rule the world,' he declared, 'does it follow that everyone else welcomes enslavement? If I had surrendered without a blow . . . neither my downfall or your triumph would have become famous. If you execute me, they will be forgotten. Spare me, and I shall be an everlasting token of your mercy!' Impressed by his bravery and frankness, Claudius allowed him to live out the rest of his days in obscurity in Rome.

Although by the mid AD 50s there was stalemate in Wales, the Romans had thrust into Devon, where they built a legionary fortress at Exeter, and were pushing against the borders of the Brigantes in Yorkshire, whose strength and warlike nature made them a formidable obstacle. There, they paused. Without the inclination, nor for the moment the capability, to attempt a conquest of the whole island, the Romans instead consolidated their position through the establishment of a series of client kingdoms, whose rulers kept their subjects quiescent in return for not suffering the full rigours of military occupation. The gradual creep forward by the Romans in many ways resembled the later British experience in India, where one victory led almost inevitably to another war to protect the gains of the first and where, in the end, it was more convenient to leave the remaining princes in a state of semi-independence than to conquer them fully.

A series of British rulers bargained away a part of their independence in exchange for Roman subsidies and the promise of being left in peace: Queen Cartimandua of the Brigantes (whose colourful marital relations with her husband Venutius would cause constant headaches for a series of Roman governors), Prasutagus of the Iceni (in East Anglia) and Togidubnus of the Regni (whose probable royal centre at the magnificent palace at Fishbourne shows the great riches that the pliant pro-Roman British elite could enjoy). The magnificent mosaic floors at Fishbourne, the gold ring found nearby inscribed with the name Tiberius Claudius Catuarus (probably a member of the royal house of the Regni), the ornate red samian ware on which the British aristocracy ate their meals, and the taste they acquired for Roman delicacies such as *garum* (a rather foul-smelling fish paste) all showed that the hunger for Roman luxuries far outweighed any thirst for independence.

This proved to be unwise. In AD 58, a new governor, Suetonius Paulinus, arrived and resumed the conquest of Wales. Two years later, he launched an attack on Anglesey, the final British stronghold. Resistance there had been marshalled by the Druids. Combining the role of prophets, poets and priests, their real beliefs have been clouded by the judgement of Roman writers such as Pliny, who accused them of 'monstrous practices, by which to kill a man was a highly religious act, and even to eat him was very salubrious'. In less histrionic form, Pliny tells us that the Druids conducted their worship in oak groves, and that they held a particular reverence for mistletoe, which they harvested with golden sickles six days after a new moon. The rites they conducted in such natural settings tally with what little we know of traditional Celtic religion in Britain – largely from dedications on stone altars – where personifications of natural features (such as the water nymph Coventina from Carrawburgh along Hadrian's Wall) and less tangible deities (such as the mysterious 'Genii cucullati' – the hooded ones) predominate.

As Paulinus' troops crossed the Menai Strait, they were faced with lines of black-clad British women and behind them the Druids, all raining down curses on the invaders. Roman javelins proved more potent than native magic, and the Druids were slaughtered and their sacred groves hacked down. Just at the moment of victory, Paulinus received news of a disaster to his rear. Prasutagus of the Iceni had died, and the procurator, Rome's chief financial official in Britain, had sent representatives to take possession of the lands of the Iceni, which he deemed to be forfeit to the empire in the absence of a male heir. The officials took to their task with a little too much relish, flogging Boudicca, the dead king's widow, and raping her daughters.

The outraged Iceni rose up in revolt, and soon other East Anglian tribes joined the rebellion. The Trinovantes, who particularly resented the implantation of a *colonia*, a settlement for legionary veterans, at Colchester (which lay within their tribal lands), fell on the town. After a spirited last stand by a group of veterans in the temple of the imperial cult, the largest stone building, Colchester was put to the torch. Largely wooden, it burned easily, and the victorious Iceni army turned westwards. Boudicca's revolt was then almost halted in its tracks by Petillius Cerialis, commander of Legio IX, the closest significant Roman unit, who had hurried south to intercept the Iceni, only to suffer a rare defeat at the hands of native forces. Battened up in a fort near Peterborough, the remnants of his legion could do nothing as Boudicca, whose fiery, red-headed depictions in a host of Victorian schoolbooks at least hint at the inspirational figure she must have been, turned on London.

As the complete collapse of the province loomed, Suetonius Paulinus turned back from north Wales. A dash southwards with his cavalry proved fruitless, as he could no longer link up with Cerialis, and Poenius Postumus, the stand-in commander of Legio II, refused orders to move out of the legionary base at Exeter. With no troops to defend it, the Romans pulled out of London, leaving it, and Verulamium (St Albans) – the next town in Boudicca's path – to be razed in turn. The damage was horrifying: the archaeologists who excavated the site found a layer of burned debris indicating widespread destruction, and Tacitus claims that 70,000 perished in the conflagration.

By the time Paulinus' infantry caught up with him, the Iceni had moved further to the west, threatening to cut the Roman province in two. Somewhere north-west of London, possibly near Towcester, Paulinus drew up his troops, his line shielded by wooded ground to prevent the British war-chariots outflanking him. Accounts of the battle are scant, but the Britons made the mistake of charging up a slope, and then their discipline broke in the face of a concerted counter-attack by the Roman infantry. As they retreated, Boudicca's warriors became caught up with their own baggage-train and were slaughtered. Although probably an exaggeration, Tacitus' figure of 80,000 British dead is some indication of how shattering a defeat the Iceni suffered. Boudicca escaped, only to commit suicide, Cleopatra-like, by poisoning soon after the battle. Paulinus' revenge was terrible; the lands of tribes who had joined the rebellion, or who had merely stayed neutral, were laid waste, and Poenius Postumus fell on his own sword to avoid the ignominy of trial for mutiny.

Seventeen years after Claudius' invasion, the Romans had almost nothing to show for their occupation of Britain save a restive population and a handful of smouldering towns. Yet in the end the Boudiccan revolt did not force the Romans to evacuate Britain. Even as the empire suffered its first significant bout of civil war following the death of Nero in AD 68, which led to the accession of four emperors in a single year, a pair of able governors, Vettius Bolanus and Petillius Cerialis – who had first-hand experience of the results of heavy-handed Roman policies – pulled Britain back from the scorched-earth retribution of Paulinus. Caution was the watch-word: several of the British legions were under suspicion for their support of opponents of Vespasian (the final victor in the civil war) and one (the XX) had its commander replaced and several cohorts transferred to other legions. The Romans were well aware that it was the harshness of their actions which had led the British tribes to rise up, and they were in no position to deal with renewed unrest on a wide scale.

The territory of the Brigantes, though, presented a particular problem, personified by Cartimandua, its mercurial queen. One of the more glamorous figures in Celtic history, she was Britain's answer to Cleopatra: both collaborator and doughty defender of her lands, her political strength was undermined by her colourful love life (though, unlike her Egyptian counterpart, her liaisons were confined to her own countrymen, and not with powerful Romans). Cartimandua's kingdom stretched right across northern England, from the North Sea to the Irish, both providing a secure buffer zone and blocking the way to further Roman expansion. The difficulty was that Brigantia, and its queen, were chronically unstable.

Cartimandua threw in her lot with the Romans in AD 51, when Caratacus, on the run from a series of defeats in Wales, fled to Brigantia. It is not clear why he did so, whether because Cartimandua represented the most powerful surviving British ruler and he thought he could win her round to his cause, or through some family link between his own dynasty and the Brigantian royal house (Welsh tradition suggested that the two were cousins, and Scottish legend even had it that Cartimandua was Caratacus' stepmother). Whatever the reason, Caratacus' faith was misplaced, and his new host had him arrested, roughly bound and handed over to the Romans.

Cartimandua's actions may have won her Roman approval, but it lost her the trust of her people and that of her own husband Venutius. His position as royal consort, and not as king in his own right, must have rankled (he may not even have been Brigantian, but from a smaller tribe such as the Carvetii, who had their power-base in Cumbria). Venutius now started plotting to overthrow his wife, leading to the arrest of his brother and several other family members. He fled and began raising warriors to launch an invasion, encouraged – as Tacitus claimed – by Brigantians who were 'infuriated and goaded by fears of humiliating feminine rule'. The Romans intervened to prop up their client, and Venutius, despite Tacitus' description of him as the 'best strategist' among the Britons, was beaten back. A furious Cartimandua then divorced her rebellious husband and began an affair with his armour-bearer Vellocatus. Finally, in AD 68, after brooding for a decade in exile, Venutius took advantage of the Roman preoccupation with the civil war to invade again, aided by a revolt inside Brigantia which he had fomented, forcing his wife out and taking the throne for himself. Cartimandua in turn appealed to the Romans, and in AD 71 Cerialis, newly arrived as governor, sent a legionary force into Brigantia, which defeated Venutius in several bloody encounters. The governor, though, did not restore the deposed queen, who had failed to perform her role as an agent of stability on the imperial frontier and whose marital strife had spilled out so disastrously into power politics. Instead he established a legionary fortress at Eboracum (York), which for over three centuries acted as the capital of the Roman north. The final fates of Venutius and Cartimandua – whose twenty-year reign makes her the longest-reigning female British monarch before Elizabeth I – are unknown, but it is to be presumed that they did not attempt a reconciliation.

North Wales – and the troublesome Silures – were finally subdued in the mid AD 70s, but the lands in the far north of the island were still unconquered. After the absorption of the Brigantians, Roman control only extended towards their former royal stronghold Stanwick, near Richmond, and possibly as far as Carlisle. It fell to Julius Agricola to complete, or almost complete, the conquest of the whole island of Britain. The most famous governor of all, he owes his fame in part to his undoubted success, but mainly to a biography written by the great historian Tacitus, who just happened to be his son-in-law.

Although *Agricola* may well exaggerate its subject's achievements, the course of the final Roman advance is clear. After arriving in summer AD 78, Agricola consolidated the conquest of Wales and then, in progressive annual campaigns, pushed the frontier ever further northwards; first to the Tyne–Solway isthmus (broadly where the Anglo-Scottish border lies today) and then in AD 80 as far as the Tay. The basis of a permanent occupation was laid the following year with the construction of forts along the Forth–Clyde isthmus, but Agricola must have known the situation was unstable. In AD 81 and 82 he attacked the lands of the Selgovae in south-eastern Scotland and the Novantae in the south-west and the following year he launched an all-out assault. A land attack, which thrust up east of the Highlands, leaving a sprinkling of encampments throughout the lowlands, as the Roman army constructed defensive marching camps each night, was accompanied by a naval force which launched raids to keep the enemy off-balance.

Somewhere in the north-eastern Lowlands, Calgacus, the leader of the British host, decided to stand and fight. As many as 30,000 warriors from both the lowlands and highlands had flocked to join him, giving him the manpower to face the Romans in a formal battle. Against him, Agricola, commanded around 8,000 Roman auxiliary infantry, 5,000 cavalry and detachments from several legions (bringing his total strength to around 20,000). Before the climactic battle at Mons Graupius – whose location is unclear – Tacitus puts a speech into the mouth of Calgacus excoriating his Roman opponents. It is a rousing affair – he exhorts his countrymen 'here at the world's end, on its last inch of liberty' to rouse themselves to the defence of their land, for 'there are not other tribes to come, nothing but sea and cliffs, and these more deadly Romans'. He invokes the spirit of Cartimandua as 'a woman who could lead the Brigantes to burn a colony, to storm a camp' and contrasts what he (rather over-optimistically) judges the unity of the Britons with the division of the Romans 'recruited from races widely separate', whose army 'is held together only by success, and will melt away with defeat'. Finally, he throws in the accusation that perhaps wounded most: that the Roman conquerors 'make a desolation and call it peace'. It was a wry comment that could just as well be directed at subsequent generations of imperialists.

The battle was close-fought and conducted on the Roman side almost completely by auxiliaries (rather than the better-trained and equipped legionaries who would normally bear the brunt of the fighting). Calgacus' men were brought to a standstill by the Roman infantry and then enveloped by Agricola's cavalry, who had first chased off the British chariots. It was a slaughter – according to Tacitus 10,000 Britons were killed, for the loss of just 360 Roman lives.

Much of the British host seems to have slipped away back into the Highlands, denying Agricola an absolutely decisive victory which would have kept the tribes submissive. The campaign was rounded off with an attack on south-western Scotland and a sally by the fleet around the Orkneys. It was the farthest north any Roman expedition is recorded as reaching, as if to show that Rome's power really did extend to the edges of the world.

The governor then set to consolidation, ordering the building of a series of forts to house auxiliary units as Scotland's garrison (including at Stracathro in Angus). Outposts were set up to block the glens and prevent hostile tribal forces from emerging from the Highlands and a legionary fortress was also constructed at Inchtuthil on the Tay. It was a moment when Britain's future lay in the balance. Had a legion been permanently stationed so far north, the subsequent fracture between England and Scotland might never have happened, as both shared the experience of three centuries as part of the Roman empire.

The whole island of Britain now lay within Agricola's grasp. From a vantage point in Galloway in south-west Scotland, he is reputed to have gazed over at Ireland – just 25 miles distant – and mused that with just a couple of auxiliary units he could conquer that, too. If the victory at Mons Graupius had been followed up with the conquest of the Highlands, there would have been no northern frontier, no unsubdued tribes. Orkney would have been as Roman as Ostia. Perhaps then Agricola might even have had a tilt at Ireland, and the whole of the British Isles would have developed a single political identity within the Roman empire (and perhaps beyond its fall).

However, it was not to be. Not for the last time, the needs of the empire and the personal preferences of an emperor outweighed the interests of a mere province. A year after Mons Graupius, Agricola's soaring reputation prompted his recall by a jealous Emperor Domitian. Having such a successful general at the head of four legions was just too risky. The Legio II Adiutrix was pulled out of Chester and sent to Dacia, where a Roman expeditionary force had been heavily defeated in 86. This left a hole in the Roman defences in western England, which was plugged by the Legio XX, originally intended as the garrison for Inchtuthil. Suddenly there were no troops to spare for an expensive occupation of lowland Scotland,

and Inchtuthil was evacuated. The withdrawal was clearly carried out in something of a hurry, as a massive hoard of seven tons of iron nails was discovered at the site. Intended to be used in the completion of the fortress, it had been buried by the retreating legionary engineers to avoid its falling into the hands of the native British and being melted down to make weapons. A number of human skulls found in pits at Newstead Fort, evacuated soon after, and the burning of several timber forts suggest that the pull-back might have been accompanied or even prompted by attacks from Scottish tribes.

'Perdomita Britannia et statim missa,' Tacitus sourly commented at the start of his *Histories*, a more general chronicle of his times: 'Britain was subdued and forthwith abandoned.' The pull-back, though, was more an act of realpolitik than a strategic blunder; a thinly spread garrison in Scotland would have been outnumbered in hostile territory, risking constant attack and quite possibly expulsion by the local tribes. An orderly withdrawal was far less damaging to Roman prestige. Step by step, the more advanced Roman positions in Scotland were abandoned; first Inchtuthil and Stracathro, then a line of forts along the Gask Ridge in Perthshire, followed by the bulk of the outposts in the southern Lowlands. Finally, early in the reign of Trajan, around AD 105, the Romans consolidated a new line along the Stanegate, a military road that ran from the Tyne to the Solway, roughly from modern Newcastle to Carlisle, defended by a string of forts from Corbridge in the east to Burgh-by-Sands, west of Carlisle.

Among these new outposts was Vindolanda, near Corbridge. It was here that one of the most stunning archaeological discoveries ever made in Britain took place. The Roman legion may have marched on its stomach, but it took an army of quartermasters and record-keepers to keep track of all that grain, pork and beer. For the most part these records have long perished, but excavations at Vindolanda in 1973 unearthed a congealed clump of woods strips. When treated, this unprepossessing mass turned out to be part of the garrison records of the fort. Written in ink on slivers of bark, they had somehow survived being thrown into a rubbish dump, where the anaerobic conditions meant many of the bacteria which would normally break down organic matter were not present, so preventing their deterioration. If history is what people in the past chose to tell us by writing it down and archaeology is what they threw away, the Vindolanda tablets are a startling combination of the two. The humdrum ephemera of military life – rosters, requisitions and supply lists – are accompanied by more personal documents: notes about mercantile contracts, and even a letter from one soldier asking for supplies of beer to his unit, and another to a homesick auxiliary telling him the sender had despatched thick socks and new underpants to protect him from the bitter British winter. Perhaps the most extraordinary is a note from Claudia Severa, an officer's wife, inviting her friend Sulpicia Lepidina (whose husband, Flavius Cerialis, was commander of the Ninth Cohort of Batavians, the Vindolanda garrison around AD 100), to her birthday party.

Roman Britain's frontier paused only briefly at the Stanegate. The death of Trajan in AD 117 was followed by a reassessment of the policy of permanent imperial expansion (shortly before his death, the emperor had defeated Parthia, which for centuries had been Rome's arch-rival on its eastern frontier, leading to a massive, but short-lived, expansion into modern Iraq). His successor, Hadrian, was an inveterate traveller with a taste for all things Greek, which won him the disparaging nickname Graeculus ('Greekling'). He was the first emperor to wear a beard (a fact most of his startled subjects would only have known through his portrait on coins) and he conducted a semi-public affair with Antinous, a young man from Bithynia (in modern Turkey), whom the emperor had deified after he mysteriously drowned during a visit to Egypt. Hadrian's travels took him to all parts of the empire: to Greece, the Balkans, the eastern frontier with Parthia, Germany and to that ill-fated trip down the Nile during which Antinous died.

In AD 122 he came to see Britannia for himself. The province had just suffered a bout of fighting, possibly a native revolt, and Hadrian installed as the new governor a close associate, Aulus Platorius Nepos, with a brief to reimpose order. He also ordered the construction of a linear barrier to mark the border between the empire and the barbarian lands beyond. The Wall (which much later took on Hadrian's name), was a novel departure. In one sense it was an admission of defeat, a sign that plans for the conquest of the whole of Scotland had now been abandoned. Yet it was also a recognition that Britannia had reached its logical shape and that ensuring the province's security and prosperity, rather than expanding its bounds, was now the imperial priority.

The Wall snakes across the narrow pinch-point of the Tyne–Solway isthmus for 80 Roman miles, beginning at Wallsend and ending near Carlisle, incorporating in its central section the dramatic landscape of the Whin Sill crags, from where nervous Roman auxiliaries would have had a grandstand view of the unsubdued, mist-shrouded land to the north. The consolidated and partially reconstructed version which can be seen today is striking enough, but in its original form, rising to over 5 metres in height and studded with forts, it must have been an awe-inspiring sight. The Wall's construction history is complex – the engineering parties from three legions who laboured for six years to complete it began with the construction of the eastern sector in stone, and then moved on to a turf barrier making up the western half of the Wall's line. There were other changes of plan, as the Wall was narrowed from an initial width of 3 metres to 2.3 metres and the fourteen forts, which had originally been built back from it, were later incorporated directly into the main barrier. Between the forts lay smaller milecastles, which, as the name suggests, were situated roughly every Roman mile, and between each of these were built two turrets, just large enough to house a small detachment of around eight troops. In front of the Wall a forward ditch protected the approach to the Wall, while to the rear another V-shaped ditch (the Vallum), flanked by earth embankments, provided a further obstacle.

In its final form the Hadrian's Wall system was a truly impressive barrier, manned by around 10,000 auxiliary troops, around a quarter of the total British garrison. But what exactly was its purpose? Although Hadrian's biographer states that the emperor built it 'to divide Romans from barbarians', the existence of gateways at milecastles which allowed passage through the Wall hints that the truth is more complex. The lack of any evidence of a wide fighting platform against the Wall also suggests that it was not ever intended to be defended in force against a large-scale attack from the north. More likely it acted as a deterrent to raiders, who would find it very difficult to sneak past it into imperial territory undetected, while the gateways and passages across the Vallum served as control points where customs duties could be levied. More serious incursions would have to be dealt with by units moving laterally along the Wall from the nearest forts and, in the case of last resort, by deploying the 5,000-strong legion based in York.

The garrison did not simply sit tight in their forts, drilling, writing tablets and glowering at what one of those referred to as 'Brittunculi' (which roughly translates as 'filthy little Britons'). The Wall and its forts also acted as jumping-off points for periodic punitive campaigns into Scotland, to demonstrate the power of Rome and prevent any of the tribes becoming over-confident. The Romans also kept a small network of outpost forts beyond the Wall, such as at High Rochester (west of Alnwick) and Newstead (near Melrose), which acted to maintain their influence among the Novantae and Selgovae, the key tribal groupings north of the frontier.

Having constructed such an imposing frontier system, the Romans promptly abandoned it. Hadrian died in 138, and his successor Antoninus Pius (r. 138–61), whose reign was afterwards remembered as a golden age of tranquil prosperity, ordered the reoccupation of large parts of the Scottish Lowlands. There is some evidence of a revolt along the frontier during which Antoninus' appointee as governor, Quintus Lollius Urbicus, was forced to 'drive back the barbarians'. The new emperor may have considered that the border tribes could be better controlled under direct Roman rule or, as Claudius had before him, he felt that a limited advance in Britain was the perfect opportunity for an easy win that would crown his new reign with an air of martial glory.

The forts along Hadrian's Wall were decommissioned, and the

army advanced to the Clyde–Forth isthmus. There, it did an extraordinary thing. The legionaries built a new barrier, this time of turf, and without the system of milecastles and turrets of its southern counterpart. This Antonine Wall (like its southern sister, it took on the name of its creator) marked a piece of both military pragmatism, as its shorter length (at 40 Roman miles) offered a more logical solution to where Roman Britain would end, and political opportunism, as it offered Antoninus a relatively risk-free win: if much of Scotland was reoccupied it would redound to his glory, but if the troops had to quietly pull back again, few in Rome would notice.

Snaking from Old Kilpatrick on the Clyde (now in the outskirts of Glasgow) to Carriden on the Forth, the Antonine Wall was fronted, just like its southern sister, by a ditch and had its own system of outpost forts, such as Ardoch in Perthshire, which projected Roman power even further north. Because it remained during its short time in commission as a turf barrier – unlike the impressive stone wall to the south – the Antonine Wall was subsequently neglected and largely forgotten, despite the decades that Roman soldiers spent there, with their forts, bath-houses (complete with the Romans' advanced plumbing systems), altars to Roman gods such as Neptune and Celtic deities like Epona, spoil heaps full of oysters, pig, cattle, deer and wild boar bones and mounds of broken pots and fine Samian ware.

Yet this new attempt to fix the frontier lasted scarcely two decades. A revolt in the mid-150s among the ever-troublesome Brigantes meant units had to be pulled back to Yorkshire to suppress it. There may have been a brief reoccupation of Hadrian's Wall around 158, followed by an even more ephemeral return to the Antonine Wall, but by the early 160s the auxiliary cohorts had marched right back down to Hadrian's Wall again, there to remain for the next 200 years.

Those two centuries of Roman rule transformed Britain. In the wake of the legions came such novelties as towns, a network of high-quality roads, a central administration, civil government and exotic additions to the British menu such as cabbage, celery and plums. Outside the new towns, the landscape was studded with villas and a sprinkling of installations where the production of goods such as pottery was carried out for the first time on an industrial scale. The network of forts housed the garrison of some 55,000 – a far heavier military presence than in any other Roman province – which provided a bulwark against rebellions, participated in civil wars on behalf of streams of pretenders to the imperial throne and guarded against incursions from the unconquered regions of northern Scotland.

As the frontier drifted backwards and forwards, the life of the Roman province of Britannia which it enclosed was transformed. The army was a key agent in this change; the 15,000 legionaries were all Roman citizens, and the auxiliary units, although composed of non-citizens, were – at least in the first generations of the occupation – recruited in a wide variety of provinces, from the Tungrians and Batavians of the Netherlands, to units of Syrian archers and even a contingent of boatmen from the Tigris in modern Iraq. It was a cosmopolitan force – though some must have bitterly regretted the freezing cold and bone-penetrating damp of the winters – and it brought with it new ideas, new religions (from altars to the spirit, or genius, of the legion, to safely Roman Jupiter, exotically Egyptian Isis and the Persian mystery cult of Mithras, as well as local Celtic deities, such as Coventina, who was worshipped at a well near Carrawburgh along the Wall) and a huge boost to the local economy from the need to supply the soldiers with food and equipment.

In the military zone of Britain, civilian encampments grew up around the auxiliary forts and legionary fortresses. These settlements (called *vici* for the forts and *canabae* for the fortresses) housed the traders who provided services to the military, retired veterans and also the soldiers' families. Although serving Roman soldiers were not legally allowed to marry until the late second century, in reality many of them took wives from among local women and maintained them in the *vicus* next to the fort. Their children provided a new generation of young men who could be recruited to their fathers' auxiliary units and bound the army more tightly in to the life of the province (where some of the units served extended periods of decades, or in the case of the Legion II Augusta, centuries, from the Claudian invasion in AD 43 until at least the early fourth century).

The Romans gave Britain a political structure for the first time. Although they had made use of client kingdoms in the initial stages of the conquest, they rapidly organized it into a regular Roman province (Britannia) under direct imperial control, governed by a *legatus* (or legate), who was based in London from around the AD 60s, and assisted by a chief financial official, or procurator. Crucially for the future of Britain, no attempt was made to reflect the system of multiple tribal kingdoms, and instead a single province was established (which was only much later, around AD 200, subdivided into two, then four mini-provinces). The figure of Britannia, or the personification of Britain, which was later to play a central role in eighteenth- and nineteenth-century mythologizing about the deep roots of the nation's identity, first appears on coins of the emperor Hadrian around AD 119, where she is shown as a martial female figure, equipped with sword and shield, in much the same shape she would appear on pre-decimal British pennies. The vagaries of Roman control in Britain are even represented in variations in Britannia's portrayal: the subjugation of the Brigantian revolt in 153–4 was celebrated by a coin issue which shows her in a distinctly subdued posture.

The Romans brought with them to Britain a cultural package which they had replicated throughout the empire: peace, prosperity and new luxuries which were an enormous inducement for local native elites to collaborate. In the *Agricola*, Tacitus wryly comments that this was the means by which the Romans enslaved those they conquered, as 'the wearing of our dress became a distinction, and the toga came into fashion, and little by little the Britons were seduced into alluring vices: to the lounge, the bath, the well-appointed dinner table. The simple natives gave the name of "culture" to this part of their slavery.'

Local elites were allowed just enough of a taste of Roman power to leave them addicted to Roman luxury. They also found their old

43

tribal centres replaced by towns. There had been none in Britain before AD 43 (although the largest of the British *oppida*, such as Colchester, came close), and so the Romans had to build up an urban network from scratch. At the top of the hierarchy were *coloniae*, established as settlements of Roman citizens (normally legionary veterans), such as Colchester and York. Next came the *municipia*, whose inhabitants had limited rights and where those who served on the town councils acquired full citizenship, such as Verulamium (St Albans), and the *civitates*, which were established as regional capitals broadly serving the old tribal divisions (such as at Canterbury, or Durovernum Cantiacorum, the capital of the Cantiaci tribe). To link these new centres, the Romans built a system of roads, which facilitated trade, as well as providing a rapid means for army units to criss-cross the province. Many probably followed pre-existing Iron Age tracks, which were rebuilt with layers of gravel topped with cobbles and metalling. Roads such as Watling Street in Kent and Ermine Street in Lincolnshire bound the province together, while others, like Dere Street (which ran north–south through Corbridge) permitted the army to react rapidly to threats on the frontier or to launch campaigns beyond it.

The larger towns like London (or Londinium), which became the provincial capital, had a full panoply of public buildings, such as the *curia* (or town council), *basilica* (or law-court), theatre, amphitheatre (where gladiatorial and beast shows were put on by rich patrons) and baths, where provincials could indulge in the curious Roman habit of public bathing through a succession of cool and warm rooms. They also possessed temples, from the Temple of the Imperial Cult at Colchester, which acted as a particular focus for the hatred of the Boudiccan rebels, to those dedicated to Roman deities such as Jupiter, Juno and Mars.

Romanitas, the sense of being Roman, though all-pervading, was only ever a surface layer grafted onto a set of much older customs which survived throughout the Roman period. This was most obviously so in the religious sphere, where local gods were conflated with their nearest Roman equivalent to create hybrid deities such as

Mars Nodens, a healing god, who was venerated at a shrine at Lydney in Gloucestershire; Mars Cocidius, a war god, who was commemorated in Birdoswald and Chesters forts along Hadrian's Wall; and Minerva Sulis, who was worshipped at the healing springs at Bath, around which a huge and much-visited complex was built (and, centuries later, revived in Georgian times). The countryside was dotted with such Romano-Celtic temples where a central building or *cella* stored a cult idol, with a surrounding, sometimes round, ambulatory, where rituals took place.

In the third and fourth centuries the religious life of Roman Britain became even more vibrant and complex with the importation of mystery cults. Some, like the Egyptian cults of Isis and Attis and Cybele (whose priests indulged in the rather off-putting practice of self-castration), must have seemed distinctly exotic in Rome's northernmost province. Others, like the cult of Mithras, an adaptation of a Persian deity who underwent a symbolic rebirth after being bathed in the blood of a slaughtered bull, were open solely to men and involved secret rites revealed only to initiates, who progressed through seven ranks from *corax* (raven) to *pater* (father). Mithraism became particularly popular among Roman soldiers, and Mithras temples (or *mithraea*) have been found at several forts near Hadrian's Wall (including Carrawburgh) as well as in London, where the *mithraeum* was operating at least as late as 308.

Mithraism ultimately lost out to another eastern cult. With its similar promise of resurrection through a blood sacrifice, Christianity benefited greatly from its openness to both sexes, wider social groups and comparative lack of secrecy (other than that imposed on it by periodic persecutions by the Roman authorities). Although there is only slight archaeological evidence for its spread in Britain, Christianity's growth there must have been eased by the toleration granted to it by Emperor Constantine by the Edict of Milan in 313, his death-bed conversion and the increasing restrictions placed on traditional paganism by subsequent emperors, which had rendered it moribund as a significant force in public life by the 390s. Hints of Christian practice have been found, such as the mid-fourth-century frescoes unearthed at a villa at Lullingstone in Kent which depict worshippers with their hands outstretched in prayer, and a possible representation of Christ (indicated by the Chi-Rho monogram, a very common early Christian symbol) in a mid fourth-century mosaic pavement at Hinton St Mary in Dorset. More definite evidence is provided by the presence of three British bishops at the Council of Arles, held in Gaul in 314. Such a tiny contingent suggests a church in an early stage of development, but the survival of Christianity among the British kingdoms which emerged after the collapse of Roman Britain in the early fifth century and the strength of a 'Celtic' form of Christianity in the north of England in the sixth and seventh centuries indicates a religion which had put down deep roots in Britain.

Roman Britain in the second century was at the peak of its prosperity. There were few hints that this would not continue indefinitely, with the persistent failure to subdue Scotland as the only blemish on Rome's achievement. The eighty years from Nerva's succession in 96, during which the throne passed from emperor to adopted son, so avoiding the hazards of hereditary succession, were a golden age, both for the empire and for Britain. All that changed within a dozen years. In 180, Commodus, the natural son of Marcus Aurelius, became emperor, turning out to be an egocentric monster with a penchant for fighting in the gladiatorial arena (his opponents, naturally, always lost). After his assassination in 192, the empire was racked by a civil war, from which Septimius Severus, the former governor of Upper Pannonia, finally emerged victorious. It had been a close-run thing, and a revolt in 196 by Clodius Albinus, the governor of Britain, whose troops declared him emperor and marched with him across the Channel to Gaul, was only put down with difficulty. It was the first ominous taste of the use of the British garrison to further a pretender's imperial ambitions, a practice that would ultimately prove the downfall of Roman Britain.

Rome's troubles attracted attention north of the border, too. The powerful Maeatae confederacy took advantage of the thinning-out of the garrison and began raiding the Wall. The disorder prompted a full-scale imperial expedition in 208, when the by-now aged Severus arrived in Britannia with his sons, Geta and Caracalla. The fighting was prolonged and relentless, punctuated by tactical truces during which the Maeatae and their Caledonian allies simply regrouped and attacked once more. In the end Severus merely declared that victory had been won and ordered the minting of a commemorative coin, before dying, exhausted, at York in February 211.

Britain had little to show for two years of concentrated imperial attention, save some reconstruction work along Hadrian's Wall and the division of the province in two: Britannia Superior, with its capital at London, and Britannia Inferior, whose governor was based at York. Although intended to prevent a single governor having command of the large British garrison, the move also confirmed Britain's position as something of a career backwater, with few really successful or ambitious men serving as governors there. While the two provinces continued in their benignly neglected prosperity, however, storm clouds were gathering elsewhere. As the third century progressed, tribal federations which had arisen along the static Roman border in Germany began pressing against it with ever greater force. Although, as an island, Britain was immune from the worst of these pressures, maritime raiders and piracy became an increasing problem. Towns, which had largely lacked defences before, began to receive them, including at St Albans in the 260s, while a city wall was constructed around London in about 200.

To face this new challenge, the Romans deployed resources away from the traditional military zone in the north and built a series of forts along the threatened coastlines. Britain's very isolation, which had long sheltered it from all but the most determined invaders, now became its weakness, as its long coastline offered easy prey for raiders who could pick their landing sites at will, while Roman resources stretched only to fortifying the most obvious promontories and the most vulnerable sectors. Beginning at Brancaster in Norfolk and Reculver in Kent, the Saxon Shore forts with their large projecting circular towers symbolize a less confident era in which Rome's frontier stance had turned from caution to despair.

47

At the imperial centre, the situation was, if anything, even worse. A succession of short-lived emperors – there were more than a dozen between 235 and 255, almost all of whom met a violent death – struggled to cope with the empire's growing problems. Usurpers, pretenders and generals seized the throne with such dizzying regularity that sculptors failed to keep up with the latest imperial image and began producing statues with replaceable heads, so that when one emperor fell, the head of the new ruler could be inserted in his place.

In the end, the empire simply fell apart: in 260 Postumus, a local army commander in Gaul, was proclaimed emperor by the troops there. Spain, parts of Germany and Britain followed suit and joined Postumus' breakaway empire. Little save the force of Postumus' personality held the rebel provinces together, and his successor, Tetricus, surrendered to the legitimate emperor Aurelian in 273. Britain, too, returned to the imperial fold, but it was clear that it could not escape the great changes which were unfolding. Pressed against by growing numbers of barbarians, the Roman empire was simply too big to govern, and the interests of the centre and of remote provinces like Britain were beginning to diverge as the age-old bargain of loss of political power in exchange for peace and prosperity became steadily less advantageous.

In 293 Diocletian brought a temporary halt to the empire's decline by instituting the Tetrarchy, a system in which there were two senior emperors (with the title Augustus) and two junior colleagues (or Caesars). He also further subdivided many provinces, including Britain, which now boasted four governors (for Maxima Caesariensis, in the south-east and East Anglia; Britannia Prima, the west of England, plus Wales; Britannia Secunda, comprising the north of England; and Flavia Caesariensis, a part of the east Midlands and Lincolnshire).

One of the less inspired decisions of Maximian, whom Diocletian had chosen as Augustus in charge of the western part of the empire, was the appointment of Mausaeus Carausius, a provincial from north-eastern Gaul, as commander of the Roman fleet in Britain. At first Carausius experienced great success in his fight-back against the pirates who had been raiding the British coastline, but his reputation was undermined by rumours – quite possibly spread by jealous rivals – that he was in league with the corsairs and was pocketing part of the loot himself. Now under imperial suspicion, Carausius took almost the only course of action available to stave off arrest and almost certain execution and declared himself emperor.

Britain now experienced its first period of independence as a separate state, but the taste of unity and freedom was fleeting. The fledgling British empire incorporated part of Gaul (including Boulogne, which housed an important naval base) and, if his coinage is anything to go by, Carausius was both an effective ruler and an able propagandist. Of far better quality than the debased imperial issues which had preceded it, his silver coinage was stamped with quotes from Virgil and stressed the notion that Carausius was a restorer of peace, not a usurper. He even cheekily issued coins depicting Diocletian and Maximian, which celebrated 'Carausius and his brothers', implying that he was an official part of the Tetrarchy. Britain's first bid for independence from the empire collapsed after Carausius was assassinated in 293. His successor Allectus proved less capable. Having recaptured Boulogne earlier that year, the Caesar Constantius launched a two-pronged attack which struck near the Isle of Wight and up the Thames Estuary. Caught between the two, Allectus was defeated and killed.

From the very beginning of the empire, it had been common for over-ambitious generals to revolt and use the legions under their command in a bid to gain the throne. By the fourth century, though, the empire was becoming more brittle, less able to cope with successive crises. For outlying provinces such as Britain, the position was worse. Its loyalty to the empire was rewarded with the gradual stripping-away of its garrison, as a series of usurpers took sections of its army with them on their marches to Rome, leaving the province even more vulnerable and prone to revolt. When the centre had been strong, Britain's security was assured, but now that Rome was weakened, it became a black hole into which taxes and troops were sucked, with little by way of return.

In 350 Emperor Constans was toppled by a rebellion by Magnentius, an army commander, who was reputed to have had a British father. When Magnentius was in turn deposed and committed suicide in 353, the revenge of Constantius II, Constans' brother, was terrible; the imperial official, Paul, who was sent to Britain to deal with defeated rebel supporters, had a dark reputation – he was nicknamed 'the Chain' from his skill at extracting confessions which implicated a web of other suspects, and his habit of crushing his victims with heavy fetters. He unleashed a reign of terror, executing many of Magnentius' former supporters, confiscating their property and even inducing one to commit suicide.

All the same, Britain had been comparatively lucky and suffered far less severely from barbarian attacks than the provinces which lay along the Rhine and Danube frontiers. That good fortune was not to last. New tribal federations had arisen on the northern frontier, and in 367 the Picts, Scotti and Attacotti launched a concerted attack southwards. The Roman historian Ammianius Marcellinus calls it 'a great barbarian conspiracy', and for a while the future of Roman Britain lay in the balance. The invaders overwhelmed Roman defences weakened by decades of neglect, the despatch of units to the Continent to support usurpers and an over-concentration on the south coast. They captured Fullofaudes, the dux Britanniarum, who was probably the officer in charge of the frontier garrison, and killed Nectaridus, the *comes litoris* ('Count of the Shore'), which indicates they had penetrated very far into the south of England. A panicked Emperor Valentinian sent an expeditionary force under Count Theodosius to restore the situation. Fortunately, he made short work of the barbarians, his task made easier by their having split up into dispersed raiding parties, who were further hampered by the weight of the plunder with which they were staggering back towards Scotland.

The moment of immediate danger had passed, but Roman Britain had less than fifty years to run. By now, the empire was pressed on so many fronts that fighting fire on one of them simply invited an outbreak on another. Usurper after usurper feasted on the diminishing spoils of a shrinking empire, ever more dependent on the rising numbers of Germanic mercenaries who filled the gaping holes in the empire's capacity to attract recruits from among its own citizens. In 383, the army in Britain raised up yet another candidate for the throne, Magnus Maximus, who promptly took a large section of the remaining garrison over to Gaul in a bid to fight his way to Rome. Predictably, he was defeated five years later, but the troops never returned to Britain. Stilicho, one of the late Roman empire's last capable commanders (and a barbarian himself, being half-Vandal), pulled out further units in 401, leaving a very diminished force to hold the line against the Picts and Scots on the northern border.

The Roman army had long guaranteed both the security and prosperity of Britain, and at about this time changes are detectable in the archaeological record which indicate that the monetary economy which had helped bond Britain into a wider imperial network was beginning to collapse. Much of the Roman coinage which reached Britain had always done so in the form of payment for the garrison. Now that garrison was much smaller, and so far less of it was needed to pay the troops. From 379, fewer and fewer coins reached the province, and after 402 none seem to have done so at all. Local copies of Roman coinage, which had previously to some extent filled the gap, also disappear.

Across the Channel the situation was deteriorating still further. In late 406, hordes of Vandals, Alans and Sueves breached the Rhine frontier and poured across into Gaul, fanning out and marauding until they reached Spain, which had up to then escaped the worst of the barbarian attacks. With little direction coming from Rome (or even Gaul), the Roman army in Britain once more raised up a series of usurpers. First was Marcus, who proved a disappointment and was deposed in favour of a civilian named Gratian, who may have been locally born, rather than an incomer from Italy or Gaul. When he, too, showed himself utterly ineffective, the soldiers selected a military man, Flavius Constantius, who took on the regnal name Constantine III as a homage to his illustrious predecessor (who had also been elevated by the British garrison).

Constantine's first, and almost only, act of policy was to take virtually the whole of what remained of the British garrison over to Gaul in a futile attempt to win the crown of the rapidly shrinking empire.

In Britain, the exasperated civilian elites did an amazing thing. As the sixth-century historian Zosimus, looking back on the events, wrote, they 'took up arms and incurred many dangerous enterprises for their own protection, until they had freed their cities from the barbarians who besieged them. In a similar manner, the whole of Armorica, with other provinces of Gaul, delivered themselves by the same means; expelling the Roman magistracies or officers, and erecting a government, such as they pleased, of their own.' It was a rare civilian rebellion, and by expelling the last imperial officials, Britain in effect declared independence from the empire.

This extraordinary rejection was not a precocious act of nation-building, and was born more out of frustration that the central authorities were not doing enough to protect Britain. Yet their actions showed that by now Britain had distinct interests and it was seen as a political unit over which control should not be imposed from elsewhere. It was the first concrete expression of a tradition that would embed itself very deeply in later centuries, through invasions by Anglo-Saxons, Vikings and Normans. The Romans had given Britain an identity, and, though their legions left and their buildings crumbled, this sense endured.

Nobody could have known at the time that the legions and auxiliary cohorts would not return to restore imperial control; after all, they always had done so in the past. In 410, though, probably in response to an appeal from Britain for aid, Emperor Honorius made it clear that the Britons could expect no aid from Rome and advised them to look to their own defences. Having taken back control, Britain was on its own, and its vulnerability was almost instantly highlighted by a large Saxon raid in 410–11, which devastated large parts of the province. Much of what had bound Roman Britain together was already dissolving, and the process now accelerated. Although provincial villas were still thriving in the late fourth century, the towns were already in decline, with municipal buildings falling into a state of disrepair and very few of the inscriptions celebrating new constructions which characterized Roman civic pride. By the 430s, many towns show layers of 'dark earth' which may represent the turning-over of areas in the centre to agricultural activities, and only a few towns, such as St Albans and Canterbury, display any sign of a significant population continuing to reside in them.

With the centre in crisis – the western Roman empire itself would collapse in 476 – very late Roman writers had far too much on their mind to be concerned about events in Britain, once again cut off beyond the bounds of Ocean, and we have very little concrete information about what was going on there. Two trips to Britain by the cleric St Germanus of Auxerre in 429 and 447 indicate some continuity with Roman culture (indeed the society is often called 'sub-Roman' by modern historians). Germanus encountered local dignitaries with Roman-sounding titles such as 'tribune', although the historical veracity of the account of his visits are somewhat cast into doubt by the alleged victory he helped win against a party of raiding Anglo-Saxons by having the Britons chant 'Hallelujah', at which the terrified pagan barbarians are said to have turned and fled.

In 446 the Britons are reported to have made one last appeal to Rome. Directed to 'Agitius' (most likely Aëtius, the western Roman empire's last really effective general, whose defeat of the Hunnish leader Attila in 451 gave the empire a couple of decades of extra life), the 'groans of the Britons' depict their plight simply, but starkly: 'The barbarians drive us to the sea, the sea drives us to the barbarians, between these two means of death, we are either killed or drowned.' No help came. The former Roman province dissolved into a patchwork of petty kingdoms, which may represent the re-emergence of long-submerged Celtic identities and the towns, the cornerstone of Roman culture, were largely abandoned. It seemed that Britain had little to show for its 367 years of Roman rule. Cut off from the larger political entity on which it had depended for so long, Britain was turning inwards at the same time as it was subjected to the external shock of barbarian invaders against whom it had no defence.

Yet not all was lost, and the Roman occupation bequeathed much to Britain (aside from fuelling Victorian historians' later obsession with measuring almost any era of history, and most notably that of the British empire, against the template of Roman constitutional and military practice). The fact that almost the whole of the island had formed part of one political unit survived in a dim sense that even if the inhabitants of 'Britannia' did not serve a single master and, indeed, spoke different languages, there was some notion of a common heritage. The implantation of Christianity in Britain also planted the seed of the idea that there was a wider community, looking to the head of the Church in Rome, in which the British played a part.

For the moment, though, the Pax Romana (the Peace of Rome) was over. Britain's precocious unity was at an end, and the map was about to undergo a radical series of changes, which would offer a tantalizing series of hints as to the final shape of the nation, with the beginnings of the emergence of England, Scotland and Wales as separate centres of political power.

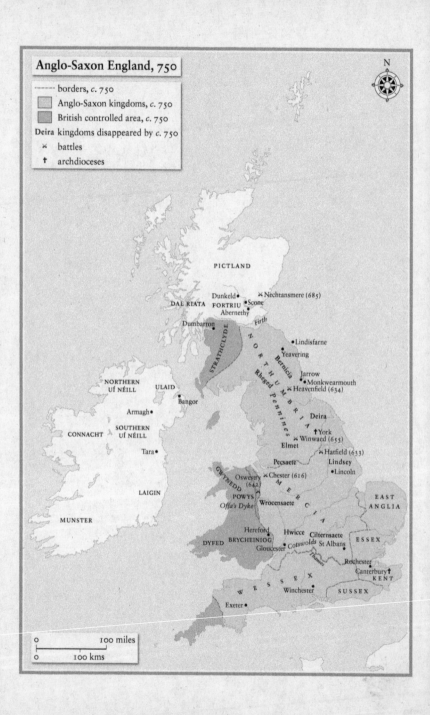

Anglo-Saxon England, 750

------ borders, c. 750

⬜ Anglo-Saxon kingdoms, c. 750

⬛ British controlled area, c. 750

Deira kingdoms disappeared by c. 750

× battles

✝ archdioceses

N

PICTLAND

Dunkeld ● ×Nechtansmere (685)
DAL RIATA FORTRIU ●Scone
Abernethy

Dumbarton ●

Firth

● Lindisfarne

Yeavering ●

STRATHCLYDE

Bernicia

Jarrow ●
● Monkwearmouth
Rheged Heavenfield (634)

NORTHERN
UÍ NÉILL   ULAID

Bangor ●

Armagh ●

CONNACHT   SOUTHERN
UÍ NÉILL

Tara ●

Pennines

Deira

✝York
× Winwaed (655)
Elmet

Elmet ×Hatfield (633)
Lindsey

Pecsaete ● Lincoln

LAIGIN

GWYNEDD
Oswestry ×Chester (616)
(642)

MERCIA

POWYS
Offa's Dyke   Wrocensaete

MUNSTER

EAST
ANGLIA

Hereford Hwicce
Cilternsaete
DYFED BRYCHEINIOG ● St Albans
Gloucester ● Cotswolds

ESSEX

Thames

Rochester ●
Canterbury ✝
KENT

W E S S E X
× Winchester
SUSSEX

Exeter ●

0 ————————— 100 miles

0 ————————— 100 kms

3 Anglo-Saxon England

If the Romans made Britain, the Anglo-Saxons created England. Or, at the very least, their coming drew a veil of historical forgetfulness over what had gone before, erasing Romans and Celts from Britain's origin narrative. The result is that all that is deemed special and particular about Britain is frequently traced to 'Anglo-Saxon' roots, despite the manifest achievements and centuries of occupation by their predecessors (and by the Celtic peoples who remained in place in Scotland, Wales and Ireland). What the Anglo-Saxons did do, though, is to give England a 'people'. No longer part of an empire, the southern part of Britain instead came to define itself with an ethnic label, as Anglo-Saxon and then as 'English'. They gave it, too, a new form of split personality, as the spread of Christianity created a mass of believers looking to a spiritual authority that lay outside the island, in Rome.

The Anglo-Saxons were just one more grouping among the waves of invaders who breached the crumbling frontiers of the Roman empire in the early fifth century. They were not even a single tribal federation (like the Goths or Franks in Europe), but a disparate group of war-bands, referred to by chroniclers variously as Angles, Saxons, Jutes and Frisians. Only much after the fact (in the eighth and ninth centuries) did they receive the unifying label Anglo-Saxon. And their conquest was a slow-motion one: it took a century and a half for the newcomers to advance from small bridgeheads on the east coast to a point where they had penned the Britons into the far south-west of England, Wales and the northern half of Scotland.

In the end Celtic Britain was more smothered than smashed. The crazy mosaic of small tribal states into which it descended after the Roman departure could offer only fitful and disorganized resistance to the newcomers. Occasionally there were victories and the odd heroic leader about whom to compose a lay or two, but only geography – the perennial difficulties faced by a power based in Britain's core in controlling its periphery – would halt the Anglo-Saxon advance.

Who, though, were these Anglo-Saxons, and how did they come to conquer much of Britain, gifting it a new language (as Latin and Celtic tongues withered away) and – in the south – a new identity as 'English'? The evidence of the brooches, pots and weaponry found in their cemeteries and of a thin dossier from contemporary chronicles suggests that they came from a strip of the north-west European coast from the Netherlands to north Germany and Denmark (and possibly southern Sweden). Like their cousins who remained in Germany and Scandinavia, they were a warrior people, whose rulers, delighting in boastful show, gloried in victory and won allegiance through generous gift-giving. The Anglo-Saxon poem *Beowulf*, whose origins stretch back into the seventh century, speaks of the king's 'large and noble feasting-hall, of whose splendours men would always speak, and there to distribute as gifts to old and young all the things that God had given him'. Power was not an intangible thing. If it could not be displayed, it did not exist.

Of course, not all the invaders were from the elite: where their dead were buried (as opposed to cremated), the grave goods were often humble, but still included jewellery for the women and weapons, such as swords and shields, for the men. Even at the lower levels of society, show was all. When such a people arrived in a strange land, they naturally began to create stories to celebrate their achievements and to justify their possession of the land they had seized. This myth-making began early and, though it obscures the exact progress of the conquests and the fate of the native Britons, it does tell us what the newcomers wanted later generations to believe.

Foundation myths are often told by people who need to create a single story around which disparate groups in society can rally, building a common narrative, or to talk up a past which is not as glorious as its tellers would like. So it was with the Anglo-Saxons. Their warring chieftains traced their genealogies from Woden, king of the gods, while even their hard-pressed opponents had their heroes: traditions about Arthur, a shadowy British war-leader whose reputed fight-back against the Anglo-Saxons won him enduring fame, created a sympathy amongst later English scholars for their Celtic foes. This confused the Victorians in particular, who – despite their general obsession with Classical history and the virtues inherent in the Roman way of life – discerned in the Anglo-Saxons the basis of what they saw as a British belief in sturdy individualism and rights independent of the whim of a monarch.

So when the Anglo-Saxons recounted the arrival of their ancestors some time in the fifth century, they saw them as sailing in unlikely flotillas of exactly three ships, each to set up their own discrete fiefdom which later blossomed into kingdoms such as Kent, Wessex (in the south and west of England), Mercia (in the Midlands) and Northumbria (in the north). The personalities which emerge from this dawn of English history are almost certainly legendary: the two Saxon brothers whom Vortigern invited to Kent, Hengist and Horsa, have names which mean 'stallion' and 'horse' and are more likely derived from tribal tradition than referring to actual people. Wessex was founded by Cynric and Cerdic (whose Celtic name suggests that there was a strong surviving British community which needed to be reflected in the foundational myth). Sussex, meanwhile, had an unusually large complement of founders, with Aelle accompanied by his three sons Cymen, Wlencing and Cissa; the latter two gave their names to Lancing and Chichester ('Cissa's fort'), showing how persistent echoes of such stories can be. Even the diminutive Jutish kingdom on the Isle of Wight was not left out and was said to have been established by a certain Stuf and Wihtgar (whose name, though in fact a corruption of Vectis, as the Romans called it, is rather too conveniently close to 'Wight').

Such bands of pioneers were implausibly small to have undertaken the conquest of most of southern England. Rather than the existing British population being virtually wiped out or fleeing from the Saxons, most of them probably remained exactly where they had always been, farming the land, marrying off their children to the newcomers and gradually discarding their own Celtic language and dress in favour of the Germanic style and tongue of the invaders. DNA analysis of the modern population of England has yielded varying results for the component contributed by the Anglo-Saxons, from suggestions as high as 38 per cent to a more modest assessment that Anglo-Saxon DNA is no higher than 15 per cent in eastern England (and about 4 per cent for England more generally). Some of this may even represent an input from later invaders, as the DNA of the Vikings, who arrived three or four centuries later, can be hard to distinguish from that of the earlier invaders. For the most part, rather than fighting the Anglo-Saxons, the British became them.

When the Anglo-Saxons arrived, some time between 420 and 450 – archaeology suggests the former, historical sources the later date – they found a land in chaos. Classical civilization had not simply vanished the moment the Roman legions left in 410, but the lack of a central authority soon took its toll. One of the few accounts we have of a visit to England in this period is that of St Germanus of Auxerre in 429, who was sent to suppress Pelagianism, a strain of fifth-century Christianity whose emphasis on the fundamental goodness of humanity was, odd though it may seem to modern tastes, regarded as heretical and in need of being stamped out. During his travels in England, Germanus encountered British notables with Roman-sounding titles such as *vir tribuniciae potestatis* ('a man with the power of a tribune'), which shows at least some memory of the old forms of organization had survived. Similarly, although urban life seems to have been in steep decline by the fifth century, some town-dwellers, at least, survived, and Germanus went to Verulamium (St Albans), where he visited the shrine of the British martyr Alban.

Education in Latin was evidently still available over a century after the arrival of the Saxons: the nearest we have to a contemporary account was compiled around 540 by Gildas, a monk who probably lived somewhere in the south-west of England. Written in a fluent and literary style, his *De Excidio Britanniae* ('On the Ruin of Britain') is as gloomy about the prospects for his fellow Britons as its name suggests. Indeed, his intention was never to provide a consistent year-by-year account of events – even if the information he had access to allowed it – but instead to demonstrate to his fellow Britons that the invading Anglo-Saxons were God's punishment for their sinfulness. His account is colourful; its tale of fire and plunder helped establish the notion that the invaders simply wiped the slate clean, destroying all traces of the British past. Typical of Gildas' doom-laden prose is his description of the Saxons as 'a pack of cubs burst forth from the lair of the lioness, who lit the fire of vengeance, justly kindled by former crimes, spread from sea to sea, fed by the hands of our foes in the east, and did not cease, until, destroying the neighbouring towns and lands, it reached the other side of the island, and dipped its red and savage tongue in the western ocean'. Little, if Gildas' account is to be believed, was left of the British kingdoms, as 'All the columns were levelled with the ground by the frequent strokes of the battering-ram . . . in the midst of the streets lay the tops of lofty towers, tumbled to the ground, stones of high walls, holy altars, fragments of human bodies, covered with livid clots of coagulated blood, looking as if they had been squeezed together in a press'. Gildas reserves his particular ire for the kings whose unjust rule has attracted the wrath of God and brought ruin to the land. Britain, he laments, 'is a land fertile in tyrants'. They, not the Saxons, are the true villains of his story.

More flesh is added to Gildas' grisly account by the *Ecclesiastical History of the English People*, written around 730 by the Jarrow-based monk Bede. Despite never straying from his remote monastic home in the north-east of England, Bede had a surprisingly wide perspective and a level head, trying to discriminate between sources he regarded as unreliable and those he trusted. Yet he, too, had an agenda – the coming of Christianity and the growth of the English Church are the centrepieces of his narrative, against which all else is framed. Almost inevitably, therefore, it is the wickedness of the Britons that causes their downfall and replacement by the (less perfidious, if still pagan) Saxons.

The invaders arrived in Britain not with a bang, but with a betrayal. The year, according to Bede, was 449, three decades after the departure of the last Roman army units, and the Britons, having given themselves to 'drunkenness, hatred, quarrelling, strife, envy' and all kinds of other vices, were afflicted by a 'virulent plague [which] suddenly fell upon these people' and 'fierce and very frequent attacks of the northern nations'. In desperation, Vortigern, the ruler of one of the British kingdoms which had sprung up in the former Roman province, invited a band of Saxons to settle in Kent. In return for supplies of food they were to keep out any other barbarians minded to continue raiding. Word of Vortigern's weakness and the 'slackness of the Britons' simply encouraged other Saxons to try their luck and demand the deal be extended to them, too. Eventually, a party at Vortigern's court objected, which led the barbarian mercenaries to revolt, ravage the countryside and then spread out in all directions, pushing the terrified Britons westwards. Those who did not succumb to fire, sword or disease were reduced to leading 'a wretched existence, always in fear and dread, among the mountains and woods and precipitous rocks'.

The scenario seems plausible. Small in number at first, the Anglo-Saxons provided convenient extra muscle in the struggles between the British kingdoms, before becoming power brokers and eventually powers in their own right. *The Anglo-Saxon Chronicle*, compiled from the late ninth century as a history of the royal house of Wessex, provides some sketchy details about the early stages of their advance. First the invaders established small bridgeheads. To add to that in Kent, another group led by Aelle landed in Sussex in 477 and before long massacred the defenders of the old Roman shore fort at Anderida (Pevensey); while in 495 Cerdic brought five shiploads of warriors and pushed out into the Upper Thames Valley and the Cotswolds to begin the conquest of what would become Wessex. Further groups landed on the east coast, seizing land in East Anglia and Northumbria, while others penetrated the Humber estuary and struck inland into the Upper Trent Valley around Lichfield and Tamworth. Their position on the exposed frontier with the remaining British-ruled territories gave the name to their kingdom, Mercia, the 'land of the border people'.

By around 600, these fluid war-bands had congealed into the nucleus of kingdoms. For the first time we read of rulers whose existence is independently verifiable. Among the most important of these was Kent, which rose to prominence under Aethelberht (r. c. 550–616). With its capital at Canterbury (the old Roman Durovernum Cantiacorum, tribal centre of the Canti people, which became corrupted in Anglo-Saxon to Cantwaraburg), Kent controlled the quickest crossing to the Continent, and so was strategically situated to take advantage of trade with Europe and to act as a conduit for cultural influence passing northwards from Gaul. Ultimately, however, its expansion was blocked to the west by the West Saxons of Wessex, who from an original base in the Thames Valley, where they were originally known as the Gewisse, expanded deep into Wiltshire under Ceawlin (r. 560–92).

Further north, East Anglia emerged under the Wuffingas, whose ruling dynasty may have been of Swedish origin. We learn surprisingly little of the East Anglian kingdom in later sources – its failure to thrive meant it was edited out of the main historical narrative – but it was clearly rich, as the stunning ship burial, excavated in 1939 at Sutton Hoo in Suffolk, showed. Among a spectacular array of treasures packed into the ship's central chamber were silver bowls from the Byzantine empire, coins from Frankish mints across the Channel and a lavish helmet, with gold-embossed nose, face and cheek-pieces, which very much resembles a late-Roman cavalry parade helmet. Trade, or at least the acquisition of desirable trinkets from far-off lands, was clearly a habit acquired very early by the Anglo-Saxon settlers. The eclectic series of influences was topped off with a set of silver christening spoons (engraved with the names Saulos – St Paul's name before his conversion – and Paulos), which suggests a Christian burial, and a tapered whetstone to which the figure of a bronze stag had been attached, which is more indicative of pagan belief. The scale of the burial indicates the deceased was of very high status, possibly even royal, and candidates for his identity have included Raedwald, the first king of East Anglia whose name we definitely know, who died around 624. The religiously ambiguous nature of the grave-goods fits in perfectly with his career: an early convert to Christianity, he later reverted to paganism when the new religion seemed to be faltering.

Raedwald was the fourth of eight rulers to whom *The Anglo-Saxon Chronicle* assigns the title 'Bretwalda' (or 'Britain-wielder'), a type of over-kingship which represented a temporary superiority over other kings, but not any kind of formal position. The Germanic tradition of warrior kingship meant that success in battle was central to gaining and retaining power, while defeat could rapidly lead to the dissolution of tribal alliances and even the disappearance of kingdoms. To be a Bretwalda was to be at the summit of a very unstable pyramid. Power shifted dramatically between the infant Anglo-Saxon states during the sixth and seventh centuries, and their numbers gradually declined as the smaller ones were eaten up by more aggressive rivals. Finally, their number was reduced to around seven (East Anglia, Essex, Kent, Sussex, Wessex, Mercia and Northumbria), a system known to historians as the Heptarchy. Those who bordered on the lands of the Britons had more room to conquer land (and win glorious victories), and by around 650, the three frontier-states, Wessex, Mercia and Northumbria, had established a clear dominance.

Yet the Heptarchy always concealed a more complex pattern of states, some of which retained a shadowy existence under their new masters. The Tribal Hidage, a compilation of tributes owed by various regional groups, which survives in a copy dating from around 1000 (but probably draws on information collected several centuries earlier), lists some thirty-five different peoples and the amount of land in hides (roughly the amount of land needed to support a single family) which each of them occupied. Included among them were leviathans such as Wessex (at 100,000 hides) and Mercia (at 30,000 hides), and smaller kingdoms, or sub-kingdoms. The Wreocensaete, Magonsaete and Hwicce in the west were ultimately absorbed by Mercia, while the Lindesfaran of Lindsey oscillated between control by the Mercians and Northumbrians. Minor peoples, such as the minuscule Pecsaete of the Peak District, who owed tribute for a mere 1,200 hides, and the East Wixna (in Cambridgeshire) who occupied just 300 hides, are probably typical of the smaller groups which had characterized the first stage of the conquest in the fifth century and had long since lost any real independence

By the time the Heptarchy was established, Celtic control over eastern England had already collapsed. There were brief respites. Bede tells us that a certain Ambrosius Aurelianus, 'the sole member of the Roman race who had survived this storm in which his parents ... had perished', won a series of victories, culminating in a battle, which he dates to 493, at a place called Mons Badonicus (Mount Badon), leading to a pause of several decades before the Saxon advance resumed. It was the kingdom of Wessex which conducted this long fight against the Britons of the south, expanding rapidly from the upper Thames Valley until a lull – whose beginning coincides with Bede's dating of Ambrosius – of about half a century. That pause also marks the appearance of one of history's most attractive, ambiguous and elusive heroes: Arthur, who became the symbol of Celtic resistance and also, by a curious process of inversion, the imagined future saviour of his Saxon foes.

We may never know for sure whether the King Arthur of fable, or someone like him, actually existed, but more important is the almost mesmerizing quality of his legend. Not mentioned by name until the ninth century (when the Welsh cleric Nennius included his tale in his *Historia Brittonum*), the bare bones of the Arthur story are unglamorous – that he first fought for the Britons at Mons Badonicus, won many victories thereafter, throwing back the Saxon advance and was then betrayed by his own nephew at the Battle of Camlann forty years later (which by Bede's reckoning would be around 540). Yet around this skeleton a glorious series of epics, tall tales and romances accumulated. In its final magnificent form, as penned by Thomas Malory in his *Morte d'Arthur* around 1470, Arthur is the grandson of a dragon, advised by a powerful wizard named Merlin, with a following of valiant (but anachronistically medieval) knights, one of whom finds the most sacred object in Christian folklore, the Holy Grail (a chalice said to have been used by Christ at the Last

Supper). At the end, the mortally wounded king is carried off by 'a barge with many fair ladies in it . . . and all they had black hoods, and all they wept and shrieked when they saw King Arthur'. It was said that Arthur was not really dead and that if the land was in peril he would arise, recover his great sword Excalibur and then save Britain, or whatever version of it might exist at the time of his resurrection.

It was all a form of wish-fulfilment, another kind of myth-making. By the ninth century, when Nennius wrote, the surviving Britons, confined to Wales and Cornwall, were in sore need of a reassuring story which spoke of resistance and the promise of future redemption. Later, the Arthur legend provided a common origin for a kingdom which in the eleventh century had become once more a hybrid, of defeated Anglo-Saxons and conquering Normans.

Whether thanks to the disappearance of some Arthur-like leader who had stiffened resistance among the Britons or simply after a period of consolidation from their strongholds in the Thames Valley, the West Saxons resumed their expansion in the mid sixth century. In 577 they won a great victory against the Britons at Dyrham, in Gloucestershire, after which Cirencester, Gloucester and Bath fell in rapid succession to Ceawlin, the first king of Wessex with anything like a solid historical existence. They overran Dorset next, slaughtering the curiously precise number of 'two thousand and sixty-five Britons' at Beandun in 614 before surging westwards into Devon. After that there was another pause, until Cenwalh defeated the Britons in 658 and drove them back to the River Parrett, opening up Somerset to Anglo-Saxon settlement. The kingdom of Dumnonia in Devon continued its resistance, but by at least 700 Exeter was in Anglo-Saxon hands, as the missionary St Boniface – who evangelized parts of Germany and Frisia – was educated at an English monastery there. Cornwall remained the last redoubt of the Britons, fighting on well into the ninth century. A campaign launched by Cuthred in 753 failed to bring them to heel, and when the Vikings appeared off the English coast in the late eighth century, the Cornish turned to them in an expedient alliance against Wessex. It was in vain, as in 815 Egbert launched a searing raid across Cornwall, harrying it from east to west and finally, in a battle at Hingston Down in 838, he defeated a joint Danish-Cornish host, reducing Cornwall to a limp dependency of Wessex. Even then, the Cornish royal house limped on, until in 936 Athelstan of Wessex expelled all the native Cornish still living in Devon, penning them west of the Tamar. Cornwall retained its sense of difference but was now firmly part of Wessex.

Although Wessex established a dominant position in the south of England, on its northern borders it jostled with Mercia, which in turn competed for land and power with Northumbria. War between this trio alternated with peace, as none proved able to achieve anything but a temporary dominance. The fifth, sixth and seventh Bretwaldas in Bede's account are all from Northumbria, established in the mid sixth century as two separate mini-states – Deira, between the Humber and Tees rivers, and Bernicia, to the north of the Tees. These were united in 604 by Aethelfrith (592–616), who enlarged its borders both to the north, where he campaigned against the Manau Gododdin, the descendants of the Votadini, who held the land above the old Roman frontier, and to the south, where he perished in battle against Raedwald of East Anglia in 616.

Aethelfrith's successor, Edwin, who came from the old royal house of Deira, continued this expansion on a much wider scale, campaigning as far as north Wales and subjugating the kingdom of Elmet, an independent British enclave in the West Riding of Yorkshire. Such a successful king needed a palace to match his pretensions, or at least a hall in the old Germanic tradition in which to reward his followers with mead and grants of land. Kingship was a very personal matter, and royal blood was not always enough to secure allegiance – there were always others who could prove or manufacture kingship to the royal dynasty, waiting to pounce at the slightest sign of weakness. It took victories, ostentatious displays and the showering of gold to secure the succession of a (preferably adult) son.

Edwin indulged all this to the full at what was probably his royal place at Yeavering (which Bede referred to as Ad Gefrin, 'the hill of the goats'). Close to an Iron Age hill-fort, one of Edwin's predecessors, probably Aethelfrith, had established the complex with the construction of a large hall studded with ox skulls (which may have been a temple). To this Edwin added a 'grandstand', a semi-circular timber structure with seats, which could have acted as a venue for large-scale assemblies, and – after a fire destroyed part of the complex – he installed an even larger hall and a huge wooden enclosure which could hold enormous herds of cattle. Building all of this required a ruler able to command the loyalty and labour of large numbers of workers over an extended period of time.

At the start of the seventh century, then, Northumbria was the most vigorous of the Anglo-Saxon kingdoms and perhaps even set to extend its hegemony into the south of England (reversing the assumption, in later English tradition, that the political powerhouse of the nation always lay in the south). All Edwin's gains, however, came crashing down when he came up against a curious alliance between Penda, the resolutely pagan king of Mercia, and Cadwallon, the Christian British ruler of Gwynedd.

Wedged between Northumbria, Wessex and the earliest Anglo-Saxon settlements in eastern England, Mercia was vulnerable to expansion by any of these, and faced the constant danger of fighting a war on two fronts (and a possible third against the Britons of Wales) which might have squeezed it out of existence. It required a ruler with very special qualities to overcome this handicap, and Mercia was fortunate to have Penda as its ruler in the mid seventh century, an able and tireless campaigner who raised his kingdom up into a military power to be reckoned with. His alliance of convenience with Cadwallon suited both parties; curbing Northumbria's ambitions would remove a threat to both of them. In 633 the allies assembled an army, marched north and somewhere near Hatfield Chase in South Yorkshire they defeated and killed Edwin. The Northumbrian kingdom fell apart into its component Deiran and Bernician kingdoms, and Cadwallon engaged in a victorious rampage through the north, which might well have resulted in a British renaissance there had it not been for his own defeat and death against the Bernician prince Oswald late in 634 at the evocatively named Battle of Heavenfield, just south of Hexham.

Although Penda stifled Oswald's restoration of the Bernician kingdom when he killed him in battle at Maserfelth (probably Oswestry in Shropshire) in 642, Mercia's insoluble geographic problem was underlined when Penda in turn perished in battle in 655. His carefully constructed coalition of Britons and subordinate Anglo-Saxon kings fell apart, leading to a swing of the pendulum once more, this time in favour of Wessex. In the three-handed chess match that was Anglo-Saxon power politics, the centre of the board was a distinctly uncomfortable position to occupy.

Anything that might cement royal power provided a distinct advantage in this complex game. From the seventh century, kings tried two new strategies, both of which involved giving up a little of their own freedom of action to produce a reason beyond brute force that their subjects should obey them. The first of these was religion, the second law. Ine (r. 688–726) ordered the compilation of Wessex's earliest law code, setting down in written form a set of customary laws and enshrining the notion that there were rules which had to be conformed to, separate from the immediate will of the king.

Many of these laws acted to royal advantage ('If anyone fights in the king's house, he shall forfeit all his property'), but they also reflect the preoccupations of a society whose security was fragile and which lived in constant fear of uncontrollable violence. Foreigners were especially suspect, so that 'If a man from afar, or a stranger, travels through a wood off the highway and neither shouts nor blows a horn, he shall be assumed to be a thief.' And being labelled a thief was a truly unfortunate event as 'He who kills a thief shall be allowed to declare on oath that the man he slew was guilty' (and so the killer would not suffer any penalty for murder). Despite the preoccupations of a predominantly rural community which needed a law to state that 'An ewe with her lamb is worth a shilling, until a fortnight after Easter', society was becoming more complex:

the law code sets out a comprehensive set of monetary fines for misdemeanours as well as a tariff of wergild, the payment due as compensation for murder, which ranged up to 1,200 shillings for a member of the king's household. Not all foreigners were immediately suspect, and there were clearly still identifiable communities of Britons living within Wessex's borders, who needed to be fitted into the social hierarchy. Ine's code lays down a separate tariff of wergild for them – they are referred to as *wealas* or 'foreigners' (the word later took on the connotation of 'slaves'). The blood-money due for their murder varied from 60 shillings for a landless man to 200 for a horswealh (a rider in the king's service). It was not as high a level as that paid for crimes against their Anglo-Saxon counterparts, showing that legally sanctioned discrimination against foreigners is nothing new, but it does indicate that, two centuries after the initial conquest, some of these could achieve relatively high social status.

Religion provided an even more potent affirmation of royal power. The early Anglo-Saxon settlers in Britain were pagans, worshippers of a pantheon of Germanic gods, but we know very little about their religious practices, and virtually the only evidence of their temples and other sacred places is in the form of place-names such as Wednesbury (named for Woden, the supreme god), Harrow (from the Old English *hearh* or 'temple') and Wye (derived from Old English *wēoh* or 'idol'). Gods like Woden and Thunor (the Anglo-Saxon version of Thor) were the subject of entertaining tales – such as that thunder was the sound of Thunor striking his war-hammer in anger against an anvil – and acted as a model against which the virtues of a king could be measured (the gods were almost a Germanic war-band in the sky). Yet while their example might enhance loyalty to a particular king, it did little to increase respect for the office of kingship as a whole.

It was a cultural influence from Europe that provided Anglo-Saxon kings with a firmer basis for their power. Christianity laid down a division of authority in which kings were supreme in secular matters, as long as they recognized the authority of Christian bishops in spiritual ones. Whereas before those who disobeyed the king faced little sanction if he were weak, now they faced the prospect of eternal damnation for opposing him.

Christianity had probably first reached Britain some time in the third century, but had lost ground in the face of the Anglo-Saxon invasions, so that what little we know of this earlier, Celtic form of Christianity comes from Ireland, Wales and northern England. The story that we are instead told, by Bede and others, is how Christianity came to England as a result of an initiative by the Pope in Rome and saved the Anglo-Saxons from their benighted heathen state. The initial conduit for the new faith was Kent, which had strong links with already Christian Frankish Gaul, and where King Aethelberht was married to Bertha, a Frankish princess, who was already a Christian and even had her own chapel at the royal court at Canterbury. In 597 St Augustine was despatched by Pope Gregory I to head a mission to convert England, after, it was said, the Pope had seen Anglo-Saxon slaves being sold in the market at Rome and, struck by their blond, youthful good looks, had punningly commented that they were 'Non Angli, sed angeli' – 'not Angles, but angels'. Augustine achieved rapid success. Aethelberht accepted baptism, and the rulers of Essex and East Anglia followed soon after. However, the mission ran into difficulties following Augustine's death in 604, and the demise of Aethelberth twelve years later deprived Christianity of an important protector and led to a wave of backsliding and a general pagan reaction. Raedwald of East Anglia was among those who apostasized.

Christianity was supposed to have offered a bargain by which accepting it meant strengthening royal power, and when the new religion proved itself weak, its adherents began to peel away. The enterprise was rescued by Paulinus, one of a new generation of missionaries who arrived in 604 and who in the 620s struck out from Kent and achieved the conversion of Edwin of Northumbria, providing a second, northern focus for the mission (Paulinus himself would become the first Archbishop of York). Although the death of Edwin in 633 caused a temporary crisis, the church in the north was saved by a series of towering personalities such as Benedict Biscop, who injected monastic rigour and pious determination into their efforts to stamp out paganism and established a functioning hierarchy for the Church. Meanwhile, in the south, Wessex was brought into the fold by Birinus, who baptized King Cynegils of Wessex in 635. Apart from the struggles with the pagan Penda of Mercia, which nearly destroyed Christian Northumbria in the 630s, the main obstacle to the spread of the brand of Christianity championed by the Papal mission came from an unexpected quarter.

Christianity had endured in the north of England and Scotland, nurtured by close connections with Ireland, which had itself been evangelized by a Romano-Briton, Patrick, who had first been taken there as a slave by pirates in the 430s. The young Patrick returned home after six years, but a vision prompted him to return to Ireland, where he began to preach Christianity. In 563, Patrick's spiritual descendant St Columba founded the Abbey of Iona, off the west coast of Scotland, and from there a brand of Celtic Christianity spread out, taking particularly strong root in Northumbria. It was a muscular faith whose spiritual centres were monasteries rather than cathedrals. St Columba was a larger-than-life figure who was said to have provoked battles in his native Ireland, raised a Pictish child from the dead, and whose voice was so powerful it could be heard at 1,500 paces and yet whose humility was such that he washed the feet of even junior monks. It was a foolish king and an even more unwise bishop who would dare cross such figures.

Under the protection of King Oswald, the Celtic Church irritated the Roman mission in the south, and its stronghold at Lindisfarne Abbey represented a particular affront. There were differences of custom between the two, such as the way in which monks were tonsured on their entry into the religious life. While 'Roman' monks had a circle shaven at the top of the head, 'Celtic' monks were shorn in a different fashion (whose shape is uncertain, although it may have been triangular).

More important were differences in the calculation of the date of Easter, which created the tricky situation in which Queen Eanflaed of Bernicia celebrated the most important Christian feast on a different day to her husband, King Oswiu: 'the king had finished the fast and was keeping Easter Sunday, while the queen and her people were still in Lent'. Most important of all was the matter of who had authority over the Church, but this was not openly discussed at a great synod convened at Whitby in 664. Weakened by the eviction of the placement of a pro-Roman abbot in Lindisfarne and after heavy prompting from Oswiu, the synod came down in favour of the Roman calculation of Easter and, implicitly, recognized the authority of the Pope and the Roman-appointed hierarchy in England. A council convened by Archbishop Theodore at Hertford in 672 consolidated the new rules and decreed that bishops should not interfere in each other's dioceses (a measure intended to stop meddling by recalcitrant Celtic bishops) and that monks should not wander from one diocese to another (similarly intended to stop any resurgence in Celtic practice, as itinerant monks had been instrumental in its spread). The Churches in Ireland, Scotland and Wales, meanwhile, stuck to their traditional practices. It was just one more way in which those areas were becoming differentiated from an England which, in religious terms at least, was acquiring a distinct identity. If the Anglo-Saxon kingdoms were still divided among warring kings, they did at least now belong to one united Church, owing obedience to Rome.

Christianity, though, had come to Britain to stay. With its simultaneous guarantee of power for kings and eternal salvation for all who obeyed its rules, it had a universal appeal and a cohesiveness which paganism lacked. There was still the tricky problem of where the boundary lay between royal authority and that of the Church, which would bedevil relations between the two for centuries (resulting in the excommunication of several English kings and, ultimately, the rupture between Henry VIII and the Papacy in the sixteenth century). Even so, adherence to the new religion was clearly often only skin-deep. In his Penitential – a set of church rules – Theodore felt it necessary to state that 'He who sacrifices to demons in trivial matters shall do a year's penance, but in serious matters shall do penance for ten years,' and that 'If any woman puts her daughter upon a roof or into an oven for the cure of a fever, she shall do penance for seven years.' Theodore also prescribed penalties for those who performed incantations, read omens from birds or ate sacrificial food. Christianity clearly still had a long way to go among the common folk.

Northumbria continued in expansive mode under Ecgfrith (r. 670–85), who suppressed a revolt in the Pictish areas of lowland Scotland, which his predecessors had acquired. He then pushed westwards over the Pennines and absorbed the British kingdom of Rheged, even sending an army to Ireland on an expedition to extract tribute. It looked as though Northumbria might revive its glory days under Edwin and sweep south to confront Mercia or Wessex. Ecgfrith's ambitions, though, were greater still. In the late spring of 685, he led an army north into Scotland, determined to smash the Picts once and for all and to conquer the entire Scottish Lowlands. His opponents, under King Bruide, carefully avoided giving battle, luring him deeper and deeper into their territory. Then, at a narrow pass near Forfar called Nechtansmere, the Picts turned and fell on the Northumbrians, massacring Ecgfrith and a good part of his host.

The death of a king was always a dangerous moment for an Anglo-Saxon kingdom, and a death after defeat in battle was a catastrophe. Northumbria would never fully recover, leaving Wessex and Mercia to tussle for supremacy unchallenged. As Bede puts it, 'the hopes and strength of the English kingdom began to fall away. For the Picts recovered their own land, which the English had formerly held'. The prospect of a northern kingdom uniting the lands of the Northumbrians and Picts faded, and instead the boundary between them was pushed south of the River Forth.

While Northumbria tried to stabilize its position, an effort not helped by a succession of usurpers who seized the throne, Mercia now became the leading Anglo-Saxon kingdom, beginning an ascendancy which it exercised for over a century. It was fortunate to enjoy rule by two long-lived and able kings, Aethelbald (716–57) and

Offa (757–96) (whereas Northumbria had a dozen different rulers during this period). Aethelbald turned his focus southwards, exerting Mercian influence over London and achieving a status which led him to describe himself in a charter of 736 as 'king not only of the Mercians but also of all the provinces which are called by the name "South English"'. Aethelbald's direct influence in Wessex was probably in reality fairly slight, although he did campaign against Cuthred of Wessex (r. 740–56), and at the other end of his realm he launched two attacks on Northumbria (in 737 and 740). Although powerful, Mercia was not yet an Anglo-Saxon superpower.

The situation was transformed during the reign of Aethelbald's successor, Offa. The change was not so much in the territorial extent of Mercian control, which was relatively unaltered (though Offa spent more time in the south, in London), but in the ways in which he reshaped notions of kingship, drawing inspiration from the model provided across the Channel by the Carolingian rulers of Francia, and in particular Charlemagne. He minted coins modelled on Carolingian originals and introduced the rite of coronation to Britain for the first time. The anointing with sacred oil of his heir, Ecgfrith, was intended to demonstrate divine approval for his son's succession and was modelled on the ritual which had been performed across the Channel since the 750s.

Offa initially struggled to assert his authority in Kent and even lost areas of Berkshire to Wessex, but once he had asserted his rule there, he was able to act more decisively. He had King Aethelberht of East Anglia executed in 794 and began to exercise direct control over the areas outside the traditional Mercian heartland which had slipped into his orbit. His use of the title king of the Mercians, as opposed to 'Rex Anglorum' (or king of the English), which appears only on a few coins minted in London, suggests that he saw his kingdom as a kind of 'Greater Mercia' and not the nucleus of an English or even pan-Anglo-Saxon state. His successful petitioning of the Pope to allow him to establish Mercia's very own archdiocese at Lichfield (to add to the existing complement of Canterbury and York) is also a sign that Offa's kingship was a very Mercian project.

To the west, Offa is traditionally associated with the massive earthwork that has borne his name from at least the ninth century (when the Welsh monk Asser, who also wrote a life of Alfred the Great, stated that the king of Mercia had constructed a great dyke between Mercia and Wales 'from sea to sea'). Although the initial stages of the Dyke may only have been about 80 miles long and intended to fend off attacks from a resurgent Welsh kingdom of Powys, the labour required to construct its 20-foot-high rampart (and 65-foot width, including the ditch) must have been enormous, needing at least 5,000 men (and possibly far more), whose marshalling and provisioning suggest a formidable organizational capacity available to the Mercian rulers. As well as its more prosaic function in setting a boundary between England and Wales – in itself an acknowledgement that the great age of Anglo-Saxon expansion was over – the Dyke is a powerful ideological statement: only the most powerful rulers could contemplate such an undertaking which rivalled that of the great Roman rulers of the past.

Offa saw himself as the equal of the Frankish Carolingian kings (even if they did not quite reciprocate the sentiment). He minted a fine new silver coinage for Mercia in imitation of the reformed Frankish coinage produced by King Pepin, and the coronation of his son Ecgfrith in 787 was a startling innovation. Previously, Anglo-Saxon custom had been that a successor be chosen from among the male relations of the king after his death. The anointing of a king's son heir in the lifetime of his father was unprecedented and a sign that kingship was taking on a new status as a hereditary office supported by the Christian Church. Things had moved a long way from the popular acclamation of the Germanic war leaders of old. The Franks, though, still looked down on their Anglo-Saxon cousins with something approaching condescension. Although Charlemagne was initially cordial in their correspondence when the Mercian king had the temerity to suggest a marriage match between his daughter Bertha and Ecgfrith, he was so angry that he imposed a trade embargo, forbidding English merchants from trading in Francia. Offa replied in kind by barring Frankish merchants, setting off a mini trade war that lasted for a decade. By 796, however, cordial relations had been restored between the two, and Charlemagne declared that relations between them should be based on 'the keeping of the laws of friendship joined in the unity of peace, and of the concord of holy love, with the deepest affection of heart'.

Offa did at least draw praise from the English cleric Alcuin who, though born in York, had decamped to Francia to take part in the spiritual and educational renewal that Charlemagne had sponsored. He also tried to act the role of international statesman by inviting Papal legates to England in 786 (the first to visit since the very early days of the conversion) and paying a yearly donation to the Papacy.

England seemed finally to be leaving the chaos of the post-Roman period behind it. It had a sense of itself as a land populated by a particular people, the 'English', who now sought to acquire as much of Britain as they could. Although still fragmented, the number of significant players had been reduced to three (Wessex and Mercia, with Northumbria struggling to retain its place) and the Mercian ascendancy seemed firmly established. If England were to be united, it would have seemed most likely, at the turn of the eighth century, to have come about by Mercia absorbing the others. Christianity had also given a new sense of unity to the English, though not one reflected in the political reality of a still fragmented nation. Had, though, Offa's successor Ecgfrith been as long-lived and capable as his father and had Mercia's greatest challenges been border skirmishes with the Northumbrians and Wessex, then Mercia (and the Midlands), not Wessex (and the south), might have been the core from which England was ultimately born.

Fate decreed otherwise, for Ecgfrith sickened and died after a reign of less than five months (Alcuin blamed the young man's early demise on God's anger at 'the blood shed by the father'). More ominous still, Britain faced its first serious external threat for three centuries. New boatloads of invaders had been seen along its coast, and raiders had struck at a scattering of vulnerable monasteries. The Vikings had arrived.

England in the Viking Age, 878

N

Viking controlled areas, 899

The Danelaw, by Treaty of Wedmore, 886

FORTRIU kingdoms

—·—·— other borders

□ Viking *longphorts* in Ireland

→ campaigns of the Great Army 865–71

reconquered by Wessex, by 919

Orkney

Hebrides

Iona

DAL RIATA

FORTRIU

Dunadd

Dunottar

Rathlin

Dumbarton/Alt Clud (878)

Lindisfarne

STRATHCLYDE

Solway

×Corbridge (918)

Carlisle

Ouse

Lough Neagh

NORTHERN UÍ NÉILL

Bangor

Armagh

Isle of Man

Ribble

KINGDOM OF YORK

×York (867)

Annagassan

CONNACHT

SOUTHERN UÍ NÉILL

Lough Reagh

Dublin

FIVE BOROUGHS

LAIGIN

Arklow

Chester

Derby

•Nottingham

Stamford

EAST ANGLIA

Leicester

Thetford

Limerick

Waterford

Tettenhall (910)×

Hoxne (869)

MUNSTER

Wexford

WALES

ENGLISH MERCIA

Tempsford (917)×

•Bedford

Mersea

Cork

Youghal

St David's

Len

Maldon (991)

Benfleet

Chippenham

London

Sheppey

Edington (878)×

×Ashdown (870)

Lympne

Athelney

WESSEX

Poole

0   100 miles

0   100 kms

4 Viking Britain

793 was the year when everything changed. The delicate balance of power between the Anglo-Saxon states was shattered by the sudden appearance of the Vikings, raiders from the north who harried, assaulted and finally overwhelmed their unsuspecting victims. Fierce warriors who were pushed to raid by harsh conditions and a lack of opportunity in their Scandinavian homeland, they were attracted to Europe's north-west coast by an abundance of lightly defended targets, in particular monasteries with their satisfying accumulation of ecclesiastical silver and jewel-encrusted treasures. Gliding across the North Sea in longships, the latest in maritime technology, whose shallow keels allowed them to beach almost anywhere, the Vikings subjected the British Isles to a 250-year-long period of trial-by-combat.

No one could have foretold that the three ships which appeared off the island-monastery of Lindisfarne were just the first wisps of a storm that would blow away old certainties and destroy long-established kingdoms. They were followed by larger and larger Viking fleets, raids which struck ever deeper inland and armies which conquered large parts of England, Scotland and Ireland. By 878 the Anglo-Saxons were reduced to a soggy refuge in the Somerset marshes, where Alfred, king of Wessex, skulked. He was a pious man and reluctant warrior, and only his stubborn refusal to admit defeat and his genius at inspiring others to resist allowed his minuscule kingdom to survive. Out of this unlikely kernel England grew. It took long and bitter years of bloodshed before the Vikings were finally expelled and England emerged as a single state ruled by a native dynasty. In the end, by destroying the parts of Anglo-Saxon England, the Vikings made it whole.

There was little warning of their coming, unless one counts the unease of the compiler of *The Anglo-Saxon Chronicle*, who notes that 'dire portents appeared over Northumbria and sorely frightened the people. They consisted of immense whirlwinds and flashes of lightning, and fiery dragons were seen flying in the air.' Despite the intermittent warfare between the Anglo-Saxon states, Britain had been free from external threats for over 200 years, and havens such as Lindisfarne Abbey, founded in 634 and home to a succession of renowned scholar-monks and hermits, must have felt themselves doubly protected by their aura of sanctity. When, on 8 June 793, several boats with dragon-headed prows (perhaps, after all, those flying dragons were prophetic) drew up on the beach, its monks might easily have mistaken them for traders. Yet instead of merchants, out of the ships poured small groups of axe-wielding foreigners speaking a barbaric tongue. As pagans, who had no qualms about desecrating a holy Christian site, they concentrated instead on ransacking the monastery and terrorizing the monks, slaughtering some and dragging others off to be sold as slaves. Then, as the practical-minded farmers they in essence were, the Vikings beat a retreat before any local forces could muster to strike back.

Among the Anglo-Saxons, the outrage was palpable. Alcuin, the York-born cleric, thundered from the safety of his refuge at Charlemagne's court in France that 'never has such a terror appeared in Britain as we have now suffered from a pagan race'. He lamented 'the church of St Cuthbert spattered with the blood of the priests of God, despoiled of all its ornaments', although rather spoiling the effect by blaming the raid on divine retribution for the sinfulness of the monks, their lewd practices, excessive drinking and adoption of foreign hairstyles.

The first raid was soon followed by others, as word spread in Scandinavia about the rich pickings to be had in Britain. Monasteries at Jarrow in north-east England, at Iona off Scotland's south-west coast and along the east coast of Ireland all suffered the same fate as Lindisfarne. At first these Viking attacks were little more than nuisance pin-pricks, which the Anglo-Saxon states did little to prevent, failing to coordinate their efforts to see off the attackers. This complacency seemed at first to be rewarded, as from 806 there was a three-decade pause with no recorded raids in Britain – though largely because the Vikings were too busy gorging on the plunder from Ireland's well-endowed monastic houses.

Then, in 835, the Vikings returned, with a raid on Sheppey in Kent. From now on, the attacks were relentless. The raiders arrived in late spring, roved across England through the summer, and in the autumn returned to Scandinavia with their booty. The Anglo-Saxon response was fitful; they possessed no fleets that could give chase, and by the time local levies were assembled to repel the raiders, the Vikings had almost invariably moved on to the next target. Occasionally the Anglo-Saxons did chalk up a minor victory, such as the stinging rebuff delivered to an overconfident Viking war-band in 845 on the River Parrett, where the men of Dorset and Somerset 'made great slaughter' of the invaders. Yet the situation deteriorated dramatically, when the Vikings began to overwinter, saving good raiding time the next spring by not having to risk the North Sea crossing. A Viking fleet did so for the first time in 850 on the Isle of Thanet in Kent, and from then on the raiding season was extended by several months.

The raids spread like an ink-stain across the south and east coasts of England, but the Viking fleets departed in the end, and the Anglo-Saxons could still believe that the attacks would abate, leaving them to concentrate on their petty border squabbles. Too late, they realized their mistake, when a much larger Viking host arrived in 865. The chroniclers called this the 'Great Army' (or in Old English *micel here*), and it probably numbered in the thousands, a huge force by the standards of the early Middle Ages. Northumbria fell first. The Vikings contrived to attack on All Saints' Day 866, when the kingdom's leading men were all gathered in York cathedral. As the raiders stormed through the city gates, the city's panicked defenders and the bulk of its nobility fled. Northumbria's quarrelsome joint kings Aelle and Osberht managed to patch up their differences long enough to launch a counter-attack the following spring and retook their capital, but the Viking horde, which had decamped only as far as the River Tyne, returned and captured York all over again. This time, Osberht was killed in battle, and Aelle, who was captured, was said to have been subjected to the 'blood eagle', a ritual in which the victim's chest was cut open, his lungs were pulled out and pinned to his torso (in grotesque mimicry of an eagle's wings). Even if such tales were slightly exaggerated, the Vikings well understood that their reputation for brutality made each of their warriors worth two in their victims' imaginings.

Mercia was raided (though not conquered) in 868, and then, two years later, the minor kingdom of East Anglia succumbed. Its ruler, Edmund, perished when the Viking war chieftain Ivar tied him to a tree and used him as an archery target, and both it and Northumbria were subjected to Viking-imposed rulers. Mercia, which under Offa just eighty years before had looked likely to subordinate the rest of England to its overlordship, suffered a crushing defeat and, though it limped on as an independent kingdom until 873, it was in no position to oppose the Great Army.

Then, in 871, it was Wessex's turn. A large Viking force struck across the border but was, to everyone's surprise, beaten back in a bloody encounter at Ashdown in Berkshire. A young Alfred the Great nearly died a premature death, when his older brother, King Aethelred, delayed joining the fighting before he had finished his morning prayers. Without the support of the royal bodyguard, Alfred's shield-wall was forced back, and only the opportune death of the Viking commander Bacsecg saved the day. Five Viking jarls were killed, and the Norsemen scurried back northwards. The respite which Wessex gained, though hard-won, was only temporary. Ominously for England's future, the Vikings began to divide out the land between them, parcelling out Northumbria, Mercia and East Anglia into little Viking lordships and earldoms, a sure sign they meant to stay. Three Christian kingdoms had suddenly returned to pagan rule. Psalms were replaced by skaldic poems glorifying the victories of Viking warriors and giving thanks to Odin and Thor. It was all part of a Viking tradition which valued the reputation of a warrior above all else – a famous Old Norse saying declared boldly that 'Cattle may die, kinsmen may die, but one thing will never die, the fame of one who has earned it' – and which included the sagas, longer oral tales which commemorated the deeds of kings and heroic figures such as Eirik the Red, the first settler of Greenland, and Yngvar the Widefarer, whose picaresque adventures included slaying a giant to use its enormous foot as a lure to draw a dragon away from its treasure-stuffed lair.

Wessex and the Vikings continued to spar. In 875, Alfred – who had by now succeeded his brother Aethelred as king – had Guthrum, the Great Army's latest leader, trapped at Wareham in Dorset but let him go on the security of an oath made on a sacred golden arm-ring not to return. It was nearly a fatal mistake. Alfred's trust was rewarded on 6 January 878, just after the feast of Twelfth Night, when his court was celebrating the end of the Christmas season at the royal estate at Chippenham in Wiltshire, and a war party of Danish Vikings led by Guthrum stole through the frozen landscape. As they burst into the palace grounds, panic erupted, and Alfred barely escaped with his life. Accompanied by just a few loyal followers, the king fled and did not stop running until he reached the safety of the Isle of Athelney, some 60 miles distant in the Somerset marshes.

There, in the unpromising setting of a little patch of sodden marshland, one of the most potent of England's national legends was born. Alfred was not a warrior king. He had only succeeded to the throne after three of his brothers succumbed to wounds and disease, and he delighted more in study than strategy. In fact, he was something of a pious prig, but he and his clerical advisers were gifted propagandists. His stint in Athelney, living 'an unquiet life among the woodland, in great tribulation', was later portrayed as almost a martyrdom. From it the king emerged, purged by his suffering, to win greater victories for Christ and for Wessex. The famous legend of his burning of a peasant woman's loaves gave the king an endearingly human quality (although it probably dates from at least a century later and has an allegorical touch, chiding Alfred for failing to tend to his realm, just as he had neglected the loaves, so is not as favourable to him as it at first sight seems).

From his refuge, Alfred issued an appeal for the Wessex levies to meet him at Egbert's Stone, just outside the marshes, a rendezvous point named for one of his more illustrious royal ancestors. His subjects came in their thousands, streaming in from all over the West Country. At the head of this unlikely host, Alfred encountered the Vikings at Edington, just outside Chippenham. The Anglo-Saxon shield wall, bristling with spears, overwhelmed Guthrum's men, and the Danish leader turned and fled. The victorious Anglo-Saxons 'pursued those who fled as far as the stronghold, hacking them down'. After two miserable, hungry weeks besieged in Chippenham, the Danish king capitulated and agreed to be baptized, with Alfred standing as his godfather. Just months before, the ruler of Wessex had been a hunted fugitive, his realm reduced to a few square miles. The unexpected nature of his victory made it all the more satisfying.

It was a moment dripping with symbolism. The pagan warrior who had nearly destroyed Wessex was accepting Christianity, and with it an implied spiritual subordination to the Wessex king. A few lapses into raiding aside, Guthrum kept his part of the bargain, but, more importantly, he made a treaty at Wedmore in about 880 which divided England into two zones. One part, to the south and west of the Rivers Lea and Ouse and Watling Street, comprising Wessex and the west of what had been Mercia, was to remain under Anglo-Saxon rule. The eastern part was the Vikings' portion. Alfred had saved Wessex, but he had condemned the rest of England to permanent alienation to Viking rule. Yet for Alfred the arrangement had its advantages. He married his sister Aethelflaed to Aethelred, the leading Mercian nobleman, so at least pulling half of Mercia firmly into the orbit of Wessex, including London, which he occupied in 886, bringing the future capital of the nation (albeit then a modest trading settlement of around a thousand souls) under his control. He had saved his kingdom, had even enlarged it and had inflicted the worst defeat the Viking invaders had suffered since their descent on Lindisfarne.

The Danish-controlled area came over time to be known as the Danelaw (though the term was not used until almost a century later).

It comprised Guthrum's realm in East Anglia, the Five Boroughs – a set of miniature fiefdoms in the East Midlands – and the Viking kingdom of York (or Jorvik, as they renamed it, unable to get their tongues around the Anglo-Saxon name of Eoforwic). The actual number of Scandinavian settlers here was comparatively light; whereas it was once thought many tens of thousands of Vikings flooded across the North Sea, swamping the indigenous Anglo-Saxons, the probable numbers are now considered to have been around 20–30,000 over the whole Viking period, with DNA analysis suggesting that the most heavy concentration was in Yorkshire (where the Scandinavian component is around 10 per cent). Just as with the Anglo-Saxons, and the Romans before them, Britain had been reshaped by a comparatively small military elite, whose rule was more like a military occupation than a full-scale colonization.

Scandinavian place-names are a good guide to the spreading influence of the new Viking ruling class. Names ending in '-by' (from the Old Norse for farmstead) and '-thorp' (meaning secondary settlement') are scattered throughout the north and east of England, with over 800 '-by' names, of which Grimsby and Derby are but the most famous. Scandinavian customs embedded themselves in northern England, some of them quite esoteric sounding, but sufficiently unlike their Anglo-Saxon equivalents to show that the Danelaw was slowly but surely differentiating itself from the rest of England. The land was not divided up for administrative purposes into 'hundreds', the smallest administrative division in the south, but into *vápnataks*, or 'weapontakes', a reference to a primitive type of Viking armed muster. A category of free peasants or *sokemen* existed in the Danelaw, who owed dues to the lords of the manor, but were at liberty to sell their land, unlike their southern counterparts. It was perhaps a sign of the fierce independence for which the Viking warriors were noted and represents a distant echo of the egalitarian spirit for which northerners would later pride themselves.

As Danish rule consolidated in the north, Alfred remained all too aware that the Viking kings in the north posed a grave threat to Wessex, not just because of the numbers of warriors who had settled there, but because they provided safe havens and bases for new Viking bands arriving from Scandinavia. Guthrum may have hung up his axe and seemed content to lord it over part of East Anglia, but other Viking warlords were not so bound. In 885 and 893 new Viking armies descended on Wessex.

Alfred had been making ready for their inevitable return. Although his preparations were mainly directed at ensuring Wessex's survival, they had the useful side-effect of consolidating royal power after the kingdom's near-death at Athelney. Alfred ordered the construction of a series of fortified towns, or *burhs*, dotted across Wessex. These could provide refuges for the populace in the event of a raid and act as strongpoints which the Vikings, who generally lacked much capability for siege warfare, would find difficult to take. Some larger towns, too, were refounded as *burhs*, including the old Saxon settlement at London, known as Lundenwic, which had suffered particularly badly from Viking raids, and was refounded as Lundenburh, further to the east within the old Roman walls.

The Vikings enjoyed two main advantages in their earlier campaigns against Wessex and the other Anglo-Saxon states. The first, their great mobility on land, Alfred had partly resolved by the building of the *burhs*, which acted as rocks against which the Viking attacks would founder. The second, the ability of the Viking longships to raid at will almost anywhere along the British coastline was harder to counter. Here, Alfred made a bold move, taking the Norsemen on at their own game by ordering the building of Wessex's very own fleet. In 896, the new vessels proved their worth, when six Danish longships were sighted off the coast of Dorset. In a confused encounter, the novice English sailors ended up grounding most of their ships, but they killed 120 Danes (for the loss of sixty-two of their own), and the remaining Vikings were forced to flee in their three remaining vessels. It was a small and hardly glorious beginning, but the encounter at Poole marked the birth of England as a maritime power. Although the Alfredian navy was left to rot away under his successors, a feeling persisted that command of the waves was a prerequisite for the country's defence, and the sense of the sea as a bulwark against England's enemies would become an essential part of the nation's identity.

Alfred also turned to his first love – of words, rather than the sword – to help consolidate his kingdom and instil in the Anglo-Saxons the sense of being one people. Although he was still illiterate when he became king, his conversion to the merits of learning was wholehearted. There was certainly a need for it: as Alfred himself wrote, 'Learning had declined so thoroughly in England that there were very few men this side of the Humber who could understand their divine services in English, or even translate a single letter from Latin into English.' More important than any generalized sense of the joy of books, though, were the very practical implications of literacy. Simply put, it enabled the government to be better run. Charters, law codes and records all acted as sinews which bound the kingdom legally together and provided proofs which could settle arguments through ink rather than bloodshed. In the pre-literate age, only those who heard the king's words directly could be sure of his commands; once they were written down, the messengers and officials who carried them could not so easily be ignored.

Alfred recruited churchmen – among the very few in the ninth century who could read and write. These men, though, were masters in Latin, the language of the Church and of almost all written documents. This was not enough for Alfred. He saw that encouraging literacy in the native Anglo-Saxon tongue would draw the people together in a way that Latin never could. To this end he sponsored the translation of a series of 'books of wisdom', which included the *Dialogues* of Pope Gregory the Great, a collection of ecclesiastical legends; the same Pope's *Pastoral Care*, a more practical manual for clerics; and *The Consolation of Philosophy*. The latter must have been particularly close to Alfred's heart. Composed by Boethius, a Roman senator and the last great philosopher of classical antiquity, as he lay in prison awaiting execution on charges of treason, it may have reminded him of his own time of trial in Athelney. Boethius' exposition of the divine order of the universe very much tallied with Alfred's sense of divine justice as it warned 'Those who have authority in this world cannot do likewise; they cannot from all their wealth grant virtue to those who love it, if they have it not by nature.' Although these books were unlikely to have been translated by Alfred himself – as was once thought – and were hardly to be found in every house in the land, it marked the elevation of Anglo-Saxon to the status of a literary language. As the national tongue of Wessex, and soon that of England, it helped shape the idea that those who spoke it constituted one nation, not many.

Another Anglo-Saxon text played an even more important role in this national consolidation. Although the oldest version of *The Anglo-Saxon Chronicle*, an account of the essential events in England each year, has entries dating back to 60 BC (the year to which it dates Julius Caesar's invasion of Britain), its initial compilation was begun in Alfred's reign and was carried out at Winchester, the royal capital of Wessex. It was undoubtedly a royal project and is biased towards events which took place in Wessex or would be of interest to the royal house of Wessex, meaning we lack a viewpoint of the Viking raids from a Mercian or Northumbrian perspective.

Reading the *Chronicle*'s account lends an air of inevitability to the final triumph of Wessex. Yet it is deceptive, as for all that Alfred had turned England's destiny away from being a Viking realm to one in which the Anglo-Saxons had the leading role, and although he had taken advantage of circumstances to create a situation in which 'king of Wessex' and the 'king of the Anglo-Saxons' were one and the same, there was a long way yet to go. The national border still remained a diagonal stripe across the Midlands, and beyond Watling Street the Danes appeared to be growing in strength. As generation succeeded generation, and the north became accustomed to its Scandinavian overlords, new political units emerged that made a reunification with the south look even less likely. In the 890s Guthfrith began a line of Viking kings of York which would last for nearly seventy years, at times uniting Dublin and York in a Viking state that straddled the Irish Sea and threatening to halt Wessex's ambitions to reclaim the north of England.

The *Chronicle*'s entry on the death of Alfred in 899 is terse, noting only that the king died 'six nights before the mass of All Saints' (i.e. 26 October) and that he 'was king over all the English nation, except for that part that was under the power of the Danes'. The conquest of the Danelaw and the pushing of England's frontiers to nearly the line with Scotland where they lie today was a task that fell to Alfred's sons and grandsons. His successor, Edward the Elder (r. 899–924) faced an immediate crisis when Alfred's cousins, the children of his brother Aethelred, sought to assert their arguably better claim to the throne. One of them, Aethelwold, struck an immediate blow by seizing a royal estate at Wimborne, to which he summoned his followers. When his bid to topple Edward failed to rally much support, he fled to the Vikings of Northumbria (abandoning a nun with whom he had eloped in severe violation of canon law). Aethelwold's new hosts were delighted to receive a pretender who might provide them with leverage in the event of a new invasion. They were even said to have accepted him as their king, but their attempt, in 903, to launch a massive raid into Mercia and northern Wessex ended in disaster. Edward reacted decisively, sending a large force into East Anglia which defeated the Vikings when a 'great slaughter was made on both sides, but more of the Danes were killed'. Crucially, among the dead was 'the atheling Aethelwold, whom they had chosen as their king'.

Wessex was still far from secure, and the English-ruled portion of Mercia was a horribly vulnerable flank. They might strike south again at any moment, and the growing links between Viking-ruled York and Dublin, which were united under a single ruler on several occasions, confirmed a new power axis, bound together by the sea-lanes of the Irish Sea, which transcended the land-based rivalries of the old Anglo-Saxon kingdoms. This danger reached a critical level after 902, when the Vikings were expelled from Dublin by the kings of Brega and Leinster, and they fled across the Irish Sea to found a new colony in north-west England. Spectacular evidence of the Viking presence in northern England comes from hoards such as the Cuerdale Hoard, found buried in the River Ribble in 1840, which included over 7,000 coins and large quantities of hack-silver (or cut-up pieces of jewellery, prized for their weight rather than workmanship), and which may have represented the pay for a Viking army intended to reconquer Dublin.

It was York, though, which remained the de facto capital of Viking England for ninety years, that provided the most intractable obstacle to Wessex's ambitions to incorporate northern England within its borders. We know a great deal about the town in the tenth century, as excavations in the 1970s at the site of the Viking settlement at Coppergate (which means 'Street of the Cup-makers' in Old Norse) unearthed tens of thousands of artefacts. Much of it is comparatively unglamorous – scraps of leather and wood which the waterlogged and oxygen-poor conditions in the sediments alongside the River Ouse allowed to survive – but it revealed a prosperous trading town with plots neatly divided by wattle fences and workshops where craftsmen worked a large variety of materials, including gold, silver, copper, lead, timber, leather, antler and bone.

Edward decided that a policy of aggression would serve far better than waiting passively for the Vikings to attack. After Aethelred's death he sent out raiding parties, turning the Vikings' own tactics back on them, for now it was the Norsemen who were forced to defend a long frontier, not knowing where the Anglo-Saxons might strike. When the Vikings retaliated with a counter-raid on Mercia in 910, Edward caught their army on its way back to York 'rejoicing in rich spoils'. During the ensuing slaughter at Tettenhall near Wolverhampton, three of their kings and eleven jarls were despatched 'to the hall of the infernal one'.

The battle marked a turning point, after which the Vikings never seriously threatened Wessex and instead had to fight a series of rearguard actions to preserve what territory they held. Edward established a series of fortified *burhs*, beginning at Hertford in 912, which pushed the borders of the land of his control ever deeper into the Viking kingdom of York. Six years later he annexed Mercia into Wessex following the death of Aethelflaed, removing the prospect that it might become a weak buffer blocking further advances northwards, while the smaller Viking enclaves in East Anglia and the

Five Boroughs had all submitted to him by 924. The divided and weakened kingdoms which had allowed the Vikings to establish themselves in England were now replaced by a single Anglo-Saxon state, whose ruler Edward referred to himself in charters and on coins as Rex Angulsaxonum ('king of the Anglo-Saxons').

Edward's son, Athelstan, took the inflation of titles even further, becoming the first to adopt the title Rex Anglorum ('king of the English') and even Rex Totius Britanniae ('king of all Britain'). Yet his ambitions outran reality, and the Vikings clung stubbornly on to York. Finally, in 927, after a marriage alliance with the Viking ruling house collapsed, Athelstan took decisive action, driving out Guthfrith and annexing the Viking kingdom. Now in control of the entire north of England, he summoned Owain of Strathclyde, King Constantine of the Scots and Ealdred the son of the English lord of Bamburgh to a meeting at Eamont (near Penrith in Cumbria) at which they were forced to declare their allegiance to him. But Athelstan had overreached himself, and an attack on Scotland in 934 provoked the Scots, the Britons from Strathclyde (who still clung on to their independent state) and Irish Vikings led by Olaf Guthfrithsson to ally to curb the ambitions of Wessex's king.

Their host clashed with the Anglo-Saxon army at a place called Brunanburh, where it suffered a catastrophic defeat in which the Viking contingent fared particularly badly, with five of their kings and seven jarls among the dead. A poem survives, embedded in *The Anglo-Saxon Chronicle*, which recounts with some relish how 'the two brothers, king and atheling, returned together to their own country, the land of the West Saxons, exulting in the battle. They left behind them the dusky-coated-one, the black raven with its horned beak, to share the corpses, and the dun-coated, white-tailed eagle, the greedy war-hawk, to enjoy the carrion, and that grey beast, the wolf of the forest,' and that 'Never yet in this island before this, by what books tell us and our ancient sages, was a greater slaughter of a host made by the edge of the sword, since the Angles and Saxons came hither from the east.'

The poet's exultation at Brunanburh proved premature, and the

Vikings soon returned, recapturing York just two years later and thrusting deep into Scotland. It looked like Athelstan's work was about to be entirely undone with the reconstitution of a substantial Viking state. Yet then the pendulum swung once again, and, with rival Viking warlords claiming its throne, in 946 Eadred of Wessex was able to occupy York and drive them both out.

Viking York still held one final surprise in the form of the most gloriously named of its warrior chieftains. In 948 its hard-pressed populace chose as their ruler Eirik Bloodaxe, a man who has been identified with a contemporary king of Norway, but who was probably a distinct figure. Neither *The Anglo-Saxon Chronicle* nor the Norse sagas recount any particular event that gave Eirik his sanguinary nickname, and the fact that he seems to have been supported by Wulfstan, the Anglo-Saxon Archbishop of York, indicates that, whatever his misdeeds, the Church erred on the side of supporting anyone who could provide a sense of stability. Eirik soon failed in this basic task, and in 949 Eadred expelled him. Three years later he was back, but his second reign was almost as short-lived as the first, and in 954 he fled another invasion launched by Eadred. A hunted fugitive, Eirik was short of friends, and he chose unwisely. Somewhere on the road north from York, at a remote and windswept place called Stainmoor, he was betrayed by Earl Oswulf of Bamburgh, whose lands he was perhaps trying to reach, and killed by a certain Earl Maccus. For his treachery, Oswulf was rewarded by Eadred with the earldom of Northumbria.

The Viking raiders were finally ousted, 160 years after their first descent on Lindisfarne (though they clung on in Ireland for over a century yet and on Orkney, in Scotland's far north, until the thirteenth century). The annexation of Viking York that followed also represents the true beginning of England, since, for the next thousand years, pretenders, rival dynasties, usurpers and invaders may have fought over it, but, even where a temporary division was mooted, everyone agreed that England constituted a single, discrete political entity.

With England united, the kings of Wessex set about giving it a form of administrative unity. The system of shires, which would characterize the map of England for the next millennium, was firmly established (each the province of an official known as an *ealdorman*), and they were sub-divided into smaller units called 'hundreds', in which monthly courts ensured the projection of royal power into the most far-flung localities. The church, too, was reformed, after the battering it had received during the period of Viking rule, when large numbers of monastic houses and even some ecclesiastical sees were abandoned. A campaign of ecclesiastical reform was spearheaded by spiritual powerhouses such as Dunstan, Archbishop of Canterbury from 959 to 988, and Aethelwold, who held the see of Winchester from 963 to 984, and who took a dim view of the laxity which had taken hold there. He found 'evil-living clerics, possessed by pride, insolence and wanton behaviour, [who] repudiated wives whom they had married unlawfully, and took others, and were continually given over to gluttony and drunkenness'. Aethelwold expelled the whole sinful confraternity and had them replaced with monks following a strict interpretation of the Code of St Benedict. In the reformed Church, there was to be no room for backsliding.

Edgar (r. 959–75), the royal patron of these reforms, pioneered a new image of kingship. Not only was he king of all England, but at his coronation at Bath in 973 he was lauded as 'above all the kings of Britain'. The site was carefully chosen to associate Edgar with the grandeur of the Roman empire (whose remains, in the shape of the baths, were still clearly visible). Unlike in modern coronations, Edgar entered the church already wearing his crown, which he removed before prostrating himself in the front of the altar. Then, garbed in a robe decorated with roses to represent martyrdom and lilies for chastity, he was presented with the rest of the royal regalia, ring, sceptre and rod. In a profoundly symbolic moment, Edgar afterwards summoned Kenneth, king of the Scots, Malcolm of Strathclyde, Maccus ('king of the Isles') and five other princes to Chester to swear fealty to him. Whether there is any truth in the twelfth-century story that he had them row him down the River Dee afterwards is uncertain, but the tale adds colour to his clear ambition to be regarded as having primacy over all the other kings in Britain (even if he was very far from being, or even trying to be, king of Britain). It was all a far cry from the distant days of Germanic warrior chiefs.

Power, in the Germanic tradition, had always been wielded at the edge of a sword. It was vital to know who one's friends were, and the warrior's code of honour, coupled with strategic marriage alliances and the occasional application of brute force had been sufficient to hold together the smaller kingdoms of the Heptarchy. The gradual ascension of the kings of Wessex from lords of a small patch of marshland to masters of the whole of England (with aspirations for an even grander status as rulers of all Britain) had required the novel assistance of law codes and charters, to provide written evidence of the king's word, and Christianity to provide a spiritual dimension that commanded obedience.

Diplomacy provided another dimension to this steady consolidation of kingship. Athelstan had already seen its advantages. His fame and reputation for martial success was such that his court became a destination of choice for foreign monarchs wishing to foster their male offspring off to a king from whom the young princelings could learn to be wise rulers and acquire a share in his glory. Thereafter, connections with continental Europe intensified, knitting the fledgling English kingdom into a network of Christian monarchs. Whereas Charlemagne had haughtily turned down Offa of Mercia's mooted marriage alliance, by 856 the status of the kings of Wessex had risen sufficiently for his grandson Charles the Bald to broker the marriage of his daughter Judith to Aethelwulf (Alfred the Great's father), while in 919 a match was arranged between Eadgifu, daughter of Edward the Elder, and the Frankish king Charles the Simple. Athelstan sent a fleet to Flanders in 939 to help Louis IV, their son (and his nephew), who was facing a rebellion there, and Edmund repeated the favour in 946. English armies may not have crossed the Channel (save a fleet which ravaged the Cotentin Peninsula around 1000 to root out a Viking band which had based itself in Normandy), but marital diplomacy created a complex web of family connections that meant exiled princes and fugitive pretenders could expect a warm welcome at the courts of their relatives.

Edgar's reign promised a new golden age for Anglo-Saxon England – his nickname 'The Peaceful' spoke eloquently of the desires of a people who had known far too much warfare. His premature death in 975, while still in his thirties, was a disaster. Edgar's son Edward was only thirteen years old, and for all the new panoply of Christian kingship, the brute fact was that a young king could not be a strong king. Soon the supporters of Edgar's half-brother Aethelred began to dispute the teenager's right to the throne. One monastic chronicler bitterly noted 'the commonwealth of the entire realm was shaken; bishops were perplexed, ealdormen were angry, monks were struck with fear, the people were terrified'. Matters were not helped when Edward was killed in suspicious circumstances in March 978 while visiting Aethelred at Corfe Castle. As *The Anglo-Saxon Chronicle* lamented, 'No worse deed for the English race was done than this, since they first sought out the land of Britain.'

Aethelred was probably too young to have played a role in the murder, but his reign began under a cloud, from which it never really escaped, and his nickname – Unraed (or 'Ill-Counselled', which became corrupted to 'Unready') – is considerably less flattering than Edgar's.

Aethelred, just eleven or twelve when he came to the throne, was badly in need of good advice, for scarcely two years after his accession the Vikings returned. Just as they had been in the first phase, the first attacks were mere probes and hit-and-run raids, but Aethelred's youth, and the fact that he was now the sole surviving male member of the House of Wessex, meant that he could not lead the resistance to the invaders, a troubling slight to his royal dignity. Then, in 991, a sea-change occurred in the nature of the raids. A huge Viking fleet of about ninety ships made its way across the North Sea and landed in Essex. At its head was Olaf Tryggvason, a Norwegian of royal blood. It was the greatest challenge England had faced since the desperate days of the Danish Great Army, and Aethelred's advisers proved unequal to the task.

The Viking host made camp near Maldon, on Northey, an island which is accessible only by a tidal causeway. The Viking's choice of base was characteristic of their tactics; sheltered from attack by land, it also allowed them to strike along a wide stretch of coastline. Byrhtnoth, Aethelred's ealdorman in Essex, made haste with the local *fyrd* (untrained levies) and his own more professional entourage. He was an experienced warrior, having served in his post for thirty-five years, and he formed a shield-wall across the shore, preventing the Vikings from making an easy crossing. Yet Byrhtnoth also faced a dilemma; although there was a theatrical series of challenges and counter-challenges yelled across the causeway, as the Vikings demanded tribute and the Anglo-Saxons rejected it – offering only 'deadly points and tried swords' – the invaders still had the option of simply boarding their ships and sailing away. It was probably for this reason, rather than, as *The Anglo-Saxon Chronicle* says, 'on account of his pride', that he allowed the Vikings to surge across the causeway.

A description of the fighting that ensued survives in a contemporary poem which gives a good sense of the martial pride, heroic posturing, chaotic manoeuvres and sickening carnage that characterized the tenth-century battlefield. Once the 'wolves of slaughter rushed forward' onto the mainland, a bloody encounter took place in which the Anglo-Saxons held their own until Byrhtnoth was wounded when 'a warrior from the sea despatched a spear of southern manufacture'. With their leader fallen, some of his chief retainers began to flee, leaving the remnant of the Anglo-Saxon host to make a last stand. In heroic fashion one of them declares 'the spirit must be the firmer, the heart the bolder, courage must be the greater as our strength diminishes', before turning to face the advancing Vikings and perishing in turn.

Aethelred – or at least his bad advisers – tried to bribe the Viking host to go away, handing over a tribute of £10,000 (a huge sum at the time, enough to buy 3,000 slaves, and around £200 million in modern terms). Predictably, this weak reaction served only to attract fresh raiders in search of a similar pay-off. In 994 Olaf appeared again, but this time he was accompanied by Swein Forkbeard, the king of Denmark. England's network of alliances in Flanders and France might deny ports there to freelance raiders but could do nothing to impede what was, in effect, a state-directed Viking raid on a grand scale. The royal pair ravaged the south coast of England, before being bought off with an even handsomer bribe of £16,000. Although Olaf accepted baptism and agreed never to return to England (a pledge which he actually kept), Swein did not feel himself similarly bound and conducted another huge raid in 1001.

The sorry cycle of paying off the Vikings followed by a brief respite, then new attacks and an even larger bribe, continued for twelve more years, until in 1012 a truly gargantuan tribute of £48,000 was paid to an army led by a Danish lieutenant of Swein's named Thorkel. The strain on the kingdom's resources was severe: in the absence of any regular procedure for taxation, the tax-gatherers simply had to enforce collection of whatever they could, giving rise to complaints of tyranny. Wulfstan, Archbishop of York, composed a sermon in which, as well as blaming the new Viking raids on the sinfulness of the English, he complained that 'houses of God are entirely despoiled of ancient privileges and stripped inside of all that is seemly'.

When Aethelred did try alternative means to scare off the Vikings, these were equally in vain. In 1002, desperate at the slow-motion dissolution of his kingdom, the king ordered the massacre of 'all the Danish men that were in England'. The resulting St Brice's Day Massacre, on 13 November, spared no one: even children 'were dashed to pieces against stones and posts'. It was brutal, and it was ineffective. The very next year, Swein Forkbeard, said to have been incensed by the slaughter of his countrymen, attacked again. The desperate English turned to prayer, and in 1009 Aethelred declared a national campaign of penance and processions to shield England from a new Viking invasion.

This display of faith may have been consoling, but it had no effect on Swein, who in 1013 came again, this time landing with a massive fleet at Gainsborough in Lincolnshire. The old Danelaw rapidly submitted to him, including senior members of the Anglo-Saxon aristocracy, and within months he was the master of all England north of Watling Street. Swein needed reliable local allies, and he cemented his position with a handy marriage alliance between his son, Cnut, and Aelfgifu, the daughter of Aelfhelm, a Northumbrian ealdorman whom Aethelred had had executed in 1006. The young man, who was in his early twenties, was serving on his first campaign abroad and now found himself tied into one of the most powerful families in Mercia (though afterwards, when he contracted a second marriage to Emma, Aethelred's widow, tongues wagged that Harold Harefoot, his son by Aelfgifu, was in fact the child of a cobbler who was smuggled into the royal bed and passed off as the heir).

If Aethelred had expected that Swein would struggle to find support beyond the Danelaw, he was mistaken. The Danes advanced into Oxfordshire, although an attempt to seize London failed when scores of Vikings drowned in a failed crossing of the Thames. But the West Country soon submitted to Swein, and a panicked Aethelred sent Queen Emma and their sons over to Normandy, before fleeing there himself. Finally, Swein had achieved what no Viking leader before him had managed, the conquest of the whole of England. The compiler of *The Anglo-Saxon Chronicle* was unimpressed, relating that 'Nothing therefore was of benefit to this nation, neither from the south, nor from the north.'

Yet the Danish kingdom of England was almost a very short-lived creature indeed, since Swein died in February 1014 after a reign of less than two months (which *The Anglo-Saxon Chronicle* refers to as 'the happy event'). The Danes were instantly thrown onto the defensive, and the Anglo-Saxon nobility invited back Aethelred as king. A chastened Cnut returned to Denmark, but events in England soon prompted him to return, as a revolt by Edmund Ironside, Aethelred's son, and then Aethelred's death in April 1016 provided another opportunity to try to seize the English throne. His cause was immeasurably aided by the support of several Anglo-Saxon noblemen, most notably Eadric Streona, the ealdorman of Mercia. A slippery opportunist, he had climbed to the top by marrying Aethelred's daughter Eadgyth around 1009 and then conniving with

Aethelred in the murders of his rival earls Sigeferth and Morcar. Perhaps Eadric had made just too many enemies at court, but he defected to Cnut, before reconciling himself with Edmund, just in time for the final clash between Danes and Anglo-Saxons at Ashingdon in Essex in October 1016. There, at the height of the battle, Eadric switched sides again, fatally undermining the Anglo-Saxon resistance.

Edmund's forces were crushed, but he still retained enough support to broker a deal with Cnut by which the kingdom was to be partitioned once more, with Edmund receiving Wessex and Cnut taking an enlarged Danelaw, which included much of Mercia (including London). This new variation on how England might be divided would probably not have lasted long, and each side was merely biding its time for a final confrontation. But a new war was rendered unnecessary by Edmund's premature death in November 1016. The Wessex *witangemot*, the council of royal advisers, had little choice but to accept Cnut as their king. The Dane secured his position by marrying Emma, Aethelred's widow (who was the daughter of Duke Richard I of Normandy), and then raised the enormous sum of £72,000 to pay off the bulk of his army. The citizens of London were forced to pay an additional levy of £10,500 to the Danish fleet which had been overwintering there. It was a far greater sum than any of the bribes paid by Aethelred to buy off Cnut's father Swein, and once again ecclesiastical treasuries had to be raided and estates were confiscated from those who were unable to satisfy the tax-gatherers' demands in a hurry.

Although Cnut purged the Anglo-Saxon ealdormen (including the treacherous Eadric Streona, whose murder he had arranged) and gifted their confiscated land to his Scandinavian followers (so that Thorkel received the whole of East Anglia, and a Norwegian called Eric gained Northumbria), his absence in Denmark meant that the government continued largely unchanged. The most troublesome area was the north, where a threat of Scottish invasion brought Cnut back to England in 1031 to lead an expedition against Malcolm II of Scotland. The most widely disseminated anecdote about Cnut, that he arrogantly ordered the tide of the Wash back so it would not wet his feet as he sat on his throne, is in fact a wry comment on the limits of royal power; Cnut knew very well that he could not force the sea to obey him – his power as king was great, but not unlimited.

Cnut's reign marked a turning point for England. Whereas large parts of the north and east had previously been occupied by Vikings, only now did the whole country become a Viking realm. Ironically, it seemed that what Alfred had made possible, and his sons achieved, now the heirs to his arch-enemy Guthrum had inherited. To complicate matters, in 1019 Cnut returned to Denmark to take up the throne vacated after his brother Harald had died. For the first time since the end of the Roman occupation, Britain found itself as part of an international state, this time a Viking empire, bound together by the North Sea, which included parts of Norway and southern Sweden, too.

In time, perhaps, a true Anglo-Danish realm might have emerged which looked eastwards to Denmark rather than south to France, and England's identity may have turned out to be a Scandinavian one. But Cnut's death in 1035 led to a division of his kingdoms. He had probably intended Harthacnut, his son by Emma, to inherit both halves of his empire, but Aelfgifu's son Harold was the only one of the brothers in England at the time, and, as with so many early medieval accessions, physical presence lent the claimant half a hand on the throne.

Harold was technically only regent – the Archbishop of Canterbury refused to perform a coronation with the royal regalia that would have confirmed him as king – and the first part of his reign was marred by a power struggle between his mother Aelfgifu and his stepmother Queen Emma. The daughter of Duke Richard I, Emma was a strong and ambitious woman, the epitome of the 'peace-weavers' who brokered alliances between warring families in the Norse sagas. Her swift marriage to Cnut, after the death of her first husband Aethelred, was intended to seal the peace between English and Danes, and Emma was a formidable champion of the interests of her children, both Harthacnut, her child by Cnut, and Alfred and Edward, her sons by Aethelred. With charge of the royal treasury,

Emma was in a good position to enforce her will and she managed to obtain an agreement, in a reprise of 1016, that she would rule south of the Thames on behalf of Harthacnut, while Harold would be sovereign north of it. The pact, though, soon collapsed, and Emma tried to break with the Danes completely by summoning Alfred, her elder son by Aethelred, who had been in exile with her family in Normandy, in 1016. The attempt ended in failure when the young prince was arrested and brutally blinded and died in agony at a monastery in Ely. Emma fled to Normandy with her surviving son, Edward, leaving Harold untroubled as king of England, save for a few border skirmishes with Gruffudd ap Llywelyn of Gwynedd, a rising Welsh prince.

Harold, who had long been sickly, died in March 1040, just in time to avert a violent confrontation with his half-brother, who was on his way from Denmark to press his claim to the throne he considered he had been denied on their father's death. England's last two years as part of a North Sea empire were inglorious. Its new king, Harthacnut, achieved very little in his reign, save to die after a heroic drinking bout during the wedding of a courtier in June 1042.

The long struggle between the Vikings and the House of Wessex was at an end. The sole plausible candidate for the throne was Emma's son Edward, whom Harthacnut had invited back to England in 1041 (and who was his half-brother). Edward was the great-great-great-grandson of Alfred the Great, and was just as pious as his illustrious ancestor, becoming known as the Confessor, but failed the test of a medieval monarch in other crucial regards: he was no warrior, not much of a leader and he failed to produce an heir. He also lacked the great strength to reconcile the competing factions who wanted a share of power now that the Danes had been driven out. The demands of the Anglo-Saxon earls, such as Godwine of Wessex, and a pro-Norman faction led by Emma proved almost irreconcilable. By the 1050s the English party was in the ascendant: Godwine's son Harold succeeded to the earldom of Wessex in 1053 upon his father's death, while his brother Tostig became earl of Northumbria two years later.

Despite the faction-fighting at court, Anglo-Saxon England had weathered the 250-year Viking phase in its history well. Whereas at its start, there had been no such thing as England, as Mercia, Wessex and Northumbria slugged it out in interminable border wars, by its end England was united, loyal to a single dynasty and with frontiers not too far removed from the modern borders between England, Wales and Scotland. It was a realm that Harold Godwineson, at the peak of his power, seemed set to inherit. With Edward the Confessor aging and heirless, he was the most obvious heir. Even though he was only a member of the royal family by marriage (as his sister Edith had married King Edward), he was the country's most successful military leader, having campaigns against Wales and Scotland under his belt, and he already had three sons (and a clutch of brothers) to ensure the new royal line would not fail. As the old king ailed in early 1066, the country's destiny seemed fixed. Yet within months the whole edifice of the Anglo-Saxon state had come crashing down.

The Normans were coming.

Medieval England, 1171

N

The Angevin empire under Henry II

inherited by Henry II 1150–54
acquired by marriage to Eleanor of Aquitaine, 1152
acquired through accession of Geoffrey as duke of Brittany, 1181
territory conquered in Ireland, early 1170s
lands of French crown, 1170
controlled by Norway
remaining English possessions in France, 1214

SCOTLAND
acknowledged
Henry II as
overlord, 1175

Perth

Edinburgh   Berwick

Carlisle   Newcastle
                 Durham

ULSTER

CONNACHT

MEATH   York
                           Lincoln
          Dublin
LEINSTER   GWYNEDD   Chester
                    POWYS   Shrewsbury

MUNSTER   DEHEUBARTH
Cork
                    Oxford
             Windsor   London
          Salisbury   Winchester   Dover
                                    Boulogne

North sea

English Channel

Rouen   VERMANDOIS
                      VEXIN
       Caen   Évreux   Paris
NORMANDY

          MAINE
Rennes   Le Mans   Orléans
                    TOURAINE
Nantes   ANJOU
POITOU

                 LIMOUSIN
          AQUITAINE   AUVERGNE

          Bordeaux

                         VERMANDOIS

GASCONY

ATLANTIC OCEAN

0   100   200 miles
0   100   200 km

5 Medieval England

England's four-century-long stint as a major continental power, occupying large tracts of France, may come as a surprise to those more accustomed to thinking of Britain as an island, and its imperial phase as one that unfolded centuries later and on other continents. Far from spending the Middle Ages in glorious isolation, Britain engaged in a series of political, military and diplomatic struggles to decide its shape, permutations of which included an Anglo-French colossus (the Angevin empire), a prematurely united Britain under Edward I and even the unrealized prospect of an Anglo-German empire which, together with the English kings' French holdings, would have anticipated the European Union by 800 years.

Looking south across the Channel was nothing new for English monarchs. Yet the Middle Ages brought a qualitative change in this relationship. Fortuitous inheritance, dynastic ties and the naked ambition of an aristocracy steeped in a martial way of life meant that English kings became much more aggressive, engaging in near-constant warfare to acquire and maintain territories in France, while struggling to balance this with equally avaricious land-grabs in the other nations of the British Isles. It was a juggling act in which they eventually failed, and when it all unwound in the fifteenth century, England found itself bounded territorially largely within its modern frontiers. How this expansion, contraction and reversion to an insular status unfolded is vital to understanding the later development of England, and then Britain.

On the surface, England enjoyed a great deal of continuity between 1066 and 1485. Apart from occasional spasms of civil war, a single monarch ruled a united land, with a largely agrarian economy, supported by a network of prosperous towns. Despite the French-speaking predilections of the Norman kings, the native language survived and developed a lively literature. Yet those four centuries also wrought fundamental changes. The growing demands of the monarchy called into being an increasingly sophisticated bureaucracy and royal power, its reach deeper into the provinces, making England the most centralized nation in Europe (its Anglo-Saxon predecessor, although comparatively sophisticated by European standards, had stood at the apprenticeship of England as a nation). Even so, English kings, for all their theoretical power, increasingly had to defer to the views of parliament, a body that first emerged in the thirteenth century. The relationships between those who worked the land and their overlords were transformed twice, once in the direction of greater servitude in the eleventh century and then, at the opposite end of the period, in the late fourteenth century, towards far greater freedom.

The most striking changes of all were in the composition of the ruling class and the orientation of England's diplomatic policy. In the mid eleventh century an Anglo-Saxon aristocracy (with a sprinkle of Anglo-Danish incomers) ruled uncontested and balanced Scandinavia and north-western Europe in its spheres of diplomatic interest. Within decades all that had changed, and the old ruling class had been swept away, to be replaced by a largely Norman elite from a tiny duchy across the English Channel. Their descendants, although increasingly anglicized, would form the backbone of the nobility for the best part of a millennium. From that time on, England and France's fates were inextricably linked, as partners, allies or opponents.

At the start of 1066 little of this could have been predicted. Edward the Confessor, ailing and childless, did not long survive the turn of the year. He died on 5 January – his biographer curiously ascribes it to 'languishing from the sickness in the soul he had contracted' on account of the disobedience of his subjects – and he was buried the very next day in Westminster Abbey, the great church which he had seen consecrated barely a week before. On his deathbed he is said to have commended his family and the kingdom to Harold Godwineson, who was, in any case, the obvious candidate for the succession (the only available member of the House of

Wessex being Edgar the Atheling, a great-grandson of Aethelred the Unready, who was unsuitable as he was only fourteen years old). Whatever Edward's dying wishes really were, Harold conveniently interpreted them as bequeathing him the crown, and he pre-empted any challengers by having himself consecrated as king in a ceremony that took place in Westminster Abbey the afternoon following Edward's funeral.

Harold may have thought his quick action had settled things, but matters were not that simple. The throne of England was a prize on which others had their eye, and his smooth accession was complicated by the existence of two other claimants. The first was Harald Hardrada, the battle-hardened king of Norway, who derived his claim from a highly creative interpretation of a deal that his predecessor (and nephew) Magnus the Good had made with Harthacnut that whichever of them died the first, the survivor would inherit the lands of the other. As Harthacnut pre-deceased Magnus in 1042, Harald maintained that he had a right to all the lands of the Danish throne, which at the time had included England.

The other threat to Harold came from William of Normandy, who had a tenuous family link to the English crown through his great-aunt Emma, who had been Aethelred the Unready's queen. More importantly, there were strong bonds between William and Edward the Confessor, who had spent much of his childhood in Normandy and who depended greatly on his Norman advisers before he was forced to expel many of them in 1052. Despite this, Edward clearly continued to cherish his links with Normandy and in 1065 he sent Harold on a diplomatic mission to France which ended in shipwreck and a period as an enforced guest of William. During that time, Norman sources conveniently insisted, Edward's envoy pledged to William that the English throne should pass to him and not to Harold. The scene is carefully portrayed on the Bayeux tapestry, a literally embroidered version of the events in 1066 from the Norman point of view, on which Harold is shown swearing an oath to William, his hands poised over sacred relics. Argument has raged ever since as to whether he did (or even had the right to) promise away the crown of England, but William and his propagandists used the incident as a platform to mount his bid for England.

Time, for William, was of the essence. The beginning of a reign was a very vulnerable time for new monarchs, when the ambitious and the disappointed jostled for preferment, and so the Norman duke had to act swiftly before Harold could establish himself and embed his supporters in positions of power. He was fortunate that when the expeditionary force he hurriedly assembled landed near Pevensey on 29 September (after a frustrating delay of several weeks caused by adverse winds) he found Harold was away in the north. His opponent was dealing with an invasion that Hardrada had mounted in cooperation with Tostig Godwineson, Harold's estranged brother, who had been expelled after a revolt the previous year against his unpopular rule as Earl of Northumbria.

For over two centuries, the principal threat to England had been from the Vikings, but this last battle was something of an anticlimax. Although the invasion force initially brushed aside local Anglo-Saxon forces, Harold saw off Hardrada and his brother with relative ease, catching the invading host unawares on 25 September at Stamford Bridge near York and delivering such a comprehensive defeat that both the Norwegian king and Tostig were killed. The survivors scuttled back to Norway in just twenty-four ships, a fraction of the fleet which had brought them.

This should have been a moment of triumph for Harold – the old Viking enemy had finally been bested – but scarcely had he dealt with Hardrada than Harold learned of William's landing. His forced march back down to Sussex is the stuff of English myth, displaying just the type of indomitable spirit preceding a heroic failure of which popular English historiography became so fond. Harold reached the vicinity of Hastings on the evening of 13 October and then made the mistake of gambling all on the chance of quick victory. The next morning, he arrayed his 8,000 Anglo-Saxon warriors on the top of a low ridge near Hastings, their shields locked into an almost impenetrable barrier. Downhill, they faced a similar number of Normans, whose superiority in cavalry and archers would not have been decisive had not Harold been killed at the height of the battle. The story soon grew up that the fatal wound was inflicted by an arrow which struck him in the eye. Harold's death caused English resistance to collapse. Unfortunately for the Anglo-Saxon cause, his brothers had also perished during the battle, and after a half-hearted attempt to rally around Edgar the Atheling failed, the leading Anglo-Saxon nobles and churchmen swiftly did homage to William. By Christmas Day, the Norman conqueror had been crowned king in Westminster Abbey. His entourage, though, were distinctly nervous at the ease of their victory, and when his guard heard noises coming from a crowd who had gathered outside the Abbey, they suspected treachery and began setting light to all the buildings in the vicinity. It was an inauspicious start for Norman England.

William soon overcame this indignity, and the 10,000 or so Normans who had come with him settled down to enjoy their prize. On the face of it they were just another set of successful military conquerors inserting themselves at the head of an existing hierarchy. However, a series of rebellions in Kent, the south-west, East Anglia and the Welsh Marches marred the first four or five years of his reign and put paid to any policy of accommodation with the English nobility. The worst of them, in the north of England in 1069–70, was especially ominous, as it threatened to unite local particularist feeling, the prospect of an Anglo-Saxon restoration in the shape of Edgar Atheling, who joined the rebels, and a Viking resurgence, as King Sweyn Estrithsson of Denmark appeared on the Humber with a fleet to support the rebels.

Although York was besieged, William finally managed to suppress the uprising. Edgar fled to Scotland, and William disposed of the Danes, whose ravages along the east coast had included the sack of Peterborough Abbey, by the time-honoured method of paying Swein a substantial bribe to return to Denmark. The Normans then engaged in such a comprehensive campaign of revenge against the rebels that the 'Harrying of the North' was still remembered generations later: lands were burned, the remaining Anglo-Saxon nobles were dispossessed, and their holdings awarded to William's leading followers, while new castles were built, including at Chester, to stamp Norman dominance on the north. By the mid 1080s there were virtually no significant Anglo-Saxon landholders left; the last native earl, Waltheof, had been removed and executed following a further revolt in 1075, ending the five-century-long dominance of the Anglo-Saxon nobility.

The confiscation of the estates of Harold Godwineson and his family meant that the king himself acquired an enormous swathe of England, amounting to 18 per cent of the land, including estates in all the counties of England save two. To his principal followers William distributed 'rich fiefs that induced men to endure toil and danger to defend them', which they held in return for the obligation to provide fighting men if called upon. The system by which William's vassals did homage to him and agreed to provide military service for their lands, in turn distributing a portion of their own holdings to lesser men in return for similar undertakings, became later known as feudalism. Although it resembled to some extent a pre-existing Anglo-Saxon tradition under which all freemen had an obligation of service to repair bridges and town walls, and serve in the fyrd when their lord required them for a campaign, feudalism, and the network of castles – at first in wood, and then in stone – which the Normans build across England and the Welsh Marches, marked a significant change in the nature of political control in England.

As well as their land, the Anglo-Saxons lost their language, or at least its position as the tongue of power. The new elite, virtually an army of occupation, spoke a different language (Norman French, a dialect of French with a few Scandinavian undertones) to that of the conquered, and their churchmen used Latin almost exclusively. The rulers were French-speaking, and laws were recorded in Norman French; it was not until 1362 that Edward III felt moved to promote the Statute of Pleading which laid down that court proceedings should be in English, as by then scarcely anyone could understand the old language. Most likely Henry IV (r. 1399–1413), who was the first monarch to take his coronation oath in English, was also the first for whom English was his mother tongue. In the meantime, Old English ceased to be used as a literary language, although the latest version of *The Anglo-Saxon Chronicle*, which was compiled at Peterborough, contains an entry as late as 1154 recording the death of King Stephen. Yet a modified version of the language did survive; the Norman incomers, who at around 10,000 men represented less than 1 per cent of the population of England, eventually lost their native tongue, just as their ancestors 150 years before in Normandy had dropped Old Norse in favour of Norman-French. After several centuries in the shadows, Middle English emerged as a fully fledged literary language in the period 1370 to 1400 with the composition of William Langland's *Piers Plowman* and Geoffrey Chaucer's *The Canterbury Tales*, both among the master-pieces of English literature.

By 1086 William's rule was firmly entrenched, and, with almost a generation having passed since the Conquest, there was little desire and no leadership among the Anglo-Saxons to promote any further revolts. External threats, too, had largely subsided: a threatened invasion that year by King Canute IV of Denmark – which would have been the last Viking attack on England – turned out to be a false alarm; on the Welsh frontier the threat of raiding had subsided after the death of Gruffudd ap Llywelyn in 1063. On the Scottish border a much more potent threat posed by Malcolm Canmore (r. 1058–93), who raided England five times, was resolved by an invasion of Scotland in 1072 which secured his submission, his homage to William and the expulsion of the troublesome Edgar Atheling, who had taken refuge at the Scottish court.

If medieval and early modern monarchs had an Achilles heel, it was the difficulty they experienced in raising money. Wars, and especially the campaigns of aggression in which English kings all too frequently found themselves embroiled, were expensive affairs and their cost often outweighed any monetary gain from plunder or tribute. The king's vassals owed knight service, but although in the later Middle Ages this could be remitted for a monetary payment (known as scutage), this was not the custom in the immediate post-Conquest period. Nor were the early Norman kings in a position to make up the shortfall by levying general taxation. Instead, they largely had to rely on the revenues from the lands which they held directly and an assortment of feudal dues, such as the relief paid by an heir on his assumption of an estate. To find more effective ways of extracting money – or simply to understand what was due from his own lands – a king needed to know precisely who was in possession of which parcels of land. So it was that in late 1085 William ordered an incredibly ambitious survey which would establish who had held the land at the time of Edward the Confessor and who owned it now. Commissioners were sent out to take sworn evidence from local panels, and the resulting returns, which were largely carried out within a single year, were compiled into county-by-county records.

The result was the Domesday Book – its name indicating the sense that the information it contained was as final as the sentence to be passed on souls at Judgement Day – the most comprehensive administrative document to survive from Britain in the Middle Ages. Although London and Winchester were omitted (as the historic capitals of England, their survey was probably intended, but never carried out) and the coverage is very thin in the north of England, the level of detail is astounding, down to the numbers of pigs which smallholders possessed (in the manor of Haversham in Buckinghamshire, William Peverel was listed as owning 300 of them, as well as 75 eels). The document also reveals the scale of the transfer of land from Anglo-Saxon to Norman since 1066: entry after entry details an Anglo-Saxon owner supplanted by a Norman between the Conquest and 1087 (the owner of the Haversham estate before the Conquest was Countess Gytha, who was married to Earl Ralph, a grandson of Aethelred the Unready). Perhaps most importantly of all, it is a sign of a kingdom coming together, of a realm that was now considered a single unit. Even though dominated by a foreign ruling caste, its economic value was clear to all.

Catalogued though it might be, England was still an occupied land, and to control it the Normans studded the landscape with castles. They began with wooden motte and bailey forts (with a fortified keep on a raised mound), such as the one constructed by William at Hastings shortly after his arrival, and then moved on to building stone castles, most grandly the Tower of London, begun in 1078. These fortified bases were used by the new elite class to impose their will on their sometimes recalcitrant subjects, and they became a potent symbol of noble power. The aristocrats who lived in them, however, had divided loyalties, since many of William's principal followers, whom he rewarded with land in England in the decades after Hastings, also held territory from him in Normandy. Grandees such as William fitz Osbert, seneschal to William, whose lands included castles at Breteuil in southern Normandy and at Chepstow, as well as on the Isle of Wight, were symbols of one possible future for England. Their interests straddled the Channel, just as William's new realm did, and with stakes in both halves of the realm they were potential agents of a convergence of interest and culture between England and Normandy.

The twin parts of the realm were awkward siblings, and it seems it was never William's intention that they remain together. Robert Curthose, his eldest son, had been recognized as heir to Normandy and he inherited it in 1087, despite being in rebellion against his father at the time of William's death (and worse, in alliance with Philip I of France). Robert's younger brother, William (who was nicknamed Rufus on account of his red hair) received England, which, though larger, was still regarded very much as the less prestigious patrimony. The result was a tussle for control of Normandy and England, during which a baronial revolt infected the highest reaches of the aristocracy, involving men such as Robert of Bellême, Earl of Shrewsbury, and Robert, Count of Mortain. The uprising came close to toppling William, and matters were only resolved (albeit temporarily) when Robert decided to go on Crusade in 1096 and pawned Normandy to his brother for 10,000 marks in order to fund the expedition. It had been a nervous time for the Anglo-Norman aristocrats, who had been forced to pick one side or the other (or to risk biding their time), and repeated temporary separations of England from Normandy in 1100–1106 and 1141–54 posed similar awkward challenges.

In the north, an invasion of Scotland in 1097 quietened the frontier by installing a pro-Norman candidate, Edgar, on the throne; the expedition was led, ironically, by a rehabilitated Edgar Atheling creating the confusing spectacle of an Anglo-Saxon pretender in the pay of a Norman king winning the crown of a kingdom (but not of England). After successful campaigns in 1097–99 which recovered parts of Maine and Vexin from the French, William Rufus seemed secure. His sudden death in August 1100 in a hunting accident in the New Forest in which he seems to have been shot by William Tyrel, one of his own entourage, ignited the conflict over Normandy once more. While William I's youngest son, Henry, seized control of England, Robert Curthose, now returned from Palestine, managed to re-establish himself in Normandy and fought off several invasions before Henry finally overwhelmed him at the Battle of Tinchebray in 1106 (after which he was imprisoned for the last twenty-eight years of his life).

England remained entwined with France and would do so for the next 350 years, its borders there expanding and contracting to the rhythm of family disputes and periodic warfare. During that time, dynastic misfortune exacted a terrible toll on the monarchy. Henry I's ambitions to add the counties of Maine and Anjou to his French possessions led him to marry his son William to the daughter of Fulk V of Anjou, but the project ended in disaster when William died in a shipwreck in 1120. Henry was left without a male heir and only one legitimate daughter, Matilda, who had married Emperor Henry V of Germany in 1114. Had this marriage produced any children, then the fate of England could have taken a very different turn. Rather than being consumed in centuries of struggle to construct an Anglo-French kingdom, England might have found itself joined to Germany, and the Hundred Years' War could have been fought along the Rhine instead of the Seine.

Instead, Henry V died in 1125, and Matilda (who ever after affected the title 'empress') was married off to Geoffrey Plantagenet,

Fulk V's son. Although Henry had recognized her as his heir, Matilda was denied her birthright on her father's death in 1135, when Stephen of Blois, whose mother Adela was the daughter of William the Conqueror, carried out an audacious coup d'état by rushing over from Boulogne and securing London and then the royal treasury at Winchester. Matilda's allies were wrongfooted, and it took more than three years to launch a counter-invasion.

The following decade, known as 'the Anarchy', gave England its first taste of a serious civil war, during which law and order broke down almost entirely as the armies of the two sides cut destructive passages through the country. Each of the contending sides came tantalizingly close to a final victory, without ever quite extinguishing the other's cause. In 1141 Stephen was captured in battle at Lincoln, despite fighting 'like a lion', and was carted off to captivity in Bristol, leading to a series of defections (including his own brother, Henry of Blois, who was Bishop of Winchester and Papal legate). The capture a few months later of Matilda's brother, Robert of Gloucester, the most able leader among her supporters, lost her side the advantage, as he had to be exchanged for Stephen, who promptly began the war again. Only the death in August 1153 of Stephen's heir, Eustace, brought hope of peace, as it was agreed that Matilda and Geoffrey's son, Henry Plantagenet, would succeed Stephen, who was to be allowed to retain his kingdom unmolested for the rest of his life.

That enjoyment was destined to be very short, for Stephen died just ten months later, in October 1154. Henry, who now took the throne as Henry II, enjoyed the first undisputed succession for over a century. He also brought with him a vast enlargement to the royal lands, since not only had he inherited the County of Anjou and the Duchy of Normandy (which his father Geoffrey had seized in 1144), but in 1152 he had married Eleanor of Aquitaine (the former wife of Louis VII of France). Through her, he acquired the vast lands of the Duchy of Aquitaine, which included Gascony, Poitou, the Limousin and the Auvergne. Henry was now the most powerful king in Europe, and his lands were vastly superior in area to those of the French royal domain, which straggled in a vulnerable arc around Paris.

Henry II spent nearly two-thirds of his thirty-four-year reign on the Continent, enjoying the economic prosperity and cultural delights of Anjou and Aquitaine (which, through its main port of Bordeaux, was the main centre of England's wine-importing trade). He also expanded the kingdom's bounds, occupying Nantes in 1158, making small gains around Toulouse in 1159 and in 1166 effectively annexing the Duchy of Brittany by deposing Duke Conan and forcing his heiress Constance to marry his son Geoffrey. His 'England' was truly a European affair, whose centre of gravity was far to the south of London.

Henry's long reign marked the beginning of the Plantagenet dynasty, which ruled England until 1485 (latterly through its Lancastrian and Yorkist cadet branches). It was also a time in which scholars began to speculate on the history of the British Isles and the origins of its peoples. A dim memory still persisted of a time when Britain had been united (under Rome) and of the struggles to maintain that unity by such heroic (and largely fictional) characters as Arthur. This recollection suited the aspirations of the Plantagenet kings to extend their territorial aggrandisement to Ireland (under Henry II) and to Scotland and Wales (under Edward I in the late thirteenth century). The post-Conquest chroniclers who turned their attention to compiling histories were under no doubt that there was such a thing as Britain and that the current version of England (or Wessex, its antecedent) were its true heirs. In the 1130s Henry of Huntingdon remarked in his *History of the English* that 'The kingdom of Wessex in course of time subjected all to itself and obtained the monarchy of all Britain.' A more ambitious attempt at manufacturing a past (and a destiny) for Britain was compiled at around the same time by Geoffrey of Monmouth. His *History of the Kings of Britain* is on the same grand scale as Bede's *Ecclesiastical History of the English People* four centuries previously, but there the comparison ends. Geoffrey's work is a collection of tall tales, all designed to burnish the antique credentials of the English crown and to bolster its claims to be the descendent of an original pan-British monarchy. Among the figures from Geoffrey's work who would be mined by later authors are Coilus, the archetype for the 'Old King Cole' of the popular nursery rhyme, and Leir, whom Shakespeare immortalized as King Lear, adding a touch of madness that was not present in Geoffrey's original (although the death of Leir's father Bladud when he tried to fly from a tower with a pair of artificial wings suggests a hint of instability in the family line). Geoffrey even gave the English rulers a fake classical lineage, which mirrored the family trees of the early Anglo-Saxon kings and their attempt to prove descent from Woden or one of the other Germanic gods. He instead traces the Plantagenets back to Brutus, an alleged refugee from the Trojan Wars, who had made landfall in Britain after a prolonged voyage following the fall of his city. As a national myth this put Britain on a par with the Romans, who claimed as their forefather Aeneas, who similarly fled Troy and started an exile colony in Italy (where sixteen generations later, his descendant Romulus founded Rome). Geoffrey also began the popularization of the Arthur myth (although it was only to reach its full flight in Thomas Malory's *Le Morte d'Arthur* in 1485), whose potency as a defender of Britain rather obscured the fact that, if anything, he was fighting against the ancestors of the English state. So popular did the Arthur legend become that artefacts started to appear which purported to confirm its reality. When Edward I conquered Wales in 1282–3 it was said that the crown of Arthur was among the plunder that the English army secured from the defeated Welsh prince Llywelyn, and in April 1278 the alleged bodies of Arthur and Guinevere, his queen, were discovered at Glastonbury Abbey in the presence of the king himself. A mania arose for knightly tournaments in commemoration of Arthur's knights, and a 'Round Table', a replica of the original from Arthur's court at Camelot, probably made around 1290 for one such tournament that Edward I held at Winchester, still hangs in the Great Hall there (the last surviving remnant of Winchester Castle).

Henry II's ambitions on the Continent, his desire to secure his dynastic legacy and his determination to strengthen the position of the crown led inexorably to the tragedy for which he is best remembered, the murder of Archbishop Thomas Becket, his former chancellor, at Canterbury Cathedral on 29 December 1170. When Henry had Becket appointed to Canterbury in 1162, he had thought his former friend would do his bidding, but the king's insistence on reforms that would allow clergy accused of serious offences to be tried in royal courts (where they were subject to capital punishment) as opposed to ecclesiastical courts (where they were not) led to an irreparable break between the two. In one sense, it was another manifestation of the longstanding English antipathy to bending to jurisdictions based outside England (in this case the Papacy), but Henry's attempt to co-opt Emperor Frederick Barbarossa by a joint recognition of an anti-Pope, Paschal III, in opposition to Alexander III, the official Pope, made matters worse. When Henry ordered Roger de Pont l'Évêque, the Archbishop of York, to carry out the coronation of Henry 'the Young King' in 1170 (in an attempt to secure a smooth succession), Becket objected, as the crowning of kings was the traditional right of the Archbishops of Canterbury. Henry's rage at Thomas' insubordination led to the Archbishop's murder by four of Henry's knights who believed they were carrying out the royal will.

Henry weathered the Becket controversy relatively unscathed (although the cult that rapidly grew up around the martyred Archbishop must have grated), but the Plantagenet monarchy very nearly did not survive the death of two of his sons in rapid succession (Henry the Young King 1183 and his brother Geoffrey in 1186). Further damage was done by the ill-tempered succession in 1189 which pitted Richard, who received the lion's share of the inheritance, against John (who received only Ireland) and little Arthur (Geoffrey's two-year-old son) who was awarded Brittany.

Richard made little impression on England, spending just a few months there before setting out on the Third Crusade and a similarly brief stay after he was finally released from the prisons of Leopold V of Austria, into whose hands he had fallen on the return trip from Palestine. The main impact of his reign was the burden of the huge ransom of 150,000 marks which had to be raised for his relief, the story of Robin Hood, which played on the alleged injustices of John's misrule while his brother was away, and the escalation in fighting in Normandy, where John lost virtually the whole duchy south of the Seine before 1194, which his brother had to win painfully back before his death in 1199.

John is one of the great villains of traditional English historiography. His nickname 'Lackland' does not refer to his final loss of Normandy, but to the humiliating arrangement after Henry II's death by which he received only the lordship of Ireland (which had fallen partially under English control after Henry II had despatched an army there in 1170 – see Chapter 6). His reign marked the collapse of the original Angevin empire and the final severing of the Duchy of Normandy from England. The prospects for the emergence of a true dual realm which united Normandy and England in a single cultural and political sphere had grown increasingly remote since the time of William the Conqueror, but the losses under John marked its death knell. Henceforth, kings of England might claim to be kings of France also, but it was clear that their primary role was as English monarch and that they came to France not as countrymen, but as conquerors.

John had seemed in a strong position in Normandy in 1202, when he captured most of his leading opponents, including his nephew Arthur of Brittany, who had been besieging his mother Isabella at Mirebeau. Yet within a year his position had collapsed. John had a knack for alienating those whom he most needed to rely on and was simply not an able war leader or a man who could inspire loyalty like his brother Richard. By 1203, Philip Augustus of France had overrun Normandy, Anjou, Maine and a good part of Poitou. John's attempts to recover the lost territory were hampered by a quarrel with the Papacy which led to England being placed under an interdict in 1208, meaning Mass could not be said. The ties of loyalty among John's barons were loosened, and the disastrous outcome and enormous cost of a French campaign which ended in a defeat at Bouvines in July 1214 proved the last straw for many.

As the price for consenting to new funds to mount yet a further expedition, the barons demanded reforms in the form of a charter intended to protect them (and it was principally designed to safeguard the interests of the high nobility, rather than the people in general) from arbitrary actions on the part of the king. John pledged 'to no one will we sell, to no one will we deny right or justice' and that all judgement should be 'by peers or by the law of the land'. Specific clauses dealt with feudal dues, which the barons feared the king would exploit to gouge ever-escalating fees from them on the occasion of succession to an inheritance or the remarriage of widows, and with a variety of special interests (such as a measure ordering the removal from the Thames of all fish weirs, which were causing a hazard to navigation on the river). To further secure their position, the barons added a clause that should the king renege on his obligations, a committee of twenty-five of them would be selected to take charge and enforce the liberties granted under the charter.

Magna Carta, as the charter became known, is a prime example of the tensions which flared up as the power of the crown waxed at the expense of the nobility. Far from a forward-looking defence of freedom, it is a conservative defence of traditional rights which the king was seen as having eroded. It also became a founding myth of English particularism, a precedent that was invoked whenever the sovereign was deemed to be encroaching too closely on his subject's freedoms, by parliamentarians opposed to Charles I in the period immediately preceding the English Civil War, and by American rebels against British rule in the late eighteenth century. That the original charter was intended to protect elite power, and not to dissolve it, did not seem to matter one jot.

John only agreed to the baron's terms after outright rebellion engulfed London in May 1215, forcing him to assent to the Charter on 19 June. No sooner had he signed, though, than he tried to wriggle free of its obligations. He induced a horrified Pope to annul the Charter, so releasing him from his promise. Faced now with a king unencumbered by Papal disapproval, the barons' position was far weaker than the previous year, and they were forced to invite Prince Louis, the son of Philip Augustus, to come to their aid (with the inducement of the English throne as a reward). He landed in Kent in May 1216 with over a thousand knights, rapidly secured London, and looked all set to topple John who had fled ignominiously to Winchester. Fourteen years earlier, the English had ruled Normandy and – under a more able ruler than John – might well have restored the Angevin empire. Now the boot was on the other foot; as John's position weakened, and with the French in control of the capital, a reprise of the Norman conquest might have made England a junior partner in a revived Anglo-French kingdom.

But then fate intervened. John's death from dysentery in October, far from making Louis' position easier, enabled the English barons to rally around John's young son Henry III (who was just nine years old). A minority, with a pliable young king, removed the threat that a vengeful John posed to the barons, and, though Louis battled on until 1217 before accepting defeat and withdrawing with the consolation prize of 10,000 marks, England settled down to the managed instability of a regency that lasted until 1232.

The loss of Normandy in 1214 had still left the English crown in possession of Gascony in the south-west. Revenues from Bordeaux wine and the need to defend royal prestige meant Henry III and his advisers clung doggedly to the territory, even though its isolation from England made it hard to defend and harder to govern. Henry made several attempts to recover territory in France, including a major expedition to Gascony in 1242–3, but loss of further ground in Poitou underlined that his was now a principally English regime. The immense cost of a quixotic attempt to secure the kingdom of Sicily for his son Edmund, which cost the huge sum of 135,542 marks, led to a humiliating agreement with Louis IX of France in 1259.

The Treaty of Paris, which marked the settlement, was a momentous occasion. For the first time since 1066, an English king formally renounced his claims over Normandy (and Maine and Anjou, too). Worse still, Henry was forced to perform homage to Louis for his position as Duke of Aquitaine (which he had formerly held as an independent fief). In the future, each time a new English king ascended to the throne, or the French king changed, the English ruler had to perform liege homage, an especially demeaning form of feudal tie which bound him personally to loyalty to the monarch of France. French kings exploited this new relationship to meddle persistently in Gascony, as appeals by the nobility from there were now in theory to be held in Paris rather than London, and on several occasions they declared it forfeit to the French crown (as in 1294, when Philip IV confiscated it after a naval skirmish between an Anglo-Gascon and Norman fleets in the Channel).

Weakened and hopelessly in debt, Henry was forced, as so many monarchs after him, to turn to the barons to bail him out. The gathering of twenty-four of them which assembled at Oxford in June 1258 made a series of provisions, including forbidding the king to alienate royal land without the permission of a new council and established inquiries into the conduct of local royal officials. Further assemblies – parliaments, as they came to be called – were to be held three times each year. It was a small start, but a sense was taking root that there should be a formal process by which the king could be forced to take counsel, and certain matters (in particular taxation) on which he had to take note of parliament's views, marking the start of its evolution into the nation's supreme law-making body.

The most immediate effect of the Provisions of Oxford, just as of the Magna Carta, was rather less positive: their sparking of a civil war between Henry and the leading barons, led by Simon de Montfort, the Earl of Leicester. Both sides sought external validation – Henry, like John before him, obtained Papal approval, absolving him from keeping to the agreement he had made, and both he and Simon submitted their cases to the king of France for arbitration. Only Simon's death in battle at Evesham in August 1265 saved England from the nightmare of a repetition of the Anarchy under Stephen.

By his death in 1272, Henry III had begun to heal the wounds of the civil war and re-established a measure of financial stability. The reign of his son Edward I was of a different measure entirely. Shorn of the Angevin empire, he was the first English king to try to make real the idea, first propagated by Geoffrey of Monmouth, that his lordship extended by right to the whole of Britain, and he was fully prepared to take military action to enforce it. Edward did make a nod in the direction of the traditional Angevin lands in France – he spent three years there, after his visit to Paris to perform homage to Philip IV, and was the last English king to hold court at Bordeaux (in 1289). However, his principal interest was in extending English power further into Wales. There, Llywelyn ap Grufudd, who had become ruler of Gwynedd in 1246, had gradually established a dominant position in Wales, securing the homage of the other Welsh princes by 1258 and in 1267 obtaining the title 'Prince of Wales' from Henry III (in exchange for an act of homage and a payment of 30,000 marks to the English king). When Edward became king, Llywelyn broke the agreement and refused to do him homage, despite three demands to do so, resulting in his being declared a rebel. In July 1277 Edward invaded Wales, and so successful was the campaign (by a 15,000-strong army including 9,000 Welsh foot soldiers) that within two months Llywelyn was forced to sue for peace. The terms of the settlement were so harsh that in 1282 the Welsh rose up in revolt again. One by one, the castles which the English had established at Hawarden, Aberystwyth and Llandovery were taken, leaving just the beleaguered garrisons at Flint and Rhudlan to maintain the English presence.

After regrouping his forces, Edward steamrollered through central Wales in the summer. The Welsh defeat of an English force in the north in November and Llywelyn's attempt to roll the English up from the south in Montgomeryshire suggested a protracted campaign, but he was killed in battle in December, and the heart fell out of the Welsh resistance. A surprise English attack on Snowdonia in January 1283, in the depths of winter, caught Dafydd, Llywelyn's brother, off guard, and with his capture in June, the Welsh revolt was finished.

This time, no mercy was shown to Wales – Edward imposed his authority much more firmly in the heartlands of Welsh resistance.

Massive stone castles were built at Harlech, Conwy, Caernarfon and Denbigh, potent symbols of the crushing of Wales' independence. The country became a military colony in which great lords such as Earl Warenne, the Earl of Lincoln, and Reginald de Grey, who had played a large part in the campaign, received great tracts of north Wales. In 1284 a Statute of Wales was issued, imposing English criminal law on Welsh courts and making clear that no further manifestations of Welsh independence would be tolerated. Further south, the Marcher lords who had step by step encroached upon the Welsh principalities there since the Norman Conquest, men such as the Earls of Hereford and Gloucester, did not receive extensive further lands, but with the crown retaining control of Snowdonia and Anglesey, the projection of English power did not require that they do so.

Predictably, the new order in Wales provoked resistance: first a minor uprising in 1287 and then in 1294–5 a larger-scale revolt, which required over 30,000 infantry and a large force of cavalry to put down (and included an attack on the Lleyn Peninsula, for which the king commanded all the brewers of Chester to produce as large a quantity of ale as possible to keep his men supplied during the raid).

By the time that the Welsh revolt collapsed in spring 1295, Edward's attention had already turned northwards to Scotland. The border between England and its northern neighbour had been fairly fluid and ill-defined in the period since the Norman Conquest. Although William I had invaded Scotland in 1072 and extracted homage from Malcolm Canmore (see p. 111), over the centuries that followed, the kings of Scotland had often had the better of the tussle over exactly where the border should lie. Frontier towns such as Berwick, Carlisle and Newcastle see-sawed between the two kingdoms.

Malcolm's attempt after the death of William the Conqueror to assert control over Northumberland and Cumberland (the old domain of the British Kingdom of Strathclyde) was rebuffed by William Rufus, who pushed north into Scotland from Durham late in 1092, forced the Scottish king to do homage and expelled the pro-Scottish lord of Cumbria. The turmoil that followed Malcolm's death the following year put a temporary end to Scottish ambitions, and it took until 1138 for David I to feel strong enough to mount an invasion to support his niece Matilda in prosecuting her claim to the English throne against Stephen. Although the Scottish army was badly beaten at the Battle of the Standard on 22 August, the English commander, Walter of Aumale, mishandled the pursuit. David regrouped in sufficient strength to occupy the whole of the north of England from the Ribble to the Tees, and in 1147 he brokered an agreement with Matilda's son, Henry, that the Scottish border would be acknowledged to be the Tyne should Henry succeed to the throne. The radical shift southwards in the border looked permanent, and in the 1140s David even held his court at Newcastle and Carlisle, but his heir Henry died prematurely in 1152, and his own death the year after left Scotland with a minor, the twelve-year-old Malcolm IV, as king. This, and the end of the Anarchy in England, forced the Scots to agree to evacuate Cumbria and Northumbria in 1157 (and young Malcolm was made to perform homage to Henry II).

William I of Scotland sought his revenge by taking advantage of a baronial rebellion against Henry II to invade Northumberland in 1174, but his capture outside Alnwick forced him to abandon the attempt and, worse, to do homage to Henry II for Scotland and to hand over the castles of Berwick, Roxburgh, Jedburgh and Edinburgh to English garrisons. The humiliation was reversed in 1189 by a payment of 10,000 marks to Richard I (who was desperate for funds to finance his crusading) and in 1216 Alexander II once again took advantage of political instability in England by intervening on behalf of the barons in their revolt against John. They recognized Scotland's claims to Northumberland, Cumberland and Westmoreland, and in August Alexander was bold enough to take an army down as far as Dover (by far the most southerly point ever reached by a Scottish king) in support of Prince Louis' attempt to seize the English crown. When the French invasion crumbled as support coalesced around the young Henry III, so too did the Scottish cause, and Alexander was forced back northwards, while the northern counties once again slipped out of Scottish control. The border was settled more or less for good by the Treaty of York in 1237, which acknowledged English overlordship over the three border counties. Even though they had failed to pull the north of England into the Scottish orbit, at least the Scottish kings could take consolation in their mastery of the Lowlands.

Although by 1296 England had been at peace with Scotland for nearly eighty years, the presence of a large rival to his north vexed Edward I. The opportunity to meddle was presented by an unfortunate series of dynastic accidents which befell the Scottish crown. Alexander III died after a riding accident in 1286. Aged just forty-four, he had been predeceased by all his three children, leaving as his only heir his granddaughter Margaret, the child of the marriage of his daughter, also named Margaret, and Eric II of Norway. The little 'Maid of Norway' remained in Norway for several years, but then in 1290 was sent by ship to Scotland to claim her crown. Tragically she died at Orkney, aged just seven, possibly from the effects of seasickness. Her demise thwarted Edward I's hopes for a marriage match between his son Edward and Margaret which would have united the two crowns three centuries before their eventual union in 1603.

A frustrated Edward instead had to settle for intervening in the disputed succession, which threw up a dozen candidates (although only two of them – John Balliol and Robert Bruce – were at all plausible). In the meantime, Edward gradually established control over Scotland, placing English garrisons in the major castles and ensuring that Balliol, his favoured candidate, was finally chosen as the victor of the 'Great Cause' in November 1292. The outbreak of war between England and France in 1294 offered the Scots the opportunity to throw off this unwanted English tutelage. Balliol was sidelined, and a treaty with Philip IV of France signed in 1295, which bound the Scots to invade England should Edward go to war with France. So began the 'Auld Alliance' which united the two countries in mutual antipathy to the English for the next 300 years.

Edward mustered the feudal host at Newcastle in March 1296, gathered a fleet and marched north. Berwick refused to surrender, and so he sacked it and then plunged on into central Scotland. The main Scottish army was defeated at Dunbar in April, and Scottish resistance collapsed. Balliol submitted soon after and was forced to abdicate, but instead of installing another king of Scots, Edward took the crown for himself, and the Scottish royal regalia was taken to Westminster (where the most sacred portion, the Stone of Scone, on which Scottish monarchs had been crowned for centuries, remained until it was returned to Edinburgh in 1996, the 700th anniversary of its removal). A rising led by William Wallace staved off a total English victory, but his defeat at Falkirk in 1298 gave Edward I the initiative, and in a grinding campaign the Scottish castles were reduced one by one. With the fall of Stirling in July 1304, Edward was the master of Scotland.

Much had changed since the Anglo-Scottish wars of the twelfth and thirteenth centuries, and Edward was not seeking, as his ancestors had done, the annexation of parts of Scotland or the imposition of homage on its kings. His ambition was both lesser – in that he did not attempt to adjust the border of the two – and greater – in that he sought the practical union of the two countries under his own personal rule. In 1305 Edward ordered an ordinance to establish a form of government under which Scotland was to be governed by a lieutenant, a chancellor and a council of twenty-two, only nine of whom would be Scottish magnates, while Scottish laws were to be revised by an assembly. A future of gradual assimilation with England beckoned.

Scotland, though, did not accept its defeat meekly, and the Scots were not to suffer the same fate as the Welsh under the Statute of Wales. In 1306 Robert Bruce was declared king (in part after revulsion at the execution of William Wallace in 1305, who was hanged, drawn and quartered, and the parts of his corpse then dispersed to four parts of Scotland to provide an example to anyone else who might be tempted to revolt). The English campaign to bring him to heel got off to a bad start in July 1307 with the death of Edward I on the march north, leaving his son Edward II to turn tail and lead the army back southwards. The seven years' grace before the English army once again entered Scotland in 1314 allowed Robert to consolidate his position. He seized a string of English-occupied castles and even engaged in some opportunistic harrying of the north of England, burning Corbridge, Hexham and Durham in 1311–12 and penetrating as far south as Hartlepool. Edward II could not stand by and see the dominant position his father had built up in Scotland crumble to dust. In the spring of 1314 Edward Bruce (Robert's brother) was besieging Stirling Castle when the English king appeared with a large relieving force. However, in the boggy ground around Bannockburn, south of Stirling, the Scottish infantry, formed up in schiltrons (a type of phalanx), held firm, and it was Edward who fled, his army in tatters, back to the English border. In the wake of the disaster, the remaining English garrisons soon surrendered, with only Berwick holding out until 1318. Scottish armies once again ravaged northern England, and the Bruces were able to engage in a piece of imperial expansion of their own, when Edward Bruce landed in Ireland in 1315 and occupied a large part of the north for three years, even having himself crowned king of Ireland before the English rallied and defeated and killed him.

The English had to wait nearly twenty years after Bannockburn for their revenge, which came when Edward III recaptured Berwick in 1333 and then, reversing his father's policy, forced Edward Balliol to do homage and grant him large parts of southern Scotland, including Wigtown, Roxburgh, Jedburgh, Edinburgh and Dumfries. The border was once more a movable thing. The Scots took advantage of the English preoccupation with a war with France after 1337 and managed to reverse most of these gains, retaking Edinburgh in 1341. David II pushed his luck too far, however, and an invasion of England ended in disaster at Neville's Cross in 1346, when he was captured and held prisoner in the Tower of London for ten years. By then Berwick, whose chief citizens must have been dizzy at dealing with such rapid changes of master, had fallen yet again to Edward III, and the border had returned more or less to where it had been since the Treaty of York in 1237.

The ability of the Plantagenet monarchs to prosecute wars in Wales, Ireland, Scotland and France (sometimes simultaneously) was striking and gave them an advantage over their opponents, in particular the French. Although at times they found themselves in financial straits as a result (and had to make a series of concessions to the barons and then to parliament which they would rather have avoided), they were able to do so with the help of a population which was growing and an expanding network of towns (of which London, with a population of around 35,000 by 1377, was by far the largest). Trade, too, was burgeoning, and by 1311–13, wool merchants, the backbone of England's prosperity, were exporting over 38,000 sacks a year to the Continent, yielding up to £70,000 a year in revenues which went a long way to keeping the crown solvent. There were, however, already danger signs. The population of England, which reached somewhere between 2 and 4 million in 1300, was not supported by a corresponding increase in cultivated land, and many peasants slipped over the line into poverty. Bad harvests in 1315, 1316, 1317, 1320 and 1321 caused enormous suffering, and epidemics which killed many sheep and cattle in 1319 and 1321 inflicted further hardship.

In 1348 calamity struck. The first cases of an affliction characterized by black blotches on the skin and raised welts (or buboes) on the glands appeared at Melcombe Regis in Dorset. The Black Death, as it became known, spread rapidly, reaching London by the end of the year and spreading its tendrils through the Midlands, the north and then into Scotland by 1349. Death came around four days after infection and, despite the efforts of physicians to prescribe a wide variety of cures, including rubbing onions on the flesh, eating crushed emeralds and smoking, nothing worked. Terrified villagers fled the plague's advance, but they merely spread the epidemic still further. Prayer was the only remedy that provided a modicum of comfort. In the absence of a census or any contemporary tally of the death toll, it is hard to establish exactly how many people died, but in the diocese of York, around 40 per cent of the parish clergy died during the course of the year. Probably at least a third of the total population perished, with the disease exacting its toll disproportionately among the young and the old.

Once the dying had subsided, society bounced back surprisingly quickly. The social landscape, though, was overturned. Younger sons, who had previously had no hope of inheritance, were now able to take up the plots of land their brothers, victims of the plague, had left vacant. Day-labourers, who had lived on the edge of subsistence, now had more work than they could handle. Apart from an outburst of morbid art that focused on the Danse Macabre – the dance of death, which struck down aristocrat and artisan, prince and peasant equally – living conditions seemed generally to have improved. There were further outbreaks of plague in 1361, 1369 and 1375, which again hit the young hardest and prevented the population from approaching pre-plague levels for over a century. As a result, many marginal villages, such as Wharram Percy in Yorkshire, were abandoned.

The labour shortages which followed the plague led to demands for increased wages (which initially rose by as much as 24 per cent). The government responded in 1351 by passing the Statute of Labourers, which decreed that wages should be pegged to the levels they had been before the pestilence and that workers should not be permitted to travel from area to area in search of better pay. In 1363 a set of sumptuary laws was passed, attempting to set down the types of clothing which each class was permitted to wear (a clear sign that the lower orders were now earning enough to ape their social superiors).

Increasingly freed from onerous feudal dues and ties which landlords could no longer enforce, the peasantry became ever more restive. In 1377 the government of Richard II, desperate for funds to finance a French campaign, came up with the expedient of a poll tax levied at the rate of fourpence on everyone in the land (which saved the trouble of land assessments and evasion by the rich). A second poll tax followed in 1379, and a third, at the penal rate of a shilling a head, was due to be collected in 1381. When the commissioners went out to begin gathering in the tax, they met with large-scale refusal. By the beginning of summer, the rebels had organized and, led by Wat Tyler, a Kentish peasant, they marched on London. There, at Blackheath, they were joined by a contingent of rebels from Essex. An alarmed Richard stood by as priories and palaces were burned and he was forced into a humiliating meeting at Mile End on 14 June, where he apparently conceded most of the rebels' demands, promising justice against officials who had oppressed the peasantry, the end of forced contracts and a general amnesty for the rebels. Although Simon Sudbury, the Archbishop of Canterbury and Richard's unpopular chancellor, and his treasurer, Sir Robert Hales, were hanged, the government almost instantly reneged on its agreements, and many of the rebels were rounded up and themselves executed.

The Peasants' Revolt, though, was a sign that the social landscape of England was evolving from the tied villeinage of the Middle Ages to the free (but still desperately poor) peasantry of the early modern period. Britain's bounds, too, were still in flux. By the time of the Peasants' Revolt, England had been at war with France for more than forty years. The Hundred Years' War – which would actually last 116 years – had its origin in the claim of Edward III on the French throne, through his mother Isabella, the sister of Charles IV of France. In many ways Edward saw this as an opportunity to escape from the indignity of his situation in Gascony, which he held as a feudal domain from the French king, making him, humiliatingly, technically his feudal subordinate. The war saw the last serious attempt by the English crown to regain its lost territories in France, and, by its end, its possessions had been diminished still further, with the loss of everything but Calais.

The initial phases of the war gave England a string of victories, including at Crécy in 1346, which became yet another stock member of the pantheon of English martial successes which punctuate the orthodox version of national history. The English (or in large part, Welsh) supremacy in archery, using the powerful longbow which scythed down the French knights as they attempted to charge, gifted Edward an initiative which he capitalized on in 1360, when the

Treaty of Brétigny enlarged his lands in Aquitaine and secured Calais and several smaller coastal ports for the English crown (together with the handy ransom of 3 million gold crowns for King John II of France, who had been captured at Poitiers in 1356). The next four decades of intermittent fighting saw heroics on the part of Edward III's eldest son, the 'Black Prince', but his death from dysentery in 1376 sapped the impetus of the English war effort, and they were gradually pushed back until they controlled scarcely more than Calais. A nasty scare in Wales, where the revolt of Owain Glyndwr in 1400 threatened to push England out of the principality (and even to extend its borders to the Mersey and the Severn) made matters worse (see Chapter 6). The situation was recovered by Henry V (r. 1413–22), who shrewdly exploited divisions in France between rival factions trying to seize power during the incapacity of Charles VI through madness. In 1414 he sent an embassy to France whose demands, for the throne of France, a marriage to the daughter of Charles IV and the restoration of the Angevin lands in Normandy and Poitou, Henry cannot have expected to be conceded. When, predictably, he was rebuffed, in 1415 he launched an invasion of northern France.

The campaign, which began with a landing at Harfleur, was crowned with unexpected success, when Henry won a crushing victory at Agincourt, again with the critical assistance of a large contingent of archers. By 1418 he had exploited this to conquer much of Normandy, which returned to full English control for the first time in two centuries. Henry's run of success continued, and in May 1420 the Treaty of Troyes, negotiated with the aid of Duke Philip of Burgundy, gave Henry almost all of his original demands; the marriage to Catherine and the affirmation of his control of northern France. He was recognized as heir to the French throne, meaning he would have to wait until Charles VI's death to receive the crown, though the French king's insanity gave him reason to hope that this would not be long delayed.

In December 1420 Henry entered Paris, which was now an English city. His triumph elevated him to one of the greatest of

English military heroes, to be celebrated in dramatic form by William Shakespeare and to be invoked whenever England's self-image as a plucky island nation needed a boost. Yet the effects of Agincourt were short-lived indeed. France was not to become an English realm, and Henry never did become king of France. His death from dysentery in August 1422 left his infant son Henry VI (who was less than a year old) as sovereign. Although the French war ground on, and in the late 1420s the English under the Duke of Bedford seemed to be close to crushing the French monarchy once and for all, the unheralded appearance of Joan of Arc changed everything. A teenage peasant girl, she had heard voices calling on her to go to Charles, the dauphin (the heir to the French throne), and encourage him to greater resistance against the English. She was an unlikely saviour of France, but Joan soon turned from intriguing curiosity into inspirational leader. Her raising of the siege of Orléans in 1429 proved a turning point, though the English gained some measure of revenge by trying their nemesis – whom the Burgundians had handed over – for heresy and burning her at the stake in 1431. Joan's legacy, though, lived on, and Charles VII was crowned king of France at Rheims, marking the symbolic start of the French fight-back.

Decades of weak leadership, regency struggles, indecision and faction-fighting sapped the English will to conduct the war, and a reinvigorated French monarchy took advantage. Paris was recaptured in 1436, and by 1442 much of the south-west had been lost, with the English left holding scarcely more than Bordeaux and Bayonne. Normandy fell to a concerted French attack in 1449–50, with the capture by the French of Harfleur, the landing site of Henry V, providing a certain symmetry to the end of the English presence. A final campaign to Gascony, led by John Talbot, Earl of Shrewsbury, ended in disaster in July 1453 at Castillon, one of the first battles in history where field guns played a decisive role. Bordeaux fell in October, and, with England's possessions in France reduced to Calais, the Hundred Years' War was over. With it disappeared any real sense that England could be a dual realm straddling the Channel.

Having lost France, England nearly lost itself. By 1453 it, too, stood on the brink of dissolution. Henry VI was a member of the House of Lancaster, a scion of the Plantagenets who claimed descent from Edward III's son John of Gaunt. His weakness and his descent into outright madness in August 1453 led the rival House of York, descendants both of Edward's fourth son Edmund and, through the female line, of his second son Lionel, Duke of Clarence, to assert their claim. During the king's invalidity, Richard, Duke of York, became Lord Protector, but when Henry recovered his senses, Richard was brushed aside, heightening factional tensions and accelerating a descent into civil war, which culminated in the Battle of St Albans in May 1455. For six years, fortunes in the Wars of the Roses – named for the red and white badges of the Lancastrians and Yorkists respectively – swung between the two sides. The Duke of York briefly regained the protectorate in 1455–6, but the Lancastrians gradually gained ground until a devastating defeat at Towton on 29 March 1461, the bloodiest battle fought in medieval England, where 28,000 men died, destroyed their cause.

Edward, Duke of York (his father Richard had been killed in battle the previous year), was now crowned king as Edward IV, but nine years later Henry VI, who had been in exile in France, returned, and the war reignited. Aided by the defection of Richard Neville, Earl of Warwick (nicknamed 'the Kingmaker'), Henry and his activist queen, Margaret of Anjou, had victory in their grasp until, in short order, Warwick was killed at the Battle of Barnet in April 1471, and then Henry's forces were overwhelmed at Tewkesbury on 4 May.

Although Henry was assassinated soon afterwards (the official story had it that he died of 'pure displeasure and melancholy'), the Wars of the Roses had one last surprise. When Edward IV died in 1483, his rightful heir, Edward V, was imprisoned in the Tower of London by his uncle Richard of Gloucester who, when the little prince and his brother Richard, Duke of York, most conveniently disappeared – almost certainly murdered on Richard's orders – had himself crowned, as Richard III. The rumours surrounding the

'Princes in the Tower' made Richard unpopular – as one chronicler put it 'he lost the hearts of his people. And thereupon many gentlemen intended his destruction' – a series of revolts broke out in October, spreading from Kent to Wiltshire. The execution of many of his opponents who had been implicated in the uprising, including most prominently the Duke of Buckingham – spread a climate of fear, further undermining Richard.

Attention turned to the leading Lancastrian pretender to the throne, Henry Tudor, Earl of Richmond. As the son of Margaret Beaufort, whose great-grandfather was John of Gaunt, Henry's claim seemed distant, but the carnage of the Wars of the Roses had left him the head of the Lancastrian house. He also had significant support in Wales, as his father's family, the Tudors, originally came from Anglesey.

So it was that a Welshman landed at Milford Haven on 7 August 1485 to claim the English crown. Henry travelled northwards along the Welsh coast and then struck east into England, gathering supporters on the way, while Richard headed off to intercept him. The two armies met at Bosworth in Leicestershire on 22 August, in a clash where Richard was undone by the defection of Sir William Stanley's contingent and the failure of the Earl of Northumberland to engage Henry's forces. During the confused mêlée, Richard was caught unguarded and cut down. With the House of York now defeated and leaderless, Henry was proclaimed king and marched on London, leaving Richard's body to be disposed of at Greyfriars Abbey in Leicester – where in 2012 a skeleton that was identified as almost certainly his through DNA analysis was discovered beneath a car park.

England's Middle Ages, which had begun with a Norman-French king overthrowing an English monarch he accused of being a usurper, ended with a Welshman toppling another Englishman whose claim to the throne was tainted by accusations of murder. Compared to its extent in 1066, England had swallowed up Calais, Wales and large parts of Ireland. Yet its shape and its centre of gravity had experienced even wilder gyrations. The 1290s had almost brought Scotland to the brink of English control, and the long engagement with France, which began with William bringing his possessions as Duke of Normandy, had at times made England a truly continental power. It was at times in those four centuries very unclear what England was, and as Henry VII took the throne in 1485 and the Tudor dynasty began, the country still teetered between plunging into further territorial engagement with Europe and a much more insular approach.

Celtic Britain and its English Fringe

The British Isles – Wales, Scotland and Ireland

N

ULSTER

CONNACHT

MEATH

•Dublin

LEINSTER

MUNSTER

Cork•

Perth •

Edinburgh •

•Berwick

•Carlisle   •Newcastle
      Durham•

York •

GWYNEDD   •Chester   Lincoln •

POWYS •Shrewsbury

DEHEUBARTH

      Oxford•
Windsor•   London•

Salisbury•   •Dover

•Boulogne

Rouen•

0   100 miles
0   100   200 km

6. Wales, Scotland and Ireland

The maps of Wales, Scotland and Ireland in AD 800 present a very different picture from those whose perspective is centred on southern Britain. They hint at the contours of those countries' future histories, while suggesting patterns which might come to influence the development of the British Isles as a whole. The prevailing sense is of fragmentation, with the Welsh principalities penned behind an expansive Anglo-Saxon England. In Ireland, a multiplicity of petty states has begun to coalesce into five main regional states. None is dominant, and their unification seems a long way off. Scotland's future is even less in focus, with a confusing mosaic of ethnic groups striving for supremacy. In the central lowlands and east, the Picts – a Celtic group – are on the retreat, their lands now encroached on by the Scots of Dál Riata (themselves a group of Irish incomers). In the south-east the Angles of Northumbria have receded from an advance which took them as far as Edinburgh in the seventh century but still occupy large parts of future Scotland. In the south-west, the kingdom of Strathclyde, peopled by Britons, descendants of the Celtic tribes who once ruled all of England, clings on, while to the north a new group has emerged: Viking raiders from Scandinavia who have occupied the Orkneys and before long will spread out in a pattern of raiding and colonization throughout the Scottish Isles and parts of the mainland.

Much of this book treats the history of the British Isles from an English perspective, or at least from a point of view in which a core state based in southern England eventually expanded to absorb Wales, Scotland and Ireland, acquiring (and then losing) an overseas empire, before facing difficult questions in the twenty-first century about its integrity as a unitary state. Yet, much as the shape of England was not inevitable for long periods of its history, so the three nations on the 'Celtic fringe' of Britain have their own pathways, their own stories of unification, civil war, state-building and resistance against English encroachment. That much of northern England was under the religious and cultural influence of Ireland in the eighth century and that a Scottish king's army reached as far as Dover in 1216 should give pause for thought. Nothing about Britain was inevitable.

Wales

From one point of view, Wales could see itself as the true heir of the pre-Roman Celtic kingdoms and their successors which emerged after the fall of Roman Britain. Fighting a losing battle against the Anglo-Saxons, the Welsh (or at least their ancestors) were gradually pushed westwards before consolidating and coming tantalizingly close to unifying, only to have their independence destroyed by renewed English aggression in the thirteenth century. In this sense, Wales is Britain.

Right from the start the Welsh proved tenacious in defending their homeland. The topography of the land, with the high mountains of Snowdonia posing a forbidding barrier to invaders (and the offshore island of Anglesey providing a handy refuge in the case that this should be penetrated) meant that occupying Wales required the deployment of considerable resources and long-term effort on the part of would-be conquerors. The Romans found this, as the Celtic tribes of Wales, particularly the Ordovices in the northern Highlands and the Silures in the south, fought a bitter, decades-long war of resistance (in part inspired by Caratacus of the Catuvellauni, who had fled his kingdom in south-eastern England to continue the fight against Rome). Despite notable successes, such as a stinging defeat inflicted on the Legio II Augusta in AD 52, a concerted campaign by governor Julius Frontinus in AD 74 to 78 finally subdued the Silures. Even then, it required the siting of a legionary fortress at Caerleon in Monmouthshire and a garrison of around 30,000 Roman troops to keep the ever-restive Welsh tribes under control.

Wales does not seem to have undergone the level of Romanization that other parts of the province experienced. There was not the same sprinkling of villas, or the development of towns which characterized the lowland zones further east. As much else about the collapse of Roman rule, the role of Wales in the twilight of Roman Britain is unclear. Later Welsh tradition lauded the usurper Magnus Maximus as a hero (strangely, as in AD 383 he denuded Britannia of much of its garrison, making it vulnerable to the Irish raiders who increasingly preyed on the western British coastline). As 'Macsen Wledig', he was assigned an entirely fictitious role as a precocious unifier of Wales, perhaps out of simple nostalgia for all things Roman in an era when new invaders threatened a fresh era of strife and subjugation.

By the mid sixth century the Anglo-Saxons, who had first arrived in great numbers around a century earlier, had pushed the British kingdoms that had emerged after the Roman departure out of most of eastern England. After a brief pause – traditionally associated with the activities of a war-leader named Arthur – the Britons suffered a devastating defeat at Dyrrham in Gloucestershire in 577. The Anglo-Saxons were then able to seize a great swathe of territory around Bath, splitting the British-controlled region in two. To the south lay Cornwall, and to the north, the Welsh Peninsula. Defined, as it would be for centuries, by its opposition to English encroachment, Wales had come into being.

That Wales, however, was not united. Like the fledgling English states which they faced to the east, medieval Welsh rulers operated in an environment where the borders of a kingdom might expand and contract according to dynastic accident or the ambition of their princes. The first king of whom we know anything was Cunedda, apparently a refugee from the post-Roman chaos in north-western England, who, according to later tradition, fled to Wales and established the kingdom of Gwynedd in the mid fifth century. A constellation of other principalities developed in the century that followed, of which Powys in the centre, and Deheubarth and Dyfed in the south-west emerged as the most powerful.

The demarcation between England and Wales became more solidly defined around 750 with the construction of a set of earthworks running from the mouth of the Wye river to Prestatyn on the north coast. Known as Offa's Dyke (or Clawdd Offa), its name associates it with the great late eighth-century king of Mercia, whose hegemony over central England certainly gave him command of the resources to build such an impressive linear barrier. Rising up to 8 feet, and with a ditch on the Welsh side, it certainly posed a significant obstacle to armies trying to pass eastwards and, though the border between English and Welsh would ebb and flow, the Dyke proved a fixed point around which it congealed.

Welsh unity first became a real prospect in the late ninth century, under Rhodri, whose nickname of Mawr ('the Great') puts him on a par with Alfred of Wessex as a nation-builder. His defeat of a Danish Viking force under Gorm in 856 and his brief stint in exile in Ireland in 877 after he was chased out of his kingdom by the Vikings reinforce the parallels. By the time of his death in 878, Rhodri had extended his overlordship in Powys and Ceredigion (which he acquired by a judicious marriage), giving him control of over half of Wales. Such early medieval empire-building often proved ephemeral, however, and despite the efforts of his son Anarawd to maintain Gwynedd's enlarged borders, most of Rhodri's conquests broke away.

Wales' next flirtation with unification took place nearly a century later, under Hywel Dda ('the Good'), the founder of the kingdom of Deheubarth (itself forged out of several smaller south-western principalities). He acquired Dyfed by marriage, Gwynedd by succession after the death of Anarawd's son Idwal Foel in 942 and for almost a decade ruled over virtually half of Wales. He even, perhaps in imitation of his Anglo-Saxon neighbours, had coins struck, including one from the mint at Chester with the legend 'Howael Rex'. After Hywel's death in 950, Wales subsided once more into a period of political instability. Unlike England, where the Viking invasions forced unity by destroying all rivals to Wessex, in Wales the lessening of external pressure (as Mercia, formerly the most expansive English power on the border, fell into decline and the English became absorbed in their two-century-long struggle with the Vikings) mitigated the consequences of dynastic squabbling.

In the mid eleventh century, Wales re-emerged from this era of disunity, driven by Gruffudd ap Llywelyn, who seized control of Gwynedd and Powys in 1039, and then over the next twenty years progressively subdued Deheubarth, Morgannwg (in the far southeast of Wales) and a number of minor principalities. In 1055 he even launched an invasion east of Offa's Dyke. As his armies penetrated as far as Hereford (which they burned), it seemed for a brief moment that not only could Wales have a future as an independent and united kingdom, but that the Welsh might even have their revenge by recovering some of the lands lost to the Anglo-Saxons centuries before.

It was not to be. Llywelyn was assassinated by one of the many enemies he had made during his rise to dominance (his severed head was sent to Harold Godwineson of England as a gruesome peace offering). This left Wales leaderless at a time of unexpected crisis. The Norman conquest of England in 1066, although it briefly destabilized Wales' neighbour, was soon followed by the arrival of a military aristocracy thirsty for land (and bent on revenge for cross-border raids by Anglo-Saxon dissidents in 1067–9). Great Norman lords such as Hugh of Avranches, Roger of Montgomery and William fitz Osbern, earl of Hereford, were granted fiefdoms on the eastern borders, and in the south, from where the castles which they constructed acted as bases for the penetration further into Welsh territory.

These Marcher lords made steady advances in the south-east, around Brecon and the River Usk, near where in 1093 'the Frenchmen who were inhabiting Brycheiniog' killed Rhys ap Tewdr of Deheubarth, who had led a successful Welsh resistance. In central and north Wales, the Normans pushed steadily beyond Offa's Dyke, occupying Rhuddlan and establishing control over Caernarfon and Bangor. By the start of the twelfth century a division was appearing between the Marchia Walliae ('March of Wales'), dominated by the

Anglo-Norman lords, and Pura Wallia ('Pure Wales') still ruled by independent Welsh princes. This uneasy equilibrium persisted – with some disturbances, as in the 1140s, when much of the land inside Offa's Dyke was reconquered by the Welsh – until the late thirteenth century, when disaster struck.

Gwynedd had experienced a resurgence from around 1200 under Llywelyn Fawr ('the Great') who imposed his overlordship on other Welsh princes, built castles in the Norman style to cement his rule (and to discourage further English incursions) and began to develop an administrative and legal system which might have given solidity to his ambitions, had he not died in 1240 and the kingdom once again fallen apart into a civil war between his sons and grandsons. One of these, Llywelyn, emerged victorious (in part through imprisoning his brother Owain for twenty-two years) and began a headlong expansion in two directions, seizing English lands in the Marches of the north-east and occupying Powys and Deheubarth in Pura Wallia. In 1258 he claimed the title 'Prince of Wales', a position which the English recognized by the Treaty of Montgomery in 1267.

By 1272, however, Llywelyn was facing a new king of England, Edward I, whose ambitions to advance English power made him a dangerous adversary. In 1277 Edward launched a massive invasion, and, with limited resources and unable to rely on the support of Welsh principalities which he had only recently conquered, Llywelyn was forced to concede the Treaty of Aberconwy, a humiliating agreement by which he forfeited much of his territory to the English crown (though he was allowed to retain his title as Prince of Wales). Edward perhaps pushed his luck too far, as the building of new castles at Aberystwyth, Flint and Rhuddlan heightened Welsh resentment, and in 1282 Dafydd ap Gruffud launched a rebellion, to be joined soon after by his reluctant brother Llywelyn. The Welsh faced overwhelming odds, and Llywelyn was killed in December in a skirmish in central Wales. His brother carried on a hopeless fight for another six months before he was captured, and then hanged, drawn and quartered to act as a savage warning to other Welsh rebels. Under the Statute of Rhuddlan (1284), Wales was parcelled up into an area in the north and west under direct royal jurisdiction (and divided up into shires on the English model), with the rest under the control of the Marcher lords.

Welsh independence and the chances of emerging as a European country of modest size had been extinguished, and, despite periodic uprisings (notably in 1287 and 1316), Wales remained largely quiescent, ruled by absentee English lords (or absentee bishops in the case of the Welsh sees) and with little hope of advancement for the native population. Discontent at this exclusion finally exploded in 1400 with the rebellion of Owain Glyn Dŵr. Claiming descent from the princes of Powys, Glyn Dŵr was declared prince of Wales on 16 September, and then his followers spread out over north Wales, laying siege to English castles (and on Good Friday 1401 even succeeding in capturing Conwy). With support from nobles such as the Percies who opposed Henry IV, and the assistance of a French fleet, Glyn Dŵr's men dominated most of Wales by 1404, even taking Harlech and Aberystwyth Castles. An able propagandist, Glyn Dŵr led his men under the banner of a golden Welsh dragon and summoned a parliament at Machynlleth to give representation to this people. For a while it looked as if the English might be driven out of Wales entirely, but by 1406, the tide had turned: the French alliance collapsed, and one by one the English recaptured the strongholds which had fallen to Glyn Dŵr's men in the previous five years. Glyn Dwr himself disappeared into the Welsh mountains in 1415, never to be heard from again.

Welsh independence finally collapsed in a distant, romantic echo. Less stirring were the ordinances passed in response to the revolt, which forbade Welshmen to carry arms, to hold any castle or fortified house, to occupy major offices or to buy land in English-controlled towns in Wales. The accession of the Tudors, a Welsh dynasty, to the English throne in 1485 promised to alleviate conditions in Wales, but it also irrevocably linked Welsh fortunes to those of England. There would be no further large-scale Welsh uprisings in favour of the restoration of the old principalities, and in 1536 Henry VIII put the final seal on Wales' political destiny when he had the Act of Union passed. By this, the old mish-mash of liberties, Marcher lordships and crown jurisdictions which had characterized the government of Wales since the thirteenth century was swept away and the country was divided up into thirteen shires (five of them new). Welsh criminal law was abolished and replaced by English customary and statute law, and English became the official language. Wales received representation in parliament – a potent means of co-opting its gentry – and, as part of the 'Kingdom of England and Wales', its people enjoyed, in theory at least, the same rights as their English cousins. Its historical course became tied to that of England.

A sense of Welsh nationhood, though, remained, nurtured by the survival of the Welsh language in the north of the country and the work of cultural enthusiasts such as Iolo Morganwg who around 1800 revived druidic ceremonies – not without a bit of judicious forgery and imaginative reconstruction – founded the Gorsedd, a community of Welsh bards and was instrumental in the movement that held the first national Eisteddfod, a celebration of Welsh literature and culture, in 1861. Although by 1951 the proportion of speakers of Welsh had declined to 29 per cent, Welsh consciousness had deep roots, and a language revival movement got underway in 1962 with the foundation of the Welsh Language Society, which helped establish Welsh language speaking in schools and greater recognition of the language in legal and administrative environments. In parallel, the Welsh nationalist party, Plaid Cymru, established in 1925, began to make electoral progress, particularly in rural areas where Welsh speakers were more numerous. In 1966 it won its first seat in parliament in a by-election for Carmarthen. Although Plaid lost a referendum in 1979 on devolving powers to a Welsh assembly, it won a second vote, held in 1997, by a wafer-thin margin (of 50.3 to 49.7 per cent).

As a result, in 1998, Wales established its first assembly since Owain Glyn Dŵr's short-lived parliament nearly 600 years before. As the use of Welsh rose, the assembly gave the country a sense of politics distinct from that being carried out in Westminster, and the

2016 vote on Britain's leaving the European Union led many to question every aspect of the British constitutional order. The idea of an independent Wales and a 'Britain' that did not include Wales within its border, once the realm of political fantasy, no longer seemed such an outlandish notion.

Scotland

For most of its history, Scotland can lay claim to a very different historical tradition to England. Much of its land was – uniquely in the island of Britain – never conquered by the Romans, and the ethnic and political mix (of Picts, Britons, Scots, Vikings and Angles) that gave birth to it was distinct from that of its southern neighbour. For many centuries it looked as if Scotland would be an entirely separate country, and at times that it might even absorb significant parts of its southern neighbour. Even after political union with England in the seventeenth century it remained restive and conscious of its roots as an ancient nation. This sentiment burst out in the twentieth century with the birth of a Scottish nationalist political party, the winning of partial autonomy and a lively debate on Scotland's re-establishment as an independent country.

Scotland has always been a vibrant place. As long ago as the Neolithic age, it was something of a cultural power-house, with even far-off Orkney playing host to one of the richest collections of standing stones and other monuments in the British Isles (such as the astonishing village at Skara Brae, with its stone beds and cabinets, which dates to the third millennium BC). Although the Romans did circumnavigate Orkney in AD 84, the northern isles, as well as the Highlands and northern Lowlands, proved a frontier too far for the legions, who had stormed north into Perthshire in AD 83 and smashed the local tribal resistance (led by their chieftain Calgacus, perhaps the first Scottish independence hero), before being forced to pull back step by step to the line of Hadrian's Wall by AD 122.

The Tyne–Solway Firth isthmus forms one of two narrow necks

of land in northern Britain (the other lying further north between the Clyde and the Forth) and could have formed the most logical dividing line between a northern British entity and a southern one. History, though, never develops along entirely rational lines, and the Romans marched back and forth across the space between the two lines, establishing a new wall (the Antonine) in AD 139, before abandoning it around twenty-five years later and reoccupying Hadrian's Wall.

To enhance security along the frontier, the Romans established frontier outposts in the area immediately beyond the two walls. They also cultivated relations with tribal groups in the area and, just as it did on the Roman empire's Rhine and Danube frontier, the inter-action between Romans and native groups led to the agglomeration of larger tribal federations, such as the Selgovae (in the south-west) and the Votadini (in the south-east). As the Roman grip on Britain weakened, tribal raids into the Roman province grew more frequent. In 367 a 'Great Barbarian Conspiracy' erupted with Saxons (from Germany), Scotti (from Ireland) and Picts (from Scotland) engaging in seemingly coordinated raids which the empire was only able to beat back with great difficulty.

The Picts, who now emerge into the historical record, were almost certainly a Celtic group. They have left no written records, only an enigmatic group of stones bearing glyph-like carvings which have not yet been satisfactorily deciphered. By the sixth century, as the chaotic aftermath of the Roman withdrawal from Britannia began to resolve itself, they formed the most powerful of a number of state-lets competing for dominance in Scotland. With their core area in the eastern Lowlands, they faced British Celtic tribes to the south, includ-ing the Gododdin, who were based around Edinburgh, and the Britons of Strathclyde (including modern Galloway) centred around their stronghold at the fortress of Alt Cluid (Dumbarton Rock). From around 600, the Angles, Germanic settlers who formed part of the wave of Anglo-Saxon invaders who had arrived in England a century earlier, began to press northwards into Scotland. In 603 their ruler Aethelfrith of Bernicia defeated Aedán mac Gabrán, the leader of yet another group, the Gaels (or Scots) who had migrated over the narrow sea-way from Galway in Ireland.

In 685 the prospect of an early English (or at least Anglian) hegemony over Scotland was ended with the defeat and death of King Ecgfrith in battle against the Picts at Nechtansmere. It seemed as though the Picts might emerge victorious in the battle for Scotland – their king, Unuist son of Uurguist (r. 729–61) sacked the capital of the Gaelic kingdom of Dál Riata on several occasions, and in 811 a Pictish dynasty was installed there. It was one of its kings, Kenneth McAlpin, who in the 840s fell on his Pictish cousins – already weakened by over forty years of Viking raiding – and defeated them, establishing the nucleus of a united Scottish kingdom which by 900 was being referred to as the Kingdom of Alba.

Although Kenneth's successors faced considerable challenges from the Viking raiders, their attacks, just as they had in England, contributed to the consolidation of Scotland by eliminating most of the rivals to Dál Riatan rule. In 870 an expedition led by Olaf and Ivar, two Norse chieftains, laid siege to and captured Dumbarton Rock, shattering the power of the British kingdom of Strathclyde. Four years earlier the Vikings had captured York, capital of the kingdom of Northumbria, which they then occupied. Only a fragment of Anglo-Saxon-ruled territory remained, in the north around Bamburgh, and its lords were in no position to provide any kind of threat to the Scottish kings.

Although the Kings of Alba were unable to exert sovereignty over the western or northern isles, or over Caithness, in all of which Viking jarls ruled, they steadily consolidated their control of central Scotland. Irish influence was strong there. Celtic Christianity, which had penetrated via the monastery at Iona which St Columba founded in 563 and from where monks radiated across lowland Scotland and into northern England (where they established the monastery at Lindisfarne in 634), formed a powerful bond linking Ireland and the northern parts of Britain in opposition to the version of Roman-linked Christianity which became dominant in southern England.

As the control of the Scottish kings moved southwards, and the sphere of influence of the English kings of Wessex expanded as they conquered the north of England from the Vikings, there were inevitable clashes. The question of where the border between the two should lie was a chronic source of conflict. In 1018 Malcolm II defeated the Northumbrians at Carham, establishing the frontier along the Tweed and definitively annexing Lothian – whose fate had lain in the balance for 400 years – to Scotland.

The process of Scottish nation-building was accelerated by the Norman conquest of England in 1066. By providing models of kingship and administration which Scottish kings imitated, it helped consolidate royal power and extend the reach of Scottish kings, so that by 1286 the whole of modern Scotland except for Orkney and Shetland acknowledged their rule (although sometimes only notionally, as in the case of much of the Highlands).

Rulers such as David I (1124–53) strengthened the diocesan structure of the Scottish church, brought the men of Moray to heel, minted the first Scottish coinage, establishing a series of royal burghs (including Berwick) and co-opting the services of Anglo-Norman nobles who were established in the Lowlands and the Borders as agents of royal control. He also, despite a defeat at the Battle of the Standard in 1138, managed to annex much of northern England beyond the Ribble and Tees to Scotland and held his court at New-castle and Carlisle (an ample revenge for William the Conqueror's invasion north in 1071). In 1149 he came tantalizingly close to cap-turing York, which might have permanently changed the balance of resources, and so of power, between England and Scotland.

As so often in Scotland's history, dynastic misfortune intervened. David's successor, Malcolm IV, was still a boy, and in 1157 the Scots were forced to retreat back to the Tweed. An ill-fated Scottish inva-sion of Northumberland by William I in 1173 resulted in a brief, technical loss of independence after he was captured at Alnwick and forced to swear homage to Henry II. With this obligation revoked by 1189, the Scots went once more on the offensive, and Alexander II took advantage of King John's troubles with his barons by invad-ing northern England and receiving baronial recognition of the

Scottish occupation of Northumberland, Cumberland and West-moreland. In 1216 he even took an army the full length of England to Dover to link up with Prince Louis, the French pretender to the English crown. The collapse of Louis' expedition when most of the English nobility recognized the young Henry III as rightful king after John's death led to the total collapse of the Scottish position. His hopes of an Anglo-Scottish frontier in Yorkshire dashed, in 1237 Alexander agreed the Treaty of York, which set the border where it still lies today (with the exception of Berwick and a small area of land in the far west whose ambiguous status led to its being called 'The Debatable Lands' and becoming a haven for brigands who ran rife in a territory where nobody's writ ran).

The truce held until 1296, the longest-ever period of peace on the frontier between the two fractious neighbours. In the meantime, the Scots kings consolidated their power, crushing a bid for freedom by Galloway, which declared allegiance to the English crown from 1174 to 1186, and gradually squeezing the Viking rulers of the Hebrides. Finally, in 1263 Alexander III's forces defeated an expedition by Hakon IV of Norway at the Battle of Largs, after which the Norwegian king agreed to the Treaty of Perth (1266) by which he ceded sovereignty over the Hebrides to Scotland.

The marriage of Alexander's daughter Margaret to King Erik of Norway in 1281 was supposed to set the seal on this peace, but it nearly provoked the end of Scottish independence. When Alexander died in 1286 after a fall from his horse, the succession fell to his grandchild, the daughter of this marriage, who, on account of her tender age, was known as Margaret, Maid of Norway. Edward I had his eye on a dynastic tie between his son and little Margaret and in 1290 signed the Treaty of Birgham to this effect. Unfortunately, Margaret's voyage back over to Scotland was a difficult one, and she died on Orkney, aged just seven.

A full-blown dynastic crisis erupted, possibly the only one in history caused by a severe bout of sea-sickness. There were more than a dozen claimants to the throne, and Edward I tried to interfere to procure the succession of John Balliol, seen as more favourable to

England, against the claim of Robert Bruce. Edward, though, pushed his hand too strongly, insisting that Balliol pay homage to him, accept English garrisons in Scotland and take part in an expedition to France. An alarmed Balliol, knowing the Scots would never accept such humiliating conditions, broke off his alliance with Edward and instead formed one with Philip IV of France in 1295 (the beginnings of the 'Auld Alliance' between the two nations that would be rear its head, in one form or another, to the intense irritation of English monarchs, right down to the eighteenth century).

Before Balliol could implement plans to invade northern England, Edward had launched a pre-emptive strike, capturing Berwick and Dunbar and then taking possession of the principal Scottish towns, including Edinburgh, Stirling and Perth. He deposed Balliol and did not replace him with another Scottish king, choosing to take direct control over Scotland for the first time. Edward thought that his task was complete and that, having twelve years earlier subdued Wales, the whole of Britain now lay at his command.

Edward did not have long to enjoy his nickname of Scottorum malleus ('the hammer of the Scots'). He had reckoned without the revolt of William Wallace, a Scottish knight, who briefly threatened to topple English rule after a victory at Stirling Bridge, before Scots hopes were crushed by his defeat at Falkirk in July 1298. Scottish resistance to the foreign occupier, though, did not simply vanish and instead coalesced around Robert Bruce, who had never reconciled himself to his loss of the throne to Balliol. In 1306 he raised his banner at Scone and had himself crowned at the traditional coronation site of the Scottish kings. The initial phases of the rebellion did not go well, but the death of Edward I in 1307 and the rather less vigorous campaigning of his son Edward II allowed the Scots to recover. In 1314 Bruce defeated an English army at Bannockburn, where his masterful deployment left the English knights wading through a waterlogged meadow before they could even engage with the Scottish army.

The English will to hold on to Scotland faltered, and the jubilant Scots in 1320 issued the Declaration of Arbroath by which they declared that 'As long as but a hundred of us remain alive, never will we on any conditions be brought under English rule. It is in truth not for glory, nor riches, nor honours, that we are fighting, but for freedom – for that alone, which no honest man gives up but with life itself.' Faced with such determination to throw off English rule, the English caved in and in 1328 Edward III signed the Treaty of Northampton, acknowledging Scottish independence.

Hard-won though peace was with England, it was easily cast off, as English monarchs meddled persistently in Scotland, often taking advantage of factional squabbles at court or royal minorities to impose their will. In 1332 Edward III invaded in a bid to place Edward Balliol, John Balliol's son, on the throne. Having taken Berwick, he pushed on even further, occupying much of the Scottish Lowlands, which were not cleared of English forces until 1340. A Scottish attempt to turn the tables in 1346 ended in disaster at Neville's Cross, where David II was captured, not to be freed until the Scots agreed a huge ransom in 1357. David rather sportingly agreed to return to London in 1363 when the ransom could not be raised but was allowed back to Scotland the following year after he agreed that a son of Edward III could succeed him in exchange for cancelling the ransom – an arrangement the Scottish parliament promptly repudiated.

With Scottish independence more or less secured, the Scots now turned to the kind of myth-making the English had indulged in a couple of centuries earlier, to discover or concoct ancient antecedents which would justify their existence as a nation. The chronicler John of Fordoun's *Chronica Gentis Scotorum* ('Chronicle of the People of Scotland'), written about 1363, traced the roots of Scotland far deeper even than the Pictish past. He assigned Scotland's foundation to Scota, the daughter of an Egyptian pharaoh who married a Greek prince and then fled from her angry father, settling first in Spain and then moving to Scotland, to which they carried the Stone of Scone, an essential part of the later Scottish royal coronation ceremonies. It neatly trumped England's pretensions to a Trojan past, as the Egyptian royal connection was both more ancient and more sacred, as it linked in to Biblical stories about the Israelite's exile in Egypt.

In 1371 the Scottish throne passed to Robert Stewart, the king's nephew, inaugurating independent Scotland's last dynasty, a ruling house which was plagued by weak rulers, minorities and periods of English captivity. Robert III (r. 1390–1406) was so debilitated by a horse-riding accident that in 1399 he ceded power to a regent, while shortly before Robert's death, his son James was captured by the English during an attempt to flee the clutches of the Duke of Albany (who wanted the throne for himself). James spent eighteen years in English exile, further undermining the authority of the Scottish crown. His unhappy reign ended with his assassination in 1437 (after an unsuccessful attempt to hide from his killers in the privy). His son, James II, was only six years old at his accession, leading to yet another Scottish regency (a pattern which would persist right up to James VI, who was just a year old when he succeeded to the throne in 1567).

If Scotland's position in respect of England weakened during this time, the Stewarts were at least able to secure possession of the final pieces of modern Scotland. In 1468 the terms of the marriage alliance between James III and Margaret, the daughter of Christian I of Denmark, included the pledging of Orkney and Shetland as security for the bride's dowry. As Christian was never able to raise the funds to pay the dowry, the pledge was considered forfeit, and in 1472 the Scottish parliament passed an act formally annexing the islands. At the other end of the kingdom, Berwick, which had passed between England and Scotland more than a dozen times since the Norman conquest, finally became an English town in 1482, when it was recaptured by Richard, Duke of Gloucester (the future Richard III). The jigsaw received its final piece in 1493, when the Lordship of the Isles, a semi-autonomous fiefdom in the Hebrides, was forfeit to the Scottish crown.

Scotland was now complete, and after centuries of neighbourly discord, peace between England and Scotland seemed also finally to have been secured. In 1502 a marriage between James IV and

Margaret Tudor, the daughter of Henry VII, was arranged by the signing of a Treaty of Perpetual Peace between the two countries. Perpetuity in this case sadly proved to be of only ten years' duration, as in 1512 James revived the Auld Alliance by siding with France against a coalition of European powers which included England. In August 1513, James took the well-trodden path southwards, crossing the Tweed, capturing several border castles, and heading for Berwick. When the English army caught up with him at Flodden Field, the resulting battle was a massacre. Among the dead were the king himself, nine earls and the Archbishop of St Andrews.

Scotland was now subjected to yet another regency and a tussle for influence between English and pro-French factions. The sorry story repeated itself when Henry VIII extended his war with France to encompass Scotland, which was still, under James V, allied with the French. In November 1542, the Scottish and English armies once again clashed, this time at Solway Moss, just on the border. The result was once again a disaster for Scotland; although James was not present at the carnage, he died, heartbroken, within weeks. His successor, Scotland's youngest ever monarch, the one-week-old Mary, was hardly in a position to lead a fight-back. With Scotland so vulnerable, Henry tried to force a marriage alliance, through which his son Edward would wed Mary, and so in due course inherit the thrones of both countries. When the Scottish parliament reneged on the agreement, Henry sent an English army north, which rampaged through the east of Scotland for the next few years. The episode is known, ironically, as the 'Rough Wooing', but Mary in the end eluded Henry's grasp and in 1548 she set sail for France, as the bride of Francis, the heir to the French throne. Instead of England and Scotland becoming united, it looked as though it was France and Scotland that would become a dual monarchy. As Henri II, the bridegroom's father, exultantly proclaimed, the two countries were now 'naught but the same thing'.

Mary became Queen of France in July 1559, but the death of her husband just sixteen months later brought her back to Scotland under difficult circumstances in 1561. Her situation was weakened by the transformation which was occurring in Europe's religious landscape, as reformed congregations grew up in opposition to the Roman Catholic Church and threw off Papal authority. While England had acquired a milder version of Protestantism, retaining bishops and much of Catholic liturgy and practice, Scotland had embraced a more radical form, encouraged by firebrand preachers such as John Knox, who denounced all Catholic vestiges and championed a Presbyterian Church, free of bishops, which was to be controlled by the elders of each congregation. As a devout Catholic, Mary was bitterly opposed to these changes, and her stormy private life – she was accused of having her second husband Lord Darnley murdered by the Earl of Bothwell, whom she then married – led to her rising unpopularity and flight to England, where her cousin Elizabeth I imprisoned her until her execution in 1587.

Once he was able to assert his independent rule from 1583, James VI, who was just a year old when his mother was deposed, ruled Scotland quietly and well until his accession to the English throne in 1603. In one sense a surprise – over the previous centuries, the most likely union had seemed to be one of violent annexation by England – James' acquisition of the English crown came about because he was the nearest relative to Elizabeth whose accession seemed likely not to cause a civil war. At a stroke, therefore, on 24 March 1603, Scotland's historical path changed – now a party to a dual monarchy, the country was, despite James' attempts to promote a 'Kingdom of Great Britain' in which all, including its citizens, were regarded as equal participants, the Scots were always regarded as junior participants. James may have had grandiose plans for a more complete merging of the two – he made sketches of a new royal seal combining national icons from both and promoted a new national flag – but he visited Scotland only once more before (in 1617), depriving the country of valuable royal patronage and leading to deep unease at the dynastic bargain which had been struck.

With the abolition of the border and the same king ruling both countries, it seemed that warfare between England and Scotland had been banished for ever. Yet it was not to be so. Charles I, though born in Scotland, was even more neglectful of Scottish interests than his father. He had himself crowned there in 1633, but in a ceremony that aped its English counterpart and annoyed even conservative Scottish nobles. His religious policy was even more inflammatory: in 1637 he imposed a new Prayer Book on Scotland, which if anything was even closer to the Catholic tradition than its English equivalent. In 1638 a 'National Covenant' was drawn up to rally resistance to Charles' policy and it drew mass support, which became even firmer once it was clear that the English king was too financially stretched to mount more than a token campaign to bring the Scots to heel. Then, in the Second Bishops' War (1640) a Scottish army occupied Northumberland (including Durham) and had to be paid off with a large subsidy, the raising of which forced Charles to summon parliament after a twelve-year break, beginning the slide into civil war.

The Scots flirted with both sides in the English Civil War (which, from a Scottish perspective is better called the Wars of the Three Kingdoms), as the Scottish Covenanters sought to extract the best possible religious settlement for Scotland. In September 1643 they signed a 'Solemn League and Covenant' by which the English parliament promised not only to respect Presbyterianism in Scotland but also to establish a similar system in England. Their army marched south, where it played a key role in the final defeats of the Royalist army in 1645 and received Charles' surrender at Newark in May 1646. Having been paid for their services (and having handed Charles over to the English, to be executed three years later), the Scottish army returned home, only to become embroiled in a second civil war on the side of the Royalists (who similarly promised to establish Presbyterianism in England, the Parliamentarians having reneged on the central tenet of the Solemn League).

At the last moment, the Scots had chosen the wrong side, with momentous consequences. The Scottish army of 'Engagers' was crushed at Preston in August 1648, Scotland was invaded by the Parliamentary army in 1650, which inflicted a severe defeat on them at Dunbar in September, while a last desperate Royalist attempt to place Charles II on the throne was crushed at Worcester in 1651. Scotland was subjected to a virtual English occupation, with commissioners appointed to run its affairs and an English garrison planted at strategic locations. Although the Union with England was now complete, it was far from happy.

Despite uprisings in 1666 and 1679 by hard-line covenanters – who were furious that Charles II reneged on his support for Presbyterianism after his restoration in 1660 – Scotland remained loyal to the Stuarts. Support there was strong for James II after his deposition in 1688 (on account of fears that he might try to re-establish Catholicism in England). Despite the significant opposition to a Catholic restoration in Scotland, where Covenanting sentiment was still widespread, dynastic loyalty trumped religious concerns. William III, England's new Dutch Protestant king, faced stubborn resistance in Scotland, and his forces were defeated at Killiecrankie in July 1689, although the death of the loyalist general Viscount Dundee from wounds he suffered at the battle meant that the Stuart cause temporarily collapsed.

The Jacobites – supporters of the Stuart cause, who took their name from Jacobus, the Latin form of James II's name – bided their time in European exile and expended their energies in colourful plotting. The near bankruptcy of Scotland following efforts to establish a Scottish colony at Darien in Panama in 1695–9 and the prospect that the death of Queen Anne might lead to the union of the crowns breaking up (with a Protestant Hanoverian on the throne in England and a Catholic Stuart restoration in Scotland) finally resulted in the kind of legal union which James I had hoped for. The passing of the Act of Union in 1707, which finally gave birth to a 'United Kingdom of Great Britain', gave Scotland representation at Westminster and economic security, and its people equal rights to those of England, but at the price of extinguishing its own parliament and separate voice within the union.

Although a French fleet lay ready in 1708 to deliver James Francis Edward Stuart (James III and VIII) to Scotland, the 'Old Pretender' had to wait to raise a significant revolt until 1715, when sentiment turned against the accession of the German Protestant George I. His supporters, led by the Earl of Mar, gathered 12,000 armed men – mostly from the Highland clans – but the military campaign was badly mishandled, and by early 1716 the uprising had collapsed. The Jacobites' next chance only came in 1745, when England's alignment against France during the Austrian War of Succession prompted hopes that Louis XV would support Charles James Stuart ('the Young Pretender') in a new bid for a Stuart restoration. The French equivocated and finally withheld their consent, and so Charles sailed to Scotland regardless, landing on the island of Eriskay in the Outer Hebrides in July 1745.

The new Jacobite uprising was far more successful than its predecessor. The clans rallied in greater numbers, and the defeat of an English army at Prestonpans in September brought further support. With the French aid he needed to secure his position in Scotland still being denied, Charles then took a calculated gamble by striking across the English border in November. He hoped to spark a pro-Stuart uprising there and then march on London, but although they met with little resistance, the Jacobites found few supporters on their long march southwards. Charles's army of Highlanders occupied Manchester and then pushed on as far as Derby, which they reached in early December. Had they pressed further, as Charles himself wanted, English morale might have collapsed – they were after all just 120 miles from the capital. His advisers, though, most notably Lord George Murray, were resolutely opposed, and so the Jacobite army turned back and began the long weary march northwards. As English reinforcements flooded into Scotland, the mistake became clear, and on 16 April 1746 the Highlanders were cut apart by a disciplined English force at Culloden, against whose artillery the Scots had no defence.

After five months as a hunted fugitive in the western Highlands, Charles fled back to Europe on a French frigate, where he remained (latterly in Italy) until his death in 1788. The English government took harsh action to extinguish the Highland way of life as a means of avoiding a future Jacobite rebellion taking root among the clans.

The Act of Proscription of 1746 forbade the carrying of arms and the wearing of traditional clan tartans, and measures were also passed to break the traditional authority of the Highland clan chieftains.

The campaign achieved its desired effect. There were no more Jacobite uprisings and, despite the widespread discontent at the Highland Clearances, which evicted thousands of smallholders from their land to make way for more profitable sheep farms, no significant acts of rebellion after 1745. Even as Irish nationalists lobbied vigorously for Home Rule in the late nineteenth century, similar movements in Scotland attracted only limited support. Feelings that London was ignoring Scottish interests never went away, however, and in 1934 the Scottish National Party was founded to lobby for independence. It achieved its first MP in 1945, but a by-election victory at Hamilton in 1967 and the discovery of oil in the North Sea, which meant that an independent Scotland stood a chance of being financially self-sufficient, raised the profile of the nationalist movement.

A referendum in March 1979 to establish a devolved Scottish parliament failed because, though a majority voted in favour, this represented only 33 per cent of the electorate, and the legislation enabling the referendum had set a 40 per cent bar which needed to be passed. The SNP continued to lobby and in 1997 won a second referendum, with 74 per cent voting to re-established a Scottish parliament with authority over a wide range of devolved powers (which in 2016 additionally gained the authority to vary taxation rates in Scotland). The final stage, full independence for Scotland, seemed an elusive goal, despite the SNP's winning of a majority in the Scottish parliament in 2011. However, in 2012 Prime Minister David Cameron conceded a further referendum, hoping that, if this were won, it would settle the independence debate for the foreseeable future.

Although the 'No' campaign won the September 2014 independence referendum by 55 to 45 per cent, that debate was almost immediately reignited by the United Kingdom referendum vote in

June 2016 to leave the European Union. A large majority of Scots (62 to 38 per cent) had voted to remain in the EU, and feelings flared up that, once again, Scotland was being led into a constitutional arrangement without its consent. The SNP demanded that Scotland have a deciding say in whether it should break with the EU, and voices were raised that there should be a new independence referendum which would, if passed, allow the country to remain as a sovereign state within the EU. Fourteen hundred years after the first English Northumbrian invasion of Scotland and over 500 years since James I united the two crowns, Scotland's relationship with England was very much still in question.

Ireland

Although the bulk of the island of Ireland does not now form part of the United Kingdom and experienced its own entirely separate political development until the twelfth century, its 800-year-long experience of English and British rule meant that for long the Irish question, of whether Ireland (or parts of it) would form part of Britain, was a vital component in the larger matter of what shape Britain would finally assume. That Ireland could be viewed by some as an essential part of Britain, which was wrongly separated from it in 1922, and by others instead as England's first colony, the victim of centuries of violent occupation, shows the passions which can be aroused by an examination of Ireland's past.

Ireland's relations with the classical world were even more fitful than Britain's. In the first century AD, the Latin Geographer Strabo refers to it as 'Ierne' but tells us little more than that the inhabitants regarded it a great honour to eat their deceased fathers. That Ireland was never conquered (or invaded) by the Romans, means that the kind of written sources we have for the province of Britannia are wholly lacking. Ireland instead only makes its entry into the historical record in AD 431, when Pope Celestine sent a certain Palladius as a missionary there. That there are no subsequent mentions of Palladius is a fair indication that the enterprise was not a success. Instead, Christianity was brought to the Irish by Patrick, a Briton from somewhere in the north of England, who was taken there as a slave and who escaped his captivity only to return in AD 432 to preach to the pagan Irish.

Ireland in Patrick's time was populated by Celtic-speaking peoples and consisted of a patchwork of states, ruled over by chieftains and kings who clustered around *crannogs* (artificial lake-dwellings) and hill-forts as their capitals. It was much the same pattern as prevailed in England before and after the Roman conquest, save that in Ireland there were no towns to speak of (although Tara in County Meath seems to have acted as a ceremonial centre for the whole of Ireland). In their absence the Christian Church coalesced around monasteries, rather than urban-based bishoprics, and these became the repositories of great wealth.

In time the eighty to 100 petty kingdoms resolved themselves into five or six, each of which held sway over a province, most notably the Ulaid in the north-east and Munster, Connacht and Leinster in the south. Over them dynasties such as the Uí Néill held sway (reputedly descended from Niall of the Nine Hostages, a king of Tara who ruled around 400). The balance of power between these kingdoms shifted regularly, with none of them able to exert dominance over the whole island. The system was destabilized in 795 by the Vikings, who began their attacks on Ireland with a raid on the island-monastery of Raithlin, off the coast of Dublin. Monasteries proved a particularly appealing target, and the most important, such as Bangor and Armagh, suffered repeated assaults (though the Vikings were not the only ones guilty of this, as in 832 the monastery at Clonmacnois was pillaged by Feidlimid mac Crimthainn, the king of Munster, and supposedly a devout Christian).

In 840, the Vikings founded a *longphort* (or fortified port) at Dublin, one of a string around Ireland's coasts, which included Waterford, Wexford and Limerick. There the Norsemen established Ireland's first towns, which began as trading outposts, but they became drawn inexorably into the politics of Ireland's feuding kingdoms. Expelled from Dublin in 902 by a coalition of Irish rulers, the Vikings returned to Ireland in 914, and in 917 they seized Dublin once more.

Although they continued to raid inland, the power of the Viking kings of Dublin was blunted by their persistent attempts to acquire the kingship of York in England and to construct a kingdom which bridged the Irish Sea. The result was that by the time the Dál Cais of northern Munster emerged to challenge the supremacy of the Uí Néill in the late tenth century, Viking power was already in decline. Brian Boruma of the Dál Cais managed to seize Limerick and Munster from the Norsemen, but his rising ambitions brought him into conflict with Máel Sechnaill II of the southern Uí Néill. The struggle between the two kings halted Brian's expansion at the Vikings' expense, until they made an agreement in 997 at Clonfert to divide Ireland between them, a pact which allowed Brian to move against the Vikings once more. Despite a desperate appeal by Sihtric Silkenbeard, the Norse ruler of Dublin, which brought Vikings flocking from as far afield as Orkney and the Isle of Man, and an alliance with Máel Morda of Leinster, the Dál Cais host crushed the Vikings at Clontarf on Good Friday 1014. Although Brian was killed – like a good Christian martyr, while at prayer in his camp, it was said – Dublin never recovered its independent power and, though still playing host to a large Scandinavian population, was ruled by Irish kings from the mid eleventh century.

The demise of the Vikings did not lessen the bitterness of the struggle for primacy between the Irish kingdoms. Máel Sechnaill had become the dominant ruler after Brian Boruma's death, and following his death in 1022 power oscillated between the Uí Néill and their rivals, until by the mid twelfth century Turlough O'Connor, king of Connacht, held sway over the other Irish kingdoms. By 1121 he had defeated Munster and shortly before he died in 1156 seemed set to unite the whole of Ireland under his kingship. His death precipitated a crisis, as a struggle erupted between Rory O'Connor, king of Connacht, and Dermot MacMurrough of Leinster. When O'Connor drove Dermot out, he fled over the Irish Sea to throw himself on the mercy of Henry II.

Henry had mooted intervening in Ireland before. Indeed, in 1155 Pope Adrian IV (who was, most conveniently, English and so well disposed to his countryman) had issued the Papal Bull *Laudabiliter* by which Henry was granted authority to rule over Ireland. Dermot's appeal gave him the perfect excuse to take action on this promise, though, nervous of the resources required, Henry initially confined himself to accepting Dermot's homage and authorizing a group of knights under Richard fitzGilbert de Clare (better known as 'Strongbow') to accompany the deposed Leinster king back to his homeland.

Strongbow was more successful than Henry II had expected and not only retook Leinster for Dermot, but gained control over Dublin and invaded and seized much of Meath. Faced with the prospect of an independent Anglo-Norman kingdom in Ireland, Henry felt that he had no choice but to step in himself. So, in October 1171, the English king landed near Waterford at the head of an army of 4,000 soldiers (including 500 knights). He stayed there six months, accepting homage from most of the native kings (including the rulers of Cork, Limerick, Leinster and Ulaid, though not that of Rory O'Connor). Ironically, the native Irish kings thought they were acquiring Henry's protection against the rapacious English barons.

They were wrong, and the English occupation lasted for nearly 750 years (the details of which are recounted in other chapters). During that time, it seemed as though Britain and Ireland would be united as one political entity (as, indeed, they formally were from 1801 to 1922 as the United Kingdom of Britain and Ireland). In the end, though, a specifically Irish political consciousness survived war, famine and dispossession, to emerge in the nineteenth century in an organized form which the British struggled to contain. In 1922 the south of Ireland achieved its independence from the United Kingdom, leaving only six counties of Ulster (where Protestants were in the majority or nearly so) under British control. Irish nationalist sentiment remains strong among Northern Ireland's Catholics, although as bitterly opposed by Protestant Unionists, and the debate over Ulster's future is far from over. While both parts of Ireland remained in the European Union, it was possible to smooth over these divisions, but the 2016 vote by Britain to leave the EU (which a majority in Northern Ireland opposed) led to concerns over the return of a hard border to Ireland, the need for military patrols to police it and a possible return to the violence of the Troubles in the 1970s. Ireland, as Wales and Scotland, remains an open question for the future shape of Britain.

Tudor Britain, 1541

under effective control of Henry VIII, *c.*1541

------- Welsh shires under act of Union, 1536

Debatable territory

routes of Pilgrimage of Grace

N

1 Anglesey
2 Caernarfonshire
3 Flint
4 Denbighshire
5 Merionethshire
6 Montgomeryshire
7 Cardiganshire
8 Radnorshire
9 Brecknockshire
10 Monmouthshire
11 Glamorganshire
12 Carmarthanshire
13 Pembrokeshire

SCOTLAND

Perth

Edinburgh
Berwick

Redesdale
Tynedale

Dumfries
Carlisle
Newcastle

Bangor

Armagh

IRELAND
Kingdom of Ireland
from 1542

Dublin

Lancaster
York

Lincoln

1 2 4 3
5
6
WALES
7 8
St David's 13 12 9
11 10

Hereford

Norwich

Bosworth 1485

London
Pale of Calais

Waterford

Cork

Bristol

Calais

Exeter

Boulogne
English
1544–49

0   100   200 miles
0   100   200 km

FRANCE

7 Tudor Britain

England reinvented itself in the Tudor Age. At its start in 1485, a country broken by decades of civil war and the cost of over a century of campaigning in France still imagined itself a continental power, its ruler forming part of a Europe-wide network of Christian, Catholic princes. By its end in 1601, England saw itself as a nation apart, a Protestant bulwark, its security protected by the sea and the valour of its navy, whose merchants and explorers were beginning to nibble at the Spanish hegemony in the New World and to venture to the fabled Spice Islands of the East. It was an act of historical escapology, as England sought to flee from its own recent past and create a new present devoid of inconvenient attachments abroad.

Within the British Isles, the Tudors compensated for their inability to recapture past glories elsewhere by a redoubled effort to create a 'British empire' within Britain itself. Wales, which since the conquest of the thirteenth century had occupied an uncertain space, in a personal union with the crown that left it half-in and half-out of the central system of administration, was now subjected to full integration. Ireland, where successive waves of English settlers had created an uneasy partition of territorial and political powers, experienced a series of largely failed experiments at resolving its relationship with the English crown. Only Scotland managed to remain aloof from the embrace of the English constrictor: too large for English armies to do more than raid and harass, it became the subject of a diplomatic tussle between England and France, in the hope that dynastic manoeuvres would deliver control of its crown, where naked force could not.

The Tudors, who made all these changes, have become enshrined in popular consciousness as virtually the originators of England, providing stability where all before had been chaos, and establishing institutions, most notably the Church of England, which were long seen as forming the core of English (though not necessarily British) national identity. This Tudor image, though, is in large part the product of luck and of its own able propagandists. Henry Tudor, the founder of the dynasty and an outsider from Wales, was fortunate in that the Wars of the Roses had led to the demise of the most plausible challengers to his rule, and the death of Richard III at Bosworth on 22 August 1485 left the way clear to declare himself king as Henry VII. He sealed the end of the long struggle between Yorkists and Lancastrians by marrying Edward IV's daughter, Elizabeth of York, in January 1486. Tolerance for his former opponents had its limits, though, and he performed a legal sleight of hand by backdating his reign to the day before Bosworth, putting any nobles who had supported Richard – and most had not committed themselves to either side – under constant threat of an act of attainder, meaning their execution, and the confiscation of all their lands to the crown.

Having seized the throne by force, Henry VII needed to make his presence felt as widely as possible in his new kingdom, and he made a triumphant tour in the spring of 1486, travelling as far north as York and visiting major towns such as Cambridge, Lincoln, Nottingham, Birmingham and Gloucester. Even so, the early part of his reign was still blighted by aftershocks from the Wars of the Roses. In the absence of genuine surviving members of the House of York or Lancaster prepared to risk their necks by fomenting uprising, these came mainly in the form of two pretenders. The first was Lambert Simnel, a youth of humble origins, whose backers claimed him to be the Earl of Warwick, Edward IV's nephew (who was in fact incarcerated in the Tower of London), and who had him crowned king as Edward VI in Dublin. In a kind of Tudor 'post-truth' moment, Henry's attempts to spike the revolt by having the real Earl paraded through the streets of London failed to convince Simnel's partisans. With the backing of the Earl of Kildare, the main Anglo-Irish magnate who was the English crown's Lord Deputy in Ireland, and John de la Pole, the Earl of Lincoln, who himself had a good claim to the throne as another of Edward IV's nephews, and who may have intended to elbow aside Simnel at a later stage, the rebels crossed the Irish Sea only to be defeated at Stoke on 16 June 1487 after a hard-won battle.

Henry was clement in victory – he could afford to be, as Lincoln had died – and instead of having Simnel executed, he put him to work as a kitchen-hand in the royal palace. Yet he still could not sit easy on his throne and for much of the 1490s was plagued by yet another pretender. Perkin Warbeck, originally from Flanders, who took service with an English merchant and caught the eye of Yorkist malcontents in Ireland, was persuaded to masquerade as Richard, Duke of York, Edward IV's younger son. He found support in Ireland and among residual Yorkists in England, but also among England's neighbours, who were more than happy to stir up trouble – including James IV of Scotland, Charles VIII of France and Duchess Margaret of Burgundy (who just happened to be Edward IV's sister). Warbeck was more of a gadfly than a real threat and, after a failed landing at Deal in Kent in 1495, flitted between Ireland and Scotland (where James IV launched a failed invasion of the north of England in 1496), before being captured at Beaulieu Abbey, where he had taken refuge after yet another failed uprising in Cornwall in September 1497.

Hardly surprisingly, given his unorthodox route to the throne and the initial troubles he had faced in keeping hold of it, Henry VII was more a consolidator than an innovator. He relied on a small number of trusted advisers, such as Richard Empson (Chancellor of the Duchy of Lancaster from 1504) and Edmund Dudley (president of the Council), and pursued an extremely parsimonious fiscal policy that squeezed the royal estates, imposed higher customs tariffs and exploited surviving feudal dues to leave the royal treasury in balance by the end of his reign. He also cut down the nobility to size by clamping down on the bands of armed retainers which many had built up since the Wars of the Roses, and levying huge fines, such as the £70,650 imposed on George Neville, Lord Bergavenny in 1507, at the rate of £5 per man per month for the 471 militiamen he was alleged to have hired between 1504 and 1506. In many cases the full amount of the fine was not collected, leaving the noblemen owing a bond which acted as a powerful incentive to loyalty, as it could always be called in in the case of future bad behaviour.

Henry's pursuit of those who had opposed him was nonetheless vigorous – it included the attainder of 136 individuals (a legal process by which an Act of Parliament simply condemned a person to death without the nicety of a trial), ninety of whom had their estates permanently confiscated – and far-reaching. In Ireland, which had long had Yorkist sympathies and where Perkin Warbeck had found sanctuary on several occasions and whose parliament had approved the claim of Lambert Simnel to be king, he was forced to take stern action. English authority was already uncertain and the area of land controlled by the crown had shrunk steadily until by the fifteenth century it had become confined to the Pale, an area defined by a makeshift fence of stakes, which enclosed County Dublin and part of Meath and Kildare. In the early part of Henry's reign authority within this area had devolved to the royal deputy, Gerald FitzGerald, eighth Earl of Kildare, whose support for Lambert Simnel shook Henry's faith in him, and whose championing of Perkin Warbeck shattered it entirely. In his place, in 1494 the king appointed Sir Edward Poynings, a military man, who passed a measure, known as Poynings' Law, which forbade the Irish parliament from passing any laws without the approval of its English counterpart. As a measure to bring England and Ireland together it was both crude and premature, and once Warbeck's revolt was suppressed, Henry returned to reliance on the Earl of Kildare, whose Irish powerbase made him a much more attractive ally. In 1496 he was reappointed governor, but Poynings' Law remained in force until 1878.

Elsewhere, Henry's foreign policy was cautious, even timid. He saw the danger of the gradual extension of French influence into Brittany, where the male line died out in 1488 and the reigning duchess, Anne, became married to Charles VIII of France in 1491. Increasing French encroachment onto Breton independence led Henry to mount several small expeditions but the token gestures did nothing to stop the eventual absorption of Brittany into France in 1514. Henry's efforts to recover the lost English territories in northern France were also perfunctory: an expedition mounted from Calais in 1492 which thrust towards Boulogne was less a bid for martial glory than an attempt to extract a payment from Charles VIII for desisting and to persuade him to withdraw his support for Perkin Warbeck, on both counts of which the French king obliged. Although it highlighted England's incapacity to mount large-scale expeditions on the Continent (Henry had been forced to confiscate Venetian galleys to transport his artillery across the Channel), the war did prove satisfyingly profitable: the pay-off from Charles VIII was £159,000 (plus an annual subsidy of £5,000 to the English, which was paid until 1511), and parliament had made grants to fund the war of over £180,000. The whole expedition, in contrast, had only cost him £49,000.

Henry's son and successor, Henry VIII, was a different man. He had never expected to be king; that accolade had been intended for his older brother. Conscious of his Welsh background, and the symbolism the name might hold for a rebirth of England under a new dynasty, Henry VII had called his first-born Arthur. The hopes vested in the young prince included a dynastic marriage with Catherine of Aragon, the daughter of Isabel of Castile and Ferdinand of Aragon, the unifiers of Spain. The marriage took place in November 1501, but Arthur died less than five months later, in April 1502, both denying England the chance of a new 'King Arthur' and sowing the seed for many of Henry VIII's later troubles.

Henry, who thus found himself the heir to the throne, was in many ways temperamentally the opposite of his father (whom he succeeded in 1509). Young, ambitious, rash and prone to chivalric gestures, he was not given to biding his time and building quietly. Instead, Henry had dreams of being a monarch on a grand scale. He was abetted in this by his chief minister, Thomas Wolsey, an ambitious and able butcher's son from Norwich, who became chancellor in 1515. He continued the policies begun under Henry VII to clamp down on magnates' abuse by summoning them to prerogative courts such as the Star Chamber and the Court of Requests, where they were fined for depopulating enclosures or keeping too many retainers. His efficient stewardship of the administration meant that the king was largely free of the need to summon parliament to vote him funds, except in the case of war.

This proved to be Henry's weak point. His decades-long rivalries with Francis I of France, an equally glamorous young monarch, and the Emperor Charles V, who by 1519 ruled over a European super-state that spanned Spain, Italy, Austria and the Netherlands, dragged him into an indelicate dance of alliances that demanded intermittent but costly warfare amid a confusing series of diplomatic volte-faces. After a disastrous first campaign in south-western France in 1512, Henry launched a much more concerted affair the next year in northern France. Henry was notionally fighting in support of Pope Julius II and Emperor Maximilian, both of whom were pleased to increase pressure on their joint enemy Louis XII of France in northern Italy, and he allowed himself to be diverted by Maximilian's pleas to attack Tournai, rather than the more logical objective of Calais. Although Henry's forces beat the French at the 'Battle of the Spurs' on 16 August – so named for the enormous numbers of spurs of fallen French knights which were gathered up from the battlefield – and captured Tournai, this left Henry with a white elephant, separated by 70 miles of hostile French territory from Calais, which was expensive to defend and lost to the French just five years later.

Wolsey brokered a seemingly greater diplomatic triumph for Henry in June 1520, when he arranged a meeting between his master and Francis I at a venue near Calais, which was so decked out with splendid pavilions and tents erected for the occasion that it became known as the 'Field of the Cloth of Gold'. An early modern equivalent of a superpower summit, it was equally full of grand proclamations and stunts – there was even a wrestling bout staged between the two kings, at which Francis, to Henry's great chagrin, threw him – but just as short in lasting effect. At the very same time, Henry was engaged in side-channel diplomacy with Charles V, and by 1522 English armies were raiding Normandy once more and launched an unsuccessful campaign into Picardy the following year. The expenses were enormous, and, much to his and Wolsey's displeasure, parliament had to be summoned in 1523 to vote further funds. When even these proved inadequate, two years later Wolsey came up with the pretext of a forced loan, which was dubbed the 'Amicable Grant', but which was anything but, as it provoked such intense resentment that parts of East Anglia and Kent were left in a state of near revolt.

Henry's cosy self-image as *primus inter pares* of European monarchs did not survive the collision of two quite separate developments, whose intertwining caused a revolution in the Tudor monarchy. There had long been calls for reforms of abuses within the Catholic Church, but the protest in 1517 by Martin Luther, a German friar, against these had led to a firestorm of dissent in Germany and the emergence of a series of reformed churches. Henry very much took the side of the Papacy in this struggle – unsurprisingly, as Wolsey had been appointed a cardinal in 1515 and was vigorously lobbying for an appointment as cardinal *a latere* (in effect head of the whole church in England). In 1521 the king penned the *Defence of the Seven Sacraments*, a condemnation of Luther, for which a grateful Pope Leo X awarded him the title of Defensor Fidei ('Defender of the Faith').

Henry had the approval of the Papacy and a fancy new title, and his meddling in the balance of power between France and the Holy Roman Empire meant England mattered in international diplomatic circles, even if not as much as the king liked to imagine. There was one thing, though, that Henry lacked and that was an heir. Catherine of Aragon, whom he had married almost immediately after becoming king, had produced only one child who survived, and that was Princess Mary (born in 1516). Henry needed a son to succeed him, and as Catherine was forty in 1526, this seemed increasingly unlikely to happen.

Henry turned to Cardinal Wolsey to negotiate with the Papacy for an annulment of his marriage, relying on a text in Leviticus which forbade a man to marry his brother's wife. Unfortunately, Pope Clement VII was not inclined to grant Henry's wishes in a hurry, as Catherine was the aunt of Emperor Charles V, on whose support he relied in Italy, and the theological waters were muddied by the deployment of a countervailing verse in Deuteronomy which seemed actually to command a man to marry his brother's widow if they had not had children.

Frustrated with Wolsey's inability to provide him with an annulment or divorce, Henry, who was already deeply involved in an affair with Anne Boleyn, removed him, had him arrested and turned to new men: Thomas Cranmer, a cleric who had developed a taste for Luther's reformed religion while serving as a diplomat in Germany, and who was consecrated Archbishop of Canterbury in March 1533; and Thomas Cromwell, from the same social milieu as Wolsey (his family were in the cloth trade), who formally became Henry's chief minister in April 1534, although he had been de facto his principal adviser for at least two years before that.

The king's 'Great Matter', the need to set aside Catherine and marry Anne Boleyn, who was by now pregnant, had become so urgent that it trumped all other considerations. As Rome remained unyielding, Cranmer and Cromwell devised a strategy to put pressure on the Papacy and ultimately to take the decision out of its hands. Beginning with the Act in Restraint of Appeals in 1533, which forbade appeals by the clergy to Rome, a series of measures were passed in parliament, culminating in the Act of Supremacy in November 1534, which declared 'The King's Majesty justfully and rightfully' to be the 'supreme head of the Church of England'. Cranmer had already obligingly ruled Henry's marriage as never having been valid, and an Act in March 1534 declared the children of Anne Boleyn would be heirs to the throne (though Anne's child born in September 1533 had proved, disappointingly, to be another girl, Elizabeth).

Although not Henry's original intention, the break with Rome marked an abrupt change in the nature of royal power in England and a serious rupture in its relations with other European powers, and it laid the foundation stone for a powerful strain of English particularism which would resonate for centuries. The canon law and feudal law which had played a key role in England's juridical history were at one stroke replaced by the 'King's Ecclesiastical Law', breaking with a centuries-old common European legal tradition. This Tudor act of taking back control imbued English law-making with a sense of being an entirely separate and indigenous tradition which defenders of English individuality would periodically invoke, from the Parliamentary side during the civil war of the 1640s to the supporters of Brexit during the 2016 Referendum on Britain's membership of the European Union. In the shorter term, England's emergence as a Protestant power meant that the threat of meddling by foreign, Catholic powers to restore Catholicism (and preferably a Catholic monarch) created a state of paranoia in which fear – albeit sometimes well founded – of invasion by France or Spain inspired the rejection of the 'enemy within' and the persecution of native Catholics, and which led to a series of wars with the 'enemy without', from the Spanish Armada of 1588 to French support for the Jacobite uprising of 1745.

The Reformation parliament which passed these Acts was conscious of its grave role in the reframing of British history to make it a thing apart and carefully validated its decisions taken during Henry's reign by reference to the far distant past. As the Act of Restraint of Appeals put it, 'where by divers sundry old authentic histories and chronicles, it is manifestly declared and expressed that this realm of England is an empire, and so hath been accepted into the world, governed by one supreme head and king, having the dignity and royal estate of the imperial crown of the same'. England's splendid isolation, a matter of shame after the loss of its French empire, was now cause for celebration.

Cromwell reshaped the administration of the realm in other ways, too. He reformed the previously unwieldy Royal Council, funnelling real power to an inner circle, or Privy Council, which began operating from around 1536, and reorganized the crown's finances on a more formal basis to avoid interference from the royal household. Before Cromwell came to power, revenues had amounted to around £100,000 and these were clearly inadequate. Henry's new status as head of the Church offered his minister a unique opportunity to resolve this shortfall. Over many centuries, England's monasteries had been the recipients of rich endowments, in land and annuities, and the temptation to annex these to the crown proved too much to resist. In 1535, Cromwell sent out surveyors to assess the financial resources of every monastic house, listing the lands and rents they controlled, and inquiring after the state of monastic observance. The *Valor Ecclesiasticus*, the report the government inspectors compiled, listed a sorry catalogue of abuses, as well as an enticing list of the landholdings and other property of the monasteries, which made the next stage of the operation all the easier. This was the dissolution of the monasteries, mandated for the smaller houses whose annual income was less than £200 by an Act of March 1536, which justified the move by condemning the 'vicious, carnal and abominable living' they had fallen prey to. The procedure was then completed for the large monasteries in 1539. The more fortunate monks received pensions, and some of the abbots were given large country houses in which to retire (and thirty became bishops). More importantly, the crown gained revenues of around £90,000 a year from the 800 dissolved houses (and an immediate bonus of £15,000 from the gold and silver plate confiscated from the monasteries and then sold on).

At one stroke the Dissolution removed potential centres of resistance to the Reformation in England, solved the increasingly pressing royal cash flow problems and provided a large pool of patronage with which the king could reward his supporters. It also provoked resistance, most notably in the north of England, where antipathy to the Reformation was most marked. A rumour that Cromwell was about to unleash his commissioners on local parish churches sparked a small uprising in October 1536, which soon spread, fuelled by hardship caused by the rising price of grain following a bad harvest. In Yorkshire, the rebels united under Robert Aske, a local lawyer, who called for the restoration of the monasteries and blamed the king's 'evil advisers' for his attack on 'Christ's Church'. Aske's 'Pilgrimage of Grace', with its banner of the five wounds of Christ, attracted religious conservatives and malcontents at an alarming rate, until between 20,000 and 40,000 supporters were encamped near Doncaster. Their numbers emboldened the rebels to make new demands, including the abolition of labour services for land, which the king could not possibly grant. In the end it was a trick that put an end to the rebellion. Just as it had during the Peasants' Revolt, the government, in the shape of the Duke of Norfolk, promised to accede to the rebel demands (or at least to place them before parliament). Aske agreed to lay down his arms, and the rebels dispersed. Once they had done so, Henry commanded Norfolk to renege on the agreement and to 'cause such dreadful execution upon a good number of the inhabitants, hanging them on trees, quartering them, and setting the quarters in every town, as shall be a fearful warning'. Over 200 rebels were put to death, including Aske and most of the Pilgrimage's leadership.

The collapse of the rebellion enabled Cromwell to pursue a reform of local administration which began with the appointment of a Council for the North, established in 1537, whose brief was to project royal power into one of the more remote parts of the realm. The north had long been a comparatively lawless place, where power resided in a small number of families, such as the Ridleys and Dacres, and where a patchwork of 'liberties', such as Redesdale and Tyndale and the County Palatine of Durham, in which the normal writ of royal authority did not run, left the king reliant on a series of compromises with feudal aristocrats. These were doubly important, given the region's Marcher status with Scotland – Berwick had only been definitively attached to the English crown in 1482, and a small area opposite Dumfries, known as the 'Debatable Land', had no clearly defined border at all, leading to endless difficulties with bandits who were able to take refuge there with little prospect of the authorities being able to apprehend them.

Trouble with Scotland was an ever-present danger, and Henry's 1512 war against France led to the revival of the Auld Alliance. James IV's contribution was to lead a huge Scottish army over the border (thereby breaching the 'Perpetual Peace' with England signed in 1502, which had lasted a paltry eleven years). In Henry's absence in France, the Earl of Surrey was despatched northwards to head off the invasion. The Scots failed to take Berwick, impeding their advance, and on 9 September 1513, at Flodden, just south of the town, their host floundered on boggy ground and was cut to pieces. Over 10,000 Scots died, including the king, leaving his one-year-old son James V to succeed him and beginning the first of a brace of minorities which hamstrung Scotland's power in the sixteenth century. In 1542 a by-then-adult James took his turn to order the Scots army into England in support of the French, who now faced a renewed Anglo-Imperial alliance. At Solway Moss on 24 November, just over the border by the River Esk, the Scots were crushed by a far inferior English force. When he heard of the scale of the defeat, James died of shock, leaving a six-day-old baby daughter, Mary, as the subject of a tussle over who should be her eventual husband. In 1544, Henry sent an army north to lay claim to little Mary as the bride for his son Edward (whose birth in 1537 to Henry's third wife, Jane Seymour, had finally provided a male heir). A successful match, whether by diplomatic choice or by force, offered the prospect of a union of the crowns after Henry's death, but the 'Rough Wooing' came to nothing. The burning of Edinburgh injected a new rancour into Anglo-Scottish relations, and in 1548 Mary was spirited away to France. There, ten years later, she married Francis, the heir to the French throne, creating just the kind of marriage alliance which Henry had so forcefully tried to avoid.

In Wales, Henry's policy was more resolute and successful. The principality had existed in a kind of administrative limbo since 1284, in which the division persisted between Marcher lordships and the shires, which were directly controlled by the crown and in both of which the worlds of the native Welsh and English incomers barely overlapped. English authority had been weakened during the Wars of the Roses, and the execution in 1531 on charges of treason of Rhys ap Gruffudd, a powerful landowner whose father-in-law was the Duke of Norfolk, led Henry VIII to take action to put a stop to the endemic disorder that was engulfing Wales. In 1534 he appointed Bishop Rowland Lee to head the Council in the Marches, who imposed a climate of fear on Wales, in which hundreds of thieves were hanged. The bishop took great delight in having made 'all the thieves in Wales quake with fear', but it was not enough. To put a final end to the ambiguous relationship between England and Wales, parliament then passed a series of statutes imposing English law on Wales and abolishing local customs. The first Act of Union in 1536 imposed English administration on the whole of Wales, replacing the medieval mixture of English lordships and native jurisdictions which had persisted since the thirteenth century with thirteen shires. By 1543, England and Wales were conjoined; though the Welsh gained representation in parliament, they lost their separate political identity entirely. For the time being the elite, at least, seem to have done so ungrudgingly; George Owen, a contemporary Welsh historian, described the transition as one in which 'the land altered in hue without, from evil to good and from bad to better'.

A rather different experiment was tried in Ireland. A rebellion by 'Silken Thomas', Lord Offaly, the heir to the Earl of Kildare, was crushed in 1535 (and Kildare himself sent to the Tower, where he was hanged two years later), but the chronic problem of the crown's reliance on overmighty Anglo-Irish magnates remained. In an attempt to resolve this, in 1541 Henry VIII had the Irish parliament change the status of Ireland into that of a kingdom, giving its inhabitants the same status as subjects of the crown as their English counterparts. Gaelic chiefs were to be deprived of their land and then regranted it under charters by which they would recognize Henry's overlordship. Native kings and princes were given peerages (such as the O'Neills, who became Earls of Tyrone). Ireland was to be divided up into shires. The experiment, though, ultimately proved hugely expensive. The sheer geographical size of Ireland made it far more difficult to control than Wales, and the rejection of the Reformation both by the native Gaelic and most of the descendants of the Anglo-Norman aristocracy provided a stubborn rallying point around which resistance to absorption by England coalesced. The costs of maintaining the English garrison rose to over £140,000 a year, and chronic opposition to English rule continued unabated into the reigns of Henry's successors.

The latter part of Henry's reign almost undid much of the work of his middle years. Having accumulated simply too many enemies, Cromwell was arrested and executed in 1540, depriving the king of an invaluable counsellor. Despite his advancing years and increasing ill health, Henry then chose to embark on a quixotic invasion of France in summer 1544. The king, at the head of some 40,000 troops, was so debilitated by his swollen legs that he had to be carried around on a litter, a humiliating contrast to the dashing and chivalrous figure he had cut during his earlier French campaigns. A two-month siege yielded the capture of Boulogne, but the war dragged on after Charles V abandoned his alliance with Henry and left the English to fight Francis I alone. With both Henry and his finances exhausted, a treaty was agreed in June 1546 by which England was allowed to keep Boulogne until 1554, when it was agreed the French would buy it back. The expedition had been ruinously expensive and together with the parallel war with the Scots had cost over £2 million. At a stroke, all Cromwell's efforts to put the royal finances on a reasonable footing were undone. Henry was forced to turn to parliament, which made five grants between 1540 and 1547, delivering £650,000, supplemented by money raised on the Antwerp money market, the debasement of the currency and forced loans. It was still not enough to cover the yawning gap in the royal accounts, and the shortfall had to be made up by selling crown lands, most of them estates which had been confiscated from the monasteries. By the end of his reign, Henry had alienated two-thirds of the monastic lands, squandering a patrimony whose loss would be sorely felt by his successors. In a final humiliation, Boulogne was handed back to the French in 1550, four years early, for the bargain price of £130,000, less than a quarter of the originally agreed sum.

Henry VIII's death in 1547 set off a decade of instability and rapid changes in religious policy that would not stabilize until the accession of his younger daughter Elizabeth in 1558. Edward VI's reign began in a series of uprisings, so serious that Exeter and Norwich were besieged, and a French expedition to Scotland in 1548 seized Mary Stewart and transported her to France and eventual marriage to the dauphin. In religious terms, Edward's advisers, such as the Duke of Somerset, pushed an increasingly radical policy in which images were removed from churches, chantries (religious foundations endowed to provide for prayers for the souls of their benefactors) dissolved, preachers licensed and a new prayer book imposed (which led to the rebellion in Cornwall in 1549, where traditional Catholic sentiment was still strong).

Edward was a sickly child and died in 1553, aged just fifteen, probably of tuberculosis. Although the Duke of Northumberland, who had supplanted Somerset in 1550, tried to have his daughter-in-law Lady Jane Grey, a great-granddaughter of Henry VII, installed as queen to secure the Protestant Reformation, the plan collapsed after just nine days, leaving the hapless Jane to be executed and Henry's elder daughter, Mary, to ascend to the throne. Mary was a devout Catholic, and a reaction soon began. Her ultimate aim was to reunite the English church with Rome, but the Reformation had become sufficiently entrenched that opposition was bitter, and prominent Protestants would not recant, leading to the burning of nearly 300 of them, including Archbishop Cranmer and Bishops Hooper, Ridley and Latimer. Mary fatally undermined her position by a decision which might have turned English history in an entirely different direction but in the end destroyed her legacy. As a female monarch, the first in English history since the troubled days of Matilda in the twelfth century, she needed a husband to provide her with an heir, and whoever she married would become king. Mary's insistence on wedding Philip II of Spain (the son of Emperor Charles V) was a disaster, as it raised the prospect both of England becoming part of a Habsburg realm that joined it to Spain and of a definitive restoration of Catholicism. At a stroke, her opponents were able to identify patriotism with opposition to the Pope. Although Mary's marriage proved childless (Philip soon became bored of his rather ambiguous status in England and returned to Spain), the fruits it did bear were bitter. England became enmired in yet another war with France in support of Philip, and in January 1558 the French captured Calais. It was said, on Mary's death, in November of the same year, that the word 'Calais' would be found graven on her heart. The shortness of her reign meant that Mary fell far short of achieving a Catholic Restoration, but the final collapse of England's French empire marked the end of a phase in England's history that had begun in 1066. Despite sporadic attempts to recover Calais (the Treaty of Cateau-Cambrésis in 1559 laid down that the French should return it after eight years, a promise that was never fulfilled), the land border with Europe now vanished, making it more than ever an island and a maritime power.

Elizabeth's path to the throne had been a troubled one – she was declared illegitimate by her father Henry VIII in 1536 to prevent her becoming queen, and only the premature deaths of her brother Edward and sister Mary had made her own succession possible. Elizabeth's reign was overshadowed, just as Mary's had been, by the question of the succession, and in particular who she would marry, a problem which she sidestepped by a deliberate policy of not committing herself, of studied hints that she might wed and of half-hearted marriage diplomacy that never led anywhere (including a mooted match in the late 1570s with the Duke of Anjou, intended to cement an anti-Spanish alliance). She satisfied herself instead with the cultivation of a series of favourites, such as Robert Dudley, Earl of Leicester, and Robert Devereux, Earl of Essex, who flattered the queen, may have dreamed of the ultimate prize themselves but ultimately fell into disfavour. In other areas, too, the queen practised studied inaction, leaving critical problems unresolved, but at least preserving her popularity as 'Good Queen Bess', the archetype of benevolent rule.

Although Elizabeth was a Protestant, she had little sympathy for the radical firebrands who had held the ear of Edward VI and initially wished for little more than a restoration of the monarch's position as the head of the church. In 1559, this was achieved by a new Act of Supremacy (in which she was termed 'Supreme Governor' of the church, rather than head, as a sop to those nervous that a woman should hold such a religious position). An Act of Uniformity ordained that everyone who attended a religious service other than those sanctioned by the Act would be fined (intended to root out Catholic recalcitrants and Protestant radicals), and the Elizabethan religious settlement was completed in 1563 by the Thirty-Nine Articles, which defined doctrine in a way which sought to appeal to moderates on both sides by steering a path between radical Protestant strains such as Calvinism and Catholicism (the doctrine of transubstantiation – which held that the communion host was literally transformed into Christ's body – was repudiated, which appealed to Calvinists, while bishops were retained in the new church structure, which made it more familiar to traditionalists). The distant past was co-opted by antiquarians to support the religious settlement, including Elizabeth's first Archbishop of Canterbury, Matthew Parker, who maintained that the reforms were not innovations at all, but simply a restoration of the Church to its pristine state in Anglo-Saxon times, when, he claimed, the use of vernacular in the liturgy and the playing of a central role in Church governance by monarchs were commonplace.

An attempt in the 1560s and 1570s by Puritans, religious radicals, to reshape the Church more to their taste was rebuffed by the queen, who declared, 'We will have no dissension or variety, for so the sovereign authority which we have under Almighty God would be made frustrate and we might be thought to wear the sword in vain.' Lest anyone forget the dangers of backsliding into Catholicism, Elizabeth had the help of able propagandists, none more influential in his adept sensationalism than John Foxe, whose *Actes and Monuments* (popularly known as *Foxe's Book of Martyrs*) memorialized the suffering of those Protestants executed under Mary. It remained a mainstay of devout Protestant households for over 300 years, in editions based on Foxe's hugely expanded 1583 version, detailing the grizzly sufferings of martyrs from the very first, St Stephen, but dwelling most particularly on the dozens burned at the stake under Queen Mary.

The series of compromises which constituted the Elizabethan religious settlement and established the Anglican Church as the centrepiece of the nation's religious life may have staved off domestic disharmony, but it did little to save Elizabeth from the gathering diplomatic storm clouds. The international struggle between Protestantism and Catholicism lay at their heart. North of the Scottish border, Mary Stewart's troubled reign entered a new phase when she returned home in 1561 after the death of her husband, Francis II of France. She entered a country transformed by the growing power of the Scottish Reformation, which had moved in a more radical direction than that in England, led by the firebrand preacher John Knox. Mary's clumsy manoeuvrings, including her marriage to the Earl of Bothwell, widely believed to have been implicated in the murder of her previous husband Lord Darnley, lost her support and led her eventually to flee to England in May 1568. There, Elizabeth had her imprisoned (in part as her Tudor blood, through her grandmother Margaret, made her a possible rival to the throne).

In 1569, the north rose up in revolt once more, inspired in part by separatist feelings, but largely by the same religious conservatism which had provoked the Pilgrimage of Grace. Bearing a banner emblazoned with the Five Wounds of Christ, the rebels occupied Durham (where they made a show of having the Mass said in Latin) and made moves to free Mary from her imprisonment at Tutbury Castle in Staffordshire. The revolt, though, lost its impetus as it moved south of York, and in December its leaders, the Earls of Westmorland and Northumberland, fled to Scotland. Hundreds were executed, the Percy Earls of Northumberland were forbidden to reside in the north, while the Earl of Westmorland and the Dacres had their lands confiscated.

With the north subdued, plots continued to swirl around Mary – some imagined, some real and all distinctly worrying to Elizabeth, such as the contacts Mary made with the Spanish through Ridolfi, a Florentine banker. Mary's position was made even worse by the Papal bull *Regnans in excelsis*, issued by Pope Pius V in 1570, which declared Elizabeth deposed (and thus made the Catholic Mary Stewart even more of a threat). Her imprisonment continued until 1587, when, after her implication in the Babington Plot, a conspiracy to assassinate the queen, Elizabeth lost patience and sanctioned the execution of her cousin.

No English monarch could ever afford to ignore events across the Channel, and Elizabeth's vulnerability to attempts at a Catholic restoration meant she almost inevitably became entangled in the revolt of the Protestant regions of the Netherlands against Spanish rule which broke out in 1568. Support for the Dutch rebels was intermittent, but irritated Philip II, and Elizabeth's sponsorship of semi-piratical voyages, such as that undertaken by Francis Drake in 1572–3 (when he attacked the Spanish-ruled isthmus of Panama) rankled even more. It mattered little that Drake's expedition was part of a pattern of increased English engagement with the wider world that had begun with John Cabot's pioneering voyage to New-foundland in 1497, and which continued with Martin Frobisher's three voyages in 1576–8 in search of a north-west passage to carry trade across the northern fringe of the Americas to the rich markets of East Asia. Walter Raleigh, another royal favourite, even received a patent to establish a colony in the Americas (though the attempt to establish a settlement at Roanoke in Virginia in 1585 was a fiasco; many colonists starved, and when a relief ship landed in 1590, it found that they had all disappeared). To the east a new breed of merchant adventurers operated through organizations such as the Muscovy Company (granted a royal charter in 1555) to pioneer trade to ever further reaches of the globe.

Philip could not tolerate Elizabeth's activities, and the prospect of England encroaching on Spain's empire was even more of an affront. An expedition mounted by the Earl of Leicester to the Netherlands in 1585, Drake's raid on Spanish America the next year (when he sacked Santo Domingo) and the execution of Mary Stewart in 1587 proved the final straws. Philip ordered the assembly of a great armada, destined to link up with a force in the Spanish Netherlands under the Duke of Parma and to transport it to mount an invasion of England which would topple Elizabeth from her throne. Delayed by an audacious raid on Cadiz in April 1587 by Drake – who impu-dently declared his intent as to 'singe the king of Spain's beard', the armada finally set out in May 1588. Leading its 130 ships was the Duke of Medina Sidonia, an efficient bureaucrat, but far from an experienced admiral (his predecessor having most unfortunately died just as the fleet was about to sail).

The defeat of the Spanish Armada became the stuff of English legend. The story that Drake refused to board ship when the enemy fleet was sighted until he had finished a game of bowls he was playing on Plymouth Hoe may have been apocryphal, but the running battles the English flotillas engaged in with the Spanish in an attempt to stop them reaching the eastern Channel were very real. On 27 July 1588 Medina Sidonia reached anchor off Calais, just a short distance from being able to rendezvous with Parma. Lord Howard of Effingham, the English admiral – who received considerably less credit in the public imagination than the self-promoting Drake – seized his chance and sent fireships, abandoned hulks packed with tar and other combustibles, careening into the mass of Spanish ships. The result was panic, as Medina Sidonia's captains scrambled to escape the fireships and exited their safe harbour into the path of the waiting English fleet. Drake's role in the battle, captaining the *Revenge*, was not as critical as he wanted others to believe, but the engagement resulted in the sinking or capture of five Spanish vessels, the crippling of several more and the scattering of the Spanish fleet as it fled northwards.

Although Medina Sidonia managed to regroup his ships, he could not return through the Channel and began a painful voyage around the east coast of Britain, Scotland and western Ireland, during which storms and shipwreck proved far more damaging than the English guns had. When the great Armada limped back into port in October 1588, it had lost over fifty ships, and half of those which remained were unfit for further service. Back in England, before the full extent of the Armada's rout became apparent, there were some nervous moments. Elizabeth travelled to Tilbury, where an army to defend against the expected Spanish invasion had been assembled under the Earl of Leicester. There, she gave the speech of her life, proclaiming 'Let tyrants fear: I have always so behaved myself that, under God, I have placed my chiefest strength and safeguard in the loyal hearts and goodwill of my subjects. I know I have the body but of a weak and feeble woman, but I have the heart and stomach of a king, and of a king of England, too.'

It was magnificent stuff, and, fortunately for Elizabeth, she did not have to follow it up with a last-ditch defence of the realm against a Spanish army. The succeeding years saw further English meddling in Europe, as contingents were sent to help the Dutch, an expeditionary force landed in Brittany, and the Earl of Essex laid siege to Rouen in 1591–2, in a reprise of the glory days of the Hundred Years' War. This, and a further attack on Cadiz in 1596, achieved very little, but they cemented Elizabeth's position as a doughty defender of England and of the rights of Protestants generally. The controversy around her refusal to marry ended up in elevation to the status of a Virgin Queen, Gloriana, whose absolute commitment to her people left no room for family life. She was compared to a variety of Biblical figures: to Moses for her deliverance of the English people from the slavery of Catholicism, and to Solomon for her wise stewardship of the nation.

By the latter part of her reign, playwrights and poets were reinforcing this myth of the Virgin Queen. Miniaturists portrayed her in the guise of the classical goddesses Diana or Cynthia and the title of Edmund Spenser's epic work *The Faerie Queene* was a thinly veiled reference to Elizabeth. As Spenser put it in his dedication of the work, 'I conceive the most excellent and glorious person of our sovereign the Queen, and her kingdom in Fairy-Land.' It was all part of a burgeoning literary culture which gave Elizabethan England another claim to be a golden age, and most particularly for its playwrights. Born of the vibrant milieu of England's growing towns, and of London in particular (which grew in size to around 200,000 by 1600), Shakespeare's plays (and the theatres which sprang up from the 1580s to put on his and others' works) answered the need of the ever-growing ranks of the urban masses for entertainment. Shakespeare's history plays, such as *Henry V*, cast their gaze back on Elizabeth's ancestors and gave them a heavily varnished aura of martial glory (or, in the case of suspect Yorkists such as Richard III, heartily vilified them).

If Elizabeth's later reign was a golden age for English literature and for her own image, it was distinctly not so for Ireland. The creation of the island as a separate kingdom under Henry VIII had done little to quell dissatisfaction with English rule or to provide the native Irish with any meaningful participation in government. The Irish parliament met only four times under the later Tudors (in 1557–8, 1560, 1569–71 and 1585–6), and what little support the regime had from longstanding 'Old English' settlers was undermined by waves of immigration of new adventure- and fortune-seekers to the Pale, beginning with the first of the 'plantations', a scheme begun under Mary in 1556 to establish English settlers in Offaly. The war with Spain and the firm resistance among the native Irish to Protestantism provided ample opportunity for malcontents to try to catch the eye of the Spanish king and invite intervention. James FitzMaurice Fitzgerald, a member of the influential Desmond family, raised the standard of revolt in 1569, appealed to the Pope and, when that failed, fled to Spain. He returned ten years later with a force of Spanish and Italian mercenaries in 1579, and it took until 1583 finally to extinguish the embers of the rebellion.

Discontent simmered, and the situation deteriorated sharply in the 1590s, with Ulster descending into a state of near-open revolt by 1596. In 1599 the Earl of Essex, Elizabeth's vain and paranoid favourite, tried to extricate himself from the queen's disfavour by having himself appointed to lead an army to finally quash the uprising. In command of 16,000 men, the largest force the Tudors ever sent to Ireland, Essex left with great fanfare. His confidence that he would beat the Earl of Tyrone, the leading rebel, was utterly misplaced. Wasting time with minor diversions and abetted by equally inexperienced young officers, he achieved nothing. Then, he made the mistake of negotiating a truce with Tyrone without seeking royal permission and the even worse misjudgement of abandoning his command, against express orders, to ride hell for leather the four days' journey down to Nonsuch in Surrey, there to burst into the royal bedchamber unannounced, where Elizabeth was 'newly up, her hair about her face'. The queen's outrage at his impertinence completed Essex's fall from grace, and, after a period in house arrest, he sealed his fate by marching through the City on 8 February 1601 in an attempt to seize control of the court. The expected crowds did not rally to his band of 140 followers, and he was arrested and incarcerated in the Tower of London. After some hesitation, the queen allowed his execution by beheading on 25 February. It was said that when word of his death was brought to her, she was playing the virginals and paused only briefly to hear the news.

Elizabeth's reign wound down to an anticlimax. The queen was ageing fast and more indecisive than ever. Essex's failure in Ireland was compounded by the landing of a Spanish army at Kinsale in 1601, but the expedition was too small: Elizabeth's new commander, Lord Mountjoy, routed it early the next year and arrested Tyrone (whose escape in 1607 would cause a scandal for Elizabeth's successor). It was the question of who would succeed Elizabeth that weighed heavily on the principal courtiers' minds. The last thing the country needed was a disputed succession, or a civil war, and the longer the queen left it, the more likely these prospects became. In the end her chief minister, Secretary Robert Cecil, opened secret contacts with Mary Stewart's son, James VI of Scotland, who was Elizabeth's closest blood relative and so her most logical heir. He could not do so in public, for fear of attracting charges of treason, but by the time the queen lay on her deathbed, arrangements had already been made. Although accounts that she openly bequeathed the throne to James before her death on 24 March were probably convenient fabrications, by then Cecil had already despatched Robert Carey, the queen's cousin, northwards to summon James to assume his new throne. The Tudor dynasty was over.

The Tudor era had seen England at its smallest geographical extent since the twelfth century. Yet within its shrunken frontiers, a process of consolidation got underway, as the administrative border with Wales was abolished. The border with Scotland finally became fixed, and largely peaceful, with an end to cross-border raiding and to formal invasions by one side or another; the last pitched battle in the long Anglo-Scottish wars took place in 1547 at Pinkie Cleugh near Musselburgh during the Rough Wooing. In Ireland the border shifted back and forth as the extent of practical English control wavered between a diminished Pale of Dublin and much greater tracts, depending on the presence of royal armies. More importantly, England became confined to the British Isles after the loss, in 1558, of Calais, its single remaining continental outpost. Its new-found insular status and its defection from the Catholic cause under Henry VIII led to the propagation of a new set of national mythologies. England, under the Tudors, really began to see itself as an island set apart, and its destiny as a very particular one. Natural mistrust of foreigners intermixed with suspicion of Catholics produced a type of xenophobia which the crown readily used to cement its power. As England's horizons shrank and its border became more defined, so too did its sense of unity as a nation. That unity, though, was still extremely fragile, as the reigns of Elizabeth's successors, the Stuarts, would demonstrate.

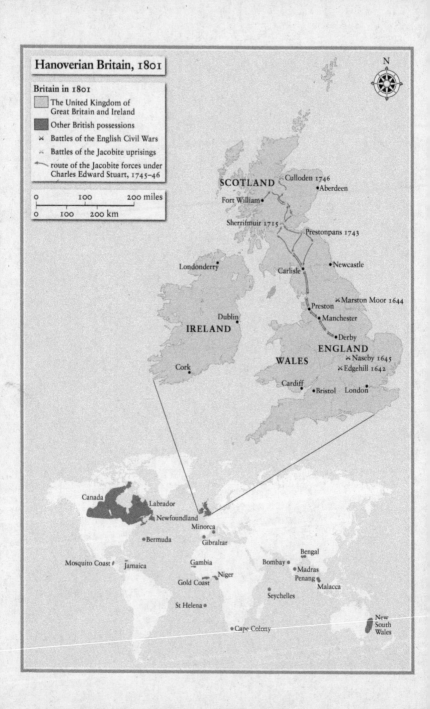

Hanoverian Britain, 1801

Britain in 1801

The United Kingdom of Great Britain and Ireland

Other British possessions

✕ Battles of the English Civil Wars

⚔ Battles of the Jacobite uprisings

→ route of the Jacobite forces under Charles Edward Stuart, 1745–46

0   100   200 miles

0   100   200 km

N

SCOTLAND

Culloden 1746
•Aberdeen

Fort William•

Sherrifmuir 1715

Prestonpans 1743

•Newcastle

Londonderry•

Carlisle•

✕Marston Moor 1644

Preston•

Dublin•

IRELAND

•Manchester

•Derby

ENGLAND

WALES

✕Naseby 1645
✕Edgehill 1642

Cork•

Cardiff•

•Bristol   London•

Canada

Labrador

Newfoundland

Minorca

•Bermuda

Gibraltar

Bengal

Mosquito Coast•

Jamaica

Gambia

Bombay•

•Madras

Gold Coast

Niger

Penang•

Malacca

Seychelles

St Helena•

Cape Colony•

New South Wales

8 Stuart and Hanoverian Britain

The accession of James VI of Scotland to the throne of England on 24 March 1603 marked a radical transformation in the relationship between the two countries. What for so long had been a troubled border between two nations whose default state was mutual suspicion and who had been intermittently at war for over 900 years was now a mere administrative line dividing two components of a greater realm. James was optimistic that the two parts of his kingdom would soon become one, indistinguishable, whole. As the new king rode south to London, he found the way lined by his new subjects 'receiving him so joyfully that all the ways betwixt Berwick and London were paved with people'. James hoped for great things from his new status, hoping to be referred to as 'King of Great Britain', designing his coronation medal to be minted with the accolade 'Caesar Augustus of Britain' and ordering that the arms of England and Scotland should be quartered together on the royal signets. He probably gained some limited satisfaction from the work of cartographers, such as the Cheshireman John Speed, whose series of maps gathered together in the Theatre of the Empire of Great Britain in 1610 not only employed the king's favoured name for his composite nation but also contained portraits of the royal family arrayed along its edges.

James also had a series of new designs made for a flag joining together the Scottish saltire and the English cross of Saint George. This 'Union Jack', which was to be flown on royal and merchant shipping, was almost all that survived of James' hopes for Great Britain, as his schemes soon met bitter resistance on both sides of the former border. In Scotland, resentment at the loss of independence grew. Trade policy, crucially, was loaded in favour of the English, who refused to open their overseas markets to Scots merchants, and their subordinate status as 'North Britain' was matched at Westminster by antipathy to the large numbers of Scottish advisers, aristocrats and hangers-on who arrived in James' wake, all anticipating honours, preferment and a share of England's much larger cake.

It must have been very disappointing to James, who had vigorously promoted the virtues of a realm united by *unus rex, unus grex, una lex* ('one king, one people, one law'). After an early outburst of enthusiasm – there was much loose talk of the new king as the successor to Brutus and Constantine as 'emperor of Britain', and the poet William Herbert wrote of a 'new found Troy' – support for an Anglo-Scottish Union foundered. Instead the two kingdoms remained in an uneasy clasp, legally distinct but sharing the same monarch. There were precedents for such multiple kingdoms – Sigismund Vasa was ruler of both Sweden and Poland-Lithuania from 1592 to 1599, and between 1519 and 1556 the Habsburg Charles V had reigned over the Holy Roman Empire, Spain and the Netherlands – but they tended to be fissile, short-lived creations with few common institutions to bring their peoples together. Great Britain, over the next century and a half, would threaten to be the same.

In general, the government of Scotland at least stayed in Scottish hands, and there was no attempt to impose a viceroy to administer it, as had been the case in Ireland. In England, the new king brought a sense of renewal, after a long period of drift in the final years of Elizabeth I. The style in which James intended to rule was set out in the *Basilikon Doron*, a handbook of advice to his son, written in 1599 in the tradition of Renaissance 'mirrors to princes'. It advised a middle road in which the monarch both laid down and respected just laws and rejected the religious extremes of 'Papism' and Puritanism, the strain of radical Protantism which was highly suspicious of the religious compromises made by the Elizabethan religious settlement. In order to be a true king, a ruler had to be mindful of his duty to God and be in all things 'temperate, merciful and magnanimous'. By the time his collected works were published in 1609, James expressed an even more stark belief that royal power came from God alone, declaring that 'Kings are justly called gods for that they exercise a manner or resemblance of divine power on earth'. This championing of the divine right of kings was not the sort of opinion that endeared kings to parliament, as his son Charles I would find to his cost.

James' hands were tied by the legacy which Elizabeth had bequeathed him, a realm both at war and with a chronic inability to raise funds. His own profligacy hardly helped – by 1610 he had doled out around £250,000 to his Scottish courtiers, and parliament was reluctant to grant the subsidies he needed to cover both the debt and his long-term expenditure. In the resulting squabble, parliament presented *The Form of Apology and Satisfaction* in 1604 as a protest against the king's contention that it derived its right from him and that it could not debate his attempts to raise money from increased customs dues. Even his own treasurer, the Earl of Salisbury, proposed a 'Great Contract' to rationalize his income by exchanging many of the traditional royal sources of revenue, such as feudal customary dues, for a fixed annual sum of £200,000. James, though, wanted more and in a fit of rage dissolved parliament, which was not recalled until 1614.

James' hopes for general religious toleration were also disappointed by the limited results of the Hampton Court Conference in 1604, held to mediate between Anglican bishops and Puritan representatives. The radicals' insistence that the authority of bishops should be diminished (or removed) and that their own ministers should be given an elevated status in the church were all rejected, and only minor changes in the Prayer Book were conceded as a sop to Puritan sentiment. About the only concrete result of the conference was the establishment of a committee which oversaw the translation of a new Authorized Version of the Bible. For many, the King James Bible, completed in 1611, with its richly modulated language that has retained its allure over four centuries, is the greatest monument to a king whose reign, in the popular imagination, is merely a punctuation mark between the grandeur of the Elizabethan age and the disasters of the reign of Charles I.

On the Catholic side, initial hopes that a more tolerant legal regime might be forthcoming were already disappointed by James' crackdown on recusants (those who refused to attend Anglican services); by February 1605, some 5,560 of them had been convicted. They were wholly undone by the effects of the Gunpowder Plot, an attempt by a group of young Catholic hotheads, led by Robert Catesby and Guy Fawkes, to assassinate James by blowing up parliament and replacing him with his nine-year-old daughter Elizabeth. The unmasking of the plot, on 5 November 1605, was followed by the killing or execution of the principal conspirators and a clampdown on the recusants, which made their plight distinctly worse than it had been before.

The latter part of James's reign foreshadowed the difficulties to come. Although peace had been made with Spain in 1604, the outbreak of the Thirty Years' War in 1618 once again threatened to involve Britain in an expensive European War. Not only was James, as a Protestant king, expected to line up against the Catholic powers (which meant, principally, Spain) and their renewed campaign against Protestants in the Holy Roman Empire, but his daughter, Elizabeth, was married to Frederick, Elector of the Palatinate, a Protestant prince whose election in 1619 as King of Bohemia ignited what had been a local conflict into a pan-European conflagration.

James listened neither to parliament, which urged him to oppose the 'strange confederacy of the princes of the popish religion', nor to public sentiment, which strongly favoured supporting Frederick against the Catholic alliance of Spanish and Austrian Habsburgs which was arrayed against Bohemia. He gave his ear instead to advisers such as George Villiers, the last in a string of young, male favourites whom James promoted to Earl, then Duke of Buckingham (in 1617 and 1623). After a quixotic – and expensive – expedition to Spain in 1623 by Buckingham and James' eldest son Charles, which agreed terms for Charles' marriage to the Spanish infanta which were simply too high for parliament to tolerate (they included removing all penal laws against Catholics), James performed an about-turn. Amidst baying for Spanish blood from a raucously anti-Catholic House of Commons, one of whose members, Sir John Eliot, proclaimed 'Spain is rich. Let her be our Indies, our storehouse of treasure', funds for a naval war – a cheaper option by far than a land campaign – were voted. Wisely, the king took the precaution of arranging a replacement marriage match between Charles and Henrietta Maria, the daughter of Henri IV of France.

James died soon after, in March 1625. The reign of his son, Charles, would prove an unmitigated disaster and one in which the unresolved tensions between the constituent parts of the United Kingdom nearly caused the infant union to break apart, while irreconcilable differences between king and parliament led to over a decade of fighting that devastated large areas of England and Ireland. Charles was the first adult male to inherit the English throne from his father since Henry VIII in 1509. Untroubled by a minority concern over a female monarch or acquiring (as his father had) a foreign throne, Charles was born to power, a fact which may have accentuated an autocratic tendency and an impatience with opposition which would serve him extremely ill.

The war with Spain dragged on until 1630. Tensions with France over Charles' failure to adhere to the treaty laying down the terms for his marriage with Henrietta Maria led in 1627 to Buckingham's failed attack on La Rochelle – whose Protestant inhabitants had rebelled against Louis XIII – which, added to a disastrous raid on Cadiz, which the duke commanded two years previously, destroyed his reputation. The cost of the war also further depleted the royal finances, which had been in almost permanent deficit for the past two decades. The 1625 parliament, on being told that the king needed over a million pounds to continue the war, voted less than a third of this. In response, Charles dissolved it and resorted to other measures, beginning with a forced loan (that raised £240,000) and moving on to the collection of Tonnage and Poundage (a medieval duty on imports and exports which had long lain dormant), none of which required parliamentary approval. All of this further inflamed parliamentary feeling against him, and in 1628 parliament drew up the Petition of Right, which called for the cessation of such extraordinary taxation, as well as ending other abuses such as extra-legal imprisonment and the billeting of troops.

Charles high-mindedly replied that he intended both to respect the 'just rights and liberties' of his subjects, but also to preserve the 'just prerogative' of the crown, and then he adjourned parliament in March 1629. He would not recall it for eleven years. For funds during the interval, the king turned to a series of precisely those forms of taxation to which parliamentarians such as John Pym and Sir Thomas Wentworth were so vehemently opposed, including Ship Money – an archaic relic by which coastal towns had paid a levy to fund the royal fleet, but which was now extended to inland areas. By 1637 Charles had largely balanced his budget and, freed of troublesome needling from the House of Commons, could pretty much rule as he pleased.

In religious terms this meant sponsoring those, such as William Laud, the Archbishop of Canterbury, whose views on the liturgy and practices of the church were seen by Puritans as dangerous backsliding in the direction of Catholicism. Laud also tried to recover lands and tithes which had been appropriated since Elizabethan times, a sure-fire method of alienating the 'Country' party of gentry and minor nobility, which had been the beneficiaries of most of them, and who were naturally suspicious of Charles' attempts to extend the royal prerogative.

In Scotland, Charles' religious policies had a far worse reception and set the first spark to the constitutional tinder which would combust so spectacularly just a few years later. Charles had already alienated many there when he chose to be crowned in Scotland in 1633, not in the traditional setting of Scone, but at Holyrood Palace in a ceremony modelled on the English coronation ceremony. Then, in October 1636, the king ordered the compilation of a new Prayer Book for Scotland which was even more conservative than the English version and upset many Scottish Protestants – who in general tended towards Presbyterianism – by such novelties as having the congregation kneel during communion as the representations of angels which it contained. In response, the Scots simply refused to obey, flocking to sign a National Covenant by which they rejected the English-imposed form of worship.

Ensuring some level of uniformity between his multiple kingdoms, while not imposing it with such insensitivity that resentment turned into outright rebellion, was not a balancing act at which Charles was temperamentally equipped to succeed. His response to the Covenanters led to the spectacle of the king ordering the invasion of his own country and twice (in 1639 and 1640) pulling back when it was clear that the Scots could mobilize a more effective force than the rag-tag royal army. He then recalled parliament to try to raise the funds to mount a more impressive invasion, but when the MPs of the 'Short Parliament' proved just as truculent as their predecessors, he dissolved it after just twenty-two days. Seizing the moment, the Scots invaded England for the first time since 1542 and marched south as far as Newcastle, which they proceeded to occupy in August 1640. They were only persuaded to budge from there and Durham in summer 1641 by a treaty under which the Scottish Church was allowed to organize itself along Presbyterian lines and the country was in effect permitted to become self-governing (together with the payment of the £850 a day that the Scots calculated that paying their troops during the occupation had cost them).

With the de facto border shifted southwards for the first time in nearly four centuries, Charles summoned yet another parliament, whose longevity gave it the nickname the Long Parliament, and which was to preside over a civil war, constitutional revolution and the near-dissolution of the union between England and Scotland. Charles' position deteriorated rapidly, as parliament grew more uncooperative, passing a Bill of Attainder against the king's hated chief minister, Strafford, a type of act which sentenced him to death without a trial, and voting by a narrow majority in favour of the Grand Remonstrance, a document which condemned royal abuses and called for the expulsion of bishops from the House of Lords. In October 1641 yet another of the cords holding the union of the three kingdoms together snapped when a Catholic revolt broke out in Ireland in a pre-emptive bid to stop the Protestant-inclined authorities from disarming the rebels.

As rumours swirled that Charles intended to ally with the Pope and Catholic Spain to invade Scotland, and as the king reneged in bad grace on almost every concession he made to parliament, the window to avoid civil war narrowed. By 22 August 1642, when the king raised the royal standard at Nottingham, it had closed completely, although the first significant clash of arms between the Royalist armies and the militias which parliament had taken under its control did not take place until 23 October at Edgehill. It began a conflict which, though traditionally called the English Civil War, might more accurately be termed the War of the Three Kingdoms, as it engulfed both Ireland (where the king found support among the Catholic population) and Scotland (where his sometimes crude diplomacy to entice the Scottish Presbyterians into his camp both prolonged the war and ultimately led to his downfall).

At the height of the civil war, in 1643–5, around 150,000 men were fighting on the two sides, with the biggest battles, such as Marston Moor (in July 1644) and Naseby (in June 1645) involving over 20,000 combatants. The Royalist forces established their strongholds in the north and south-west of England, but, although the fortunes of war swung between the two parties, the king's failure to secure London and the resources of the south-east and the reorganization in 1645 of the parliamentary forces into the New Model Army, led by Thomas Fairfax and Oliver Cromwell, finally turned the tide of war against Charles.

The king's last effective army, led by his able but impetuous nephew, Prince Rupert of the Rhine, was smashed by the New Model Army at Naseby. As well as the loss of all his guns, the capture of his correspondence and the publication of the most damaging and salacious letters as *The King's Cabinet Opened* also proved an enormous propaganda coup for the parliamentary side. In despair, Charles turned to the Scots, surrendering himself to them at Newark in May 1646, but their conditions, which included the dismantling of the Anglican Church and the establishment of Presbyterianism in England, were too much for the king to agree to, and they handed him back to parliament the following January. Even in captivity, Charles sought to manoeuvre, trying to drive wedges between moderate and radical parliamentarians and to negotiate with the Scots. Leading opinion in the House of Commons was becoming increasingly radicalized. Charles finally did persuade a faction of the Scottish Covenanters (who became known as the 'Engagers') to believe his promises that he would now consent to impose Presbyterianism in England for a trial period of three years, and in April 1648 the Scots mounted another invasion. By then, impatient with his equivocation and fearful that he might escape (as he had done so briefly in November 1647), Cromwell, who had become the dominant figure on the parliamentary side, condemned the king as 'so great a dissembler and so false a man that he was not to be so trusted'. Royalist risings in the south-east and Wales were put down, and in August Cromwell defeated the Scots at Preston, ending the second phase of the civil war. He despaired of parliament's continued insistence on negotiating with the king and had it purged of all but his die-hard supporters (causing it to be nicknamed the Rump). Even of this reduced complement of six dozen members, just twenty-nine voted to order the trial of the king at Westminster Hall on charges of his abuse of his 'unlimited and tyrannical power'.

It was a moment of high drama. Kings had faced usurpers, rebels and foreign invasions, but never before had one been hauled before the common people to account for his actions. Charles put up a spirited defence, refusing to acknowledge the court and positioning himself as a defender of the 'liberty and freedom' of the people in opposition to the anarchy caused by parliament. It was all in vain, and he was condemned to death as a 'tyrant, traitor, murderer and public enemy to the good people of this nation' and on the afternoon of 30 January 1649 was beheaded outside the Banqueting House on Whitehall. When the executioner severed his head, a huge groan went up from the large crowd which had assembled to watch.

It was an extraordinary and shocking act and represented a very real rupture in the nation's history. The eleven centuries of royal rule over one version or another of England (and then of Britain) had never been broken in this manner, for Cromwell did not recognize the king's son, Charles, as his heir, or indeed choose another king, but determined that the nation should be ruled without a monarch, as a Republic. In the aftermath of the revolution, ever more radical political and religious strains prospered, such as the Quakers, founded by George Fox, the Levellers, led by John Lilburne, who called for annual parliaments and universal franchise, the Diggers, who championed the communal ownership of land, and the Fifth Monarchy Men, who believed that the reign of Christ was about to begin and that the godly (which essentially meant members of their own sect) should rule.

With total anarchy looming, Cromwell was persuaded to accept the position of Lord Protector in December 1653, retaining most of the powers of the king, but shorn of the ceremony (or the need to rely on parliament, which was reduced to a body of compliant appointees). The Protectorate appealed to moderates who had been horrified at the religious and political anarchy which seemed to be engulfing England, but the religious reforms of the previous few years were not undone, and a relatively tolerant regime permitted local communities to decide on their religious practices. In political terms, however, Cromwell's rule became progressively harsher, impelled by a series of Royalist plots, and in 1655 he appointed eleven major-generals with a brief to root out remaining Royalists, whose activities did much to undermine support for his regime. There was even less tolerance extended to those parts of the kingdom which were seen to have been particularly complicit with the Royalist cause. In Ireland, Cromwell mounted a campaign of revenge in which the Catholic Confederate forces which had allied with the Royalist cause were defeated in a series of sieges, at Drogheda, Waterford and Wexford, after which the garrisons and citizens of the towns were brutally massacred. By 1653 resistance had been ended, and Irish landowners had two-thirds of their estates confiscated and handed over to English settlers or soldiers.

The Republican religious settlement gave the Scots Presbyterians much of what they had wanted in 1646. It did not, though, win Scotland's loyalty. The Scots had not played any part in Charles' trial, nor had they even been consulted, and in February 1649 they proclaimed his son, Charles II, as king of Scotland. The price, the recognition of the Presbyterian Church, was one Charles was reluctantly prepared to pay to smooth his return from exile in the Netherlands. Cromwell's reaction to his landing in Scotland in June 1650 was swift. He crushed the Scottish Covenanter army at Dunbar in September and then occupied Edinburgh and much of southern Scotland. Uncharacteristically, Cromwell failed to press home his advantage, as he had done in Ireland, allowing Charles to evade the English armies and strike south across the border in August 1651 with a Covenanter and Royalist army. Far from meeting with the general uprising in his favour that he had imagined, the king found almost total indifference to his cause. Cromwell's pursuing forces caught up with Charles on 3 September at Worcester, where the royal forces were finally overwhelmed in a hard-fought battle. Charles himself was one of the very few Royalist leaders to escape the battlefield. Tradition had it that he hid himself up an oak tree to avoid capture, before zig-zagging across the West Country for six weeks and then finally taking ship from Shoreham-by-Sea for nine more interminable years of exile and plotting.

Cromwell exacted terrible revenge on Scotland and Ireland – where opponents of the Republic had also risen in support of Charles. The brutality of the Republican army in massacring the populations of Drogheda and Wexford in 1649 certainly kept Ireland cowed, but it reinforced nostalgia for the Stuarts, which would erupt with serious consequences forty years later. The Republican authorities briefly flirted with the idea of allowing the Scots to retain a monarchy, as long as they chose a king other than Charles Stuart (his brother, Henry, the Duke of Gloucester, was suggested), but the Royalist defeat at Worcester ushered in a much harsher policy. In 1651 parliament issued a Tender of Union abolishing the Scottish parliament and in effect annexing Scotland. The measure was confirmed by an Act of Union in 1657, which meant that for three brief years all of the three kingdoms (of Ireland, Scotland and England) were ruled as one, anticipating the better-known Acts of Union with Scotland and Ireland by fifty and 144 years.

In England only the strength of Cromwell's personality held the Republic together. The mechanisms of repression became harsher as radical sentiment proliferated, Royalist plots mushroomed, and general disenchantment with the regime festered. By the time Cromwell finally died in September 1658, a new war with Spain had once again widened the gap between national income and expenditure to over £1 million, leaving the Protectorate in much the same parlous financial position as Charles I's monarchy had been at its nadir. About the only concrete result of the conflict was the acquisition of Jamaica in 1655 – in a campaign in which thousands of English troops sickened and died of fever – giving Britain a solid base in the Caribbean to add to Bermuda (1609) and Barbados (1625), which it had acquired before the civil war. The war also yielded possession of Dunkirk, which a Cromwellian army captured from the Spanish in 1658, providing the tantalizing prospect of a revival of Britain's European possessions, until, short of money and tired of the cost of permanently garrisoning the town (which cost £70,000 a year), Charles II sold it to the French in 1662 for 5 million livres.

Oliver Cromwell's son Richard succeeded him as Lord Protector in September 1658, but he was entirely unfitted to take his father's place (his popular nickname of 'Tumbledown Dick' is an indication both of his abilities and of the contempt in which he was held). Within months, the excluded members of the Long Parliament had been restored, and, with the strong encouragement of General Monck, the Protectorate's military commander in Scotland, who marched south with his army, an invitation was sent to Charles II to return from the Netherlands, and the king arrived back in England in May 1660.

The monarchy had been restored bloodlessly and unconditionally, but it was not unchanged. The king's initial attempts to establish a religious settlement in which all strains of Christianity – Puritanism, the independent churches which the Republic had spawned,

Catholicism and traditional Anglicanism – were tolerated met with rebuffs in parliament, and the Act of Uniformity passed in 1662 imposed a profoundly conservative settlement under which those clergy who refused to take oaths of conformity – and around a fifth did not – were expelled from the Church. In general, though, Charles was a laissez-faire monarch; his sole ambition for the previous thirteen years had been the restoration of the monarchy, and once this was achieved he left the matter of government to ministers such as the Earl of Clarendon and Lord Danby, while his string of mistresses, including most notoriously the former actress Nell Gwyn, lent a permissive edge to his court.

The reign's middle years delivered a series of blows: the final outbreak of the Plague, which hit London in 1665; the Great Fire, which left much of the city a smoking ruin (though ripe for reconstruction and adornment with Wren's fine churches); and a disastrous war with the Dutch, in which the enemy fleet managed to creep up the Medway and fall on Chatham Dockyard in June 1667, burning three ships and towing away two more (including the flagship *Royal Charles*), in the worst naval humiliation the nation ever experienced.

More serious still, for the future of the house of Stuart and the relationship between the constituent parts of Great Britain, was the issue of the succession. Although Charles had over a dozen illegitimate children, he had none by his wife, Catherine of Braganza. The most fruitful result of the marriage was the British acquisition of Bombay (Mumbai) in India and Tangier in Morocco as part of the queen's dowry, but it opened Charles to constant accusations that he favoured his wife's Catholic co-religionists or that he himself was indeed a closet Catholic. Charles did convert to Catholicism on his death-bed in 1685, and by a secret clause in the 1670 Treaty of Dover agreed to help Louis XIV prosecute his war against the Netherlands in exchange for a hefty subsidy and a promise to become a Catholic (though the text specified rather vaguely that he should make a public declaration at a time 'left absolutely to his own pleasure'), so the accusations had some substance.

Charles' brother James, the Duke of York, most certainly was a

Catholic and an overt one. The prospect of his becoming king opened up the still-raw wounds of the Reformation and roused fears that Britain's very particular brand of religious settlement would be overwhelmed by foreign influence should a Catholic monarch be allowed to take the throne. A series of plots attempted to smear James, the most notable one concocted in 1679 by Titus Oates, a preacher of doubtful character, in which he was accused of involvement in a plot to murder the king. As a result, attempts were made in parliament to exclude the Duke of York from the succession, and the Duke of Monmouth, Charles' most prominent bastard, and James' satisfyingly Protestant (and legitimate) daughter Mary – who was married to an equal paragon of Protestantism, William of Orange, the Stadtholder of Holland – were all touted as possible successors. Charles, though, remained resolute that his brother must succeed.

When James did become king in 1685, he consumed virtually his entire reign in a tussle to induce parliament to repeal the penal laws which fined those who did not attend Anglican service and the Test Acts, which imposed an oath which Protestant non-conformists and Catholics could not take (among other things it repudiated the doctrine of transubstantiation), and which in effect excluded them from becoming MPs or holding public office. Opposition to the return of Catholicism encouraged the Duke of Monmouth to make a bid for the throne, but his invasion, mounted with just 82 followers, gathered limited support and was crushed at Sedgemoor in Somerset on 6 July.

While James had no heir, Anglican traditionalists then bided their time – he was already fifty-one years old at the time of his accession, and Mary, the heir apparent, would provide for a Protestant succession. All that changed in June 1688. After a string of miscarriages and stillbirths, the birth of James Francis Edward Stuart to James' wife, Mary of Modena, transformed the dynastic calculus and offered the prospect that the next king would be brought up a Catholic. Plotting went into overdrive, and on 30 June an invitation was sent to William of Orange, asking him to intervene to save the Protestant settlement. The prospects for such an enterprise were not necessarily good – the fate of Monmouth's rebellion had shown that, and the savage crackdown which followed it, headed by Judge Jeffreys, who sentenced 300 rebels to death and hundreds more to transportation to the new British colonies in the West Indies, acted as a further deterrent.

After some hesitation, on 1 November William finally set sail with around 15,000 troops. A strong adverse wind stopped James' fleet from coming out to intercept him (it was later mythologized as the 'Protestant wind', which saved Britain from a Catholic future) and the Dutch army landed at Torbay four days later. James held most of the cards, including a disinclination to treasonous conduct on the part of the majority of parliament and the nobility. James, though, did not march out to squash the invasion but wavered, and his irresolution – he spent days immobilized by nose-bleeds – led to support ebbing away from him. With officers and ministers such as his second-in-command Lord Churchill (an ancestor of Winston Churchill) and even family members such as his brother-in-law Prince George of Denmark defecting to William's cause, James panicked, turned tail and returned to London, before finally fleeing to France on Christmas Day.

The 'Glorious Revolution' as James' removal came to be called, created a dilemma. It was resolved by the fiction that the king had left the throne vacant and so did not even need to be deposed. A Commons resolution that James, 'having withdrawn himself out of his kingdom, had abdicated the government and that the throne is thereby vacant' allowed parliament a clear constitutional conscience when it invited William, in association with his wife Mary (a genuine Stuart), to take the crown. The Bill of Rights by which parliament sanctified its abandonment of James did impose some constraints on William's exercise of power, in particular that he was not to suspend parliament, and not to levy taxes save by parliamentary consent, and that no attempt was to be made to constrain freedom of speech. Catholics were formally excluded from the succession to the throne, and the general legal restrictions on them went unmodified (whereas those on Protestant nonconformists were slightly loosened).

William's general preoccupation with affairs in the Netherlands and his protracted war with Louis XIV (which only came to an end with the Treaty of Ryswick in 1697) meant that he came to rely heavily on his English advisers, beginning the trend to parliamentary government in which an inner circle of ministers ('the Cabinet') determined the direction of policy. The beginnings of party politics emerged, too, with the coalescence of competing 'Tories', who tended to favour a traditional view of the importance of the royal prerogative, and the more radical 'Whigs', who took the position that there existed such a thing as traditional liberties which the king must respect.

The Glorious Revolution was less well received in Scotland and Ireland, where pro-Stuart sentiment remained strong (the Stuarts were, after all, a Scottish dynasty). There had been no consultation with the Scots regarding James' deposition, and he continued to receive recognition there (as James VII) among Highlanders and Scottish Episcopalian clergy (those who adhered to a form of Protestantism which, like the Anglican Church, retained bishops). The Stuart loyalists, who came to be called Jacobites (from Jacobus, the Latin version of James' name), gathered a small army around Viscount Dundee, who engaged in a guerrilla war against the Williamite forces. But they were too few, and in June 1691 a truce was agreed which marked the end of the first Jacobite uprising in Scotland.

In Ireland matters proceeded differently. The antipathy to the Protestant William III was strong among the Catholic Irish, and when James called them to arms in 1689 they responded enthusiastically; by the spring the area under William's control had been reduced virtually to Londonderry and Enniskillen. Yet once again, James proved himself a poor leader, failing to impose discipline or direction on his army, and, as William sent over reinforcements, including 15,000 hardened mercenaries, the initiative rapidly swung away from the Jacobites. On 1 July 1690 William, at the head of a 35,000-strong army, crushed James' force of Irish Catholics, bolstered by a few French regiments sent over by Louis XIV. The victory of 'King Billy' at the Battle of the Boyne would be celebrated down the ages by

Protestants in Ireland in marches which continued to aggravate the rift with the Catholic community well into the twenty-first century.

William had saved the Union, but at the cost of an even closer identification with a Protestant settlement and the reinforcement of Britain's sense of its insular status and antipathy to influences from Europe. The ties of that Union came to bind even closer in the reign of his successor Anne (r. 1701–14). Save for a brief period under Cromwell, Scotland had retained a separate legal identity, with the right to a separate foreign and mercantile policy. The establishment in 1695 of a Bank of Scotland and the setting-up in the same year of Company of Scotland Trading to Africa and the Indies formed part of a concerted effort to assert this right. The enormous sum of £400,000 was raised in Scotland to back the Company, and a scheme devised to establish a colony at Darien (in modern Panama). England, after all, had founded a series of colonies in North America, beginning with the establishment of Jamestown in Virginia, in 1607, and the Scots saw no reason why they should be left out.

The Darien experiment was a fiasco. The colony was hard to supply, and the Spanish were none too keen on another power lodging a stronghold in the underbelly of their empire. Three expeditions sailed to 'New Caledonia', but under heavy Spanish attack the final fleet was forced to evacuate the fledging settlement in 1699. Scotland was virtually bankrupted by the enterprise, just at the moment that concern was rising over who would inherit the throne when Anne, whose many pregnancies had all ended in miscarriages, stillbirths or infants who did not survive long, finally died. Her lack of an heir revived the spectre of Jacobitism, with real fears that James II's son, James Francis Edward Stuart (the 'Old Pretender') might return to claim the throne. The only obvious alternative was through the line of the Protestant descendants of Elizabeth, James I's daughter (who had married Frederick, the Elector Palatine), whose grandson George had inherited the Electorate of Hanover, in north Germany.

Pressure grew for a legislative union between England and Scotland which would help avoid the scenario in which a Hanoverian succeeded to the throne in England, but a Stuart was proclaimed in Scotland. A serious breakdown almost occurred in 1703 when the Scottish parliament passed an Act of Security laying down that the successor to Anne in Scotland should not be the same person chosen to succeed her in England unless Scotland received a settlement which gave it improved religious and trading freedoms. It was a piece of brinkmanship that almost backfired badly. After initially withholding her royal assent, Anne finally gave it, but tempers were so inflamed that in 1705 the English parliament threatened to pass an Alien Act which would instantly have made the Scots aliens and prohibited trade between the two nations. It was the eighteenth-century equivalent of a no-deal divorce.

Scotland in the end capitulated, thanks to a generous financial settlement (the handing over of £398,000 as compensation for Scotland's taking on a portion of the national debt and exempting it from some trade excises, stamp duties and the hated window tax), and the incorporation of a contingent of forty-five Scottish MPs into the House of Commons and sixteen Scottish nobles into the House of Lords. Both Scottish and English parliaments passed an Act of Union, which came into effect in 1707, creating the United Kingdom of Great Britain, in fulfilment of the hopes of James I, and extinguishing the Scottish parliament for the next 292 years.

England, Wales and Scotland were now a united realm (with Ireland for the time being remaining on one side as, in theory, a separate kingdom). It was also a much more assertive one. The first glimmerings of the future British empire had begun with the Jamestown Settlement in 1607, rapidly followed by expansion into the Caribbean with the settlement of Bermuda in 1609, and then the expansion of the North American colonies, with the foundation of Massachusetts, Maryland, Rhode Island and Maine by the 1630s. The foundation of the East India Company in 1600 to break into the lucrative spice trade which had hitherto been the monopoly of the Spanish and Portuguese extended Britain's reach into Asia, with the planting of a trading outpost at Surat in Gujarat in 1618, while the chartering of the Royal Adventurers into Africa in 1660 began the establishment of British possessions along the coast of west Africa, as well as the start of a longstanding British involvement in the slave trade.

In 1703 Britain, which had been politically marginal in European terms for centuries (its increasingly imposing naval presence aside), announced its arrival as a land power by despatching a series of armies to oppose Louis XIV's ambitions to unite the crowns of Spain and France. A series of dazzling victories at Blenheim and Ramillies by Anne's chief general John Churchill (who was created the Duke of Marlborough by a grateful queen) stifled Louis' hopes and the Treaty of Utrecht, which ended the War of the Spanish Succession in 1713, recognized the rights of his grandson, Philip, Duke of Anjou, to be king of Spain, as long as he renounced any claim to the French throne. Utrecht also restored a string of possessions which the French had captured in North America, including the Hudson Bay Forts, centres for the lucrative fur trade, and Newfoundland, as well as giving Britain control of Gibraltar and Minorca, so extending Britain's frontier for the first time into the Mediterranean. The latter would remain British until 1756, the former into the twenty-first century, creating a persistent thorn in Anglo-Spanish relations.

George I's accession to the throne in 1714 reignited an array of constitutional concerns. The convenient fiction by which William (who was married to a Stuart) and Anne (who genuinely was one) were maintained on the throne to the exclusion of James II and his descendants was dangerously strained by the arrival of a very distant German cousin whose first love was his Electoral territory of Hanover. The Welsh Tudors had been succeeded by the Scottish Stuarts and now – after a Dutch interlude with William III – a German (who could barely speak English) was on the throne. It was hard to raise much patriotic fervour for George, especially in Scotland, where Jacobite feeling was running high after the Union with England. The Old Pretender had planned a landing in 1708, but an inopportune bout of measles and a strong Royal Navy flotilla had led him to abort his plans. In 1715, with the 'usurpation' of the Hanoverians, he seized his moment. Unfortunately, the conspiracy in England was riddled with informers, and only a token uprising took place in the north. In Scotland, the rebellion's military leader, the Earl of Mar, was inept, and when his 10,000 highlanders charged the Duke of Argyll's small force of regulars at Sherrifmuir on 13 November, he failed to exploit their initial success, and the battle was indecisive. By the time James Francis Stuart landed in Scotland on 22 December, the rebellion was already in effect defeated, and Scotland relapsed into thirty years of disillusionment, repression and fruitless plotting.

The reigns of the first two Georges provided Britain with a measure of political stability it had rarely known, as the party system matured and the position of prime minister emerged under Robert Walpole's extended ministry from 1721 to 1742. The country's financial equilibrium was threatened by the South Sea Bubble, a scheme to pay off the burgeoning national debt through the medium of a company notionally making vast profits through its trade in the South Seas. It was a sign of growing financial sophistication in that such complex measures could now be contemplated to fund national expenditure, but also of naivety, as the promised trade bonanza did not exist. After a wild speculative frenzy, the South Sea Company's stock rose to £1,050 in June 1720 and then by October had collapsed to £135. All but the most fleet-footed (or well-informed) investors lost the substantial capital they had invested in it.

Britain was helped by the need not to fight expensive foreign wars, a boon which ended when George II's concern to defend his interests in Hanover caused the country to become involved in the War of the Austrian Succession (1740–48), sparked by a French attempt to remove the Austrian ruler Maria-Theresa, which, as well as involving extensive fighting between the French, Prussians and Austrians in Europe, also extended to side-campaigns between the English and French in North America and India. The war also provided an opportunity for Charles Edward Stuart (the 'Young Pretender'), James II's grandson and the new leader of the Jacobite cause, to launch a new uprising in Scotland.

Although the original plan for a large-scale French landing in

Essex was cancelled in February 1744 after a storm destroyed most of the invasion fleet, Charles still managed to muster 700 volunteers and, after evading a Royal Navy frigate, landed on Eriskay in the Hebrides on 23 July. Support for him was muted in the Lowlands, but Charles managed to recruit large numbers of Highland clansmen and smashed the main loyalist force of Sir John Cope at Prestonpans on 20 September. The effect was electrifying, and doubters flocked to his standard. Against the advice of many of his advisers, Charles then ordered his army south. On 8 November, a Scottish army advanced into England for the first time since the 1650s. Faced with the prospect of the Jacobite invasion, there was an outbreak of ostentatious patriotism in London, and in late September the cast of the Drury Lane Theatre gave the first known public rendition of 'God Save the King', which then began its ascent to acceptance as the national anthem.

Promised French support failed to materialize, and by the time the Jacobites reached Derby on 3 December serious doubts were mounting among his generals about the wisdom of proceeding further, despite the fact that only a modest Hanoverian military force lay between Charles and London. The demoralized army of clansmen began the long march back to Scotland, where on 16 April 1746 at Culloden Moor it was battered by the Duke of Cumberland's artillery, and the last great highland charge was blunted and smashed apart by the British redcoats. Charles fled the battlefield and then after an odyssey which mirrored that of his great uncle following the Battle of Worcester, he took ship from the Isle of Skye back into an exile from which he never returned. Jacobitism was to all intents and purposes a spent force – although pretenders lingered on until the death in 1807 of Henry Benedict Stuart (or 'Henry IX'), who as a cardinal was childless. In Scotland a period of repression followed which spelled the death of the traditional highland way of life, as the Act of Proscription (1746) banned the wearing of highland dress and outlawed the possession of weapons; further measures diluted the power highland chiefs had exercised over their clansmen, and the beginnings of the Highland Clearances in the decades following Culloden evicted many smaller tenants from their land-holding, beginning waves of emigration and the depopulation of the Highlands.

The next great test for Britain's capacity to maintain a global empire came in 1756 with the outbreak of the Seven Years' War. Yet another round in the country's centuries-long tussle for supremacy with France, the conflict saw the British ally with Frederick the Great's Prussia against a coalition of the French and Austrians. British fortunes in Europe were mixed; a campaign in Germany ended in defeat but secured the neutrality of Hanover; and Minorca was lost in 1756 following Rear Admiral Byng's tactical act of cowardice in failing to attack a French fleet delivering an invasion force there (he was subsequently court-martialled and hanged, leading Voltaire to comment that the English 'every so often kill an admiral to encourage the others').

Far more important for the future were the campaigns which took place outside Europe. In North America, the British colonies fought off a French attempt to advance from Canada into New England, and a counter-attack in summer 1759 on Quebec, the capital of French Canada, succeeded resoundingly, although it cost the life of both the British commander, General James Wolfe (who became a national hero for his calm acceptance both of victory and death), and his French counterpart, the Marquis de Montcalm. Montreal, the other French stronghold in Canada, fell in September 1760, and the Treaty of Paris, which ended the war in 1763, affirmed British control over virtually the whole of former French Canada and secured its position in New England.

In India, French intriguing with Suraj-ud-Daulah, the nawab of Bengal, threatened to push the British East India Company out of its most valuable station in Calcutta. The nawab's forces succeeded in taking it in June 1756, but their treatment of the British captives – some 146 of them imprisoned in a tiny, chokingly hot room for a night which few of them survived – led to revulsion in London at the 'Black Hole of Calcutta' and the sending of reinforcements to Robert Clive, the company's military commander. In June 1757 he defeated Suraj-ud-Daulah and installed his own puppet nawab of Bengal. By 1761 the French had been driven out of most of their possessions in India. It was the first time Britain had ruled over a substantial non-European population with political traditions of its own, and the gradual acquisition and defence of what became seen as the 'jewel in the crown' of its overseas possessions shaped British imperial policy for almost 200 years.

Great Britain was forged in war and by the need to create enduring myths to gloss over fundamental fault lines in the nation. The country had rallied around the Protestant Hanoverian succession (and the Dutch Protestant William of Orange before them) because the alternatives, a dynastic civil war, a constitutional upheaval along the lines of the Republic or foreign invasions to install a Catholic monarch, had all proven themselves catastrophic failures and threatened the position of the landed gentry class which by the eighteenth century had become the arbiters of power, as the practical authority of the sovereigns waned.

That nation was changing in other ways, which made it both more prosperous and more divided. A series of agricultural depressions from the 1730s helped stimulate moves to improve the level of agricultural production and, under the influence of men such as Charles, Viscount Townshend (who was nicknamed 'Turnip' Townshend because of his promotion of the use of turnips in crop rotation, so significantly increasing crop yields), Britain moved closer to banishing the blight of rural famine. As towns grew in size – London reached a population of around 700,000 in 1760 – and the numbers of consumers grew, the need for methods to ensure larger-scale production of manufactured goods increased. The inventions of men such as James Watt, who developed an improved steam engine in 1765, originally for use in pumping water from mines, but which was later adapted to a whole range of industrial uses, and Richard Arkwright, whose water frame (patented in 1769) harnessed the power of water to vastly increase the output of cotton yarn, helped lay the base for Britain's industrial dominance in the nineteenth century.

An upsurge in manufacturing led to an increase in goods which

Britain could export to her burgeoning colonies in exchange for raw materials to process to create more goods. It was a very satisfying equation, but one which depended on the quiescent acceptance of their role by the colonists, above all those in North America, to where around 300,000 people had emigrated by the mid eighteenth century. Their constitutional status was significantly inferior to that of their British cousins – the Thirteen Colonies which had sprung up along North America's eastern seaboard had been established by royal charter, either directly as royal enterprises or by private entrepreneurs, and the inhabitants had no right to political representation in parliament. They were also far more difficult to tax directly, owing allegiance to their own colonial assemblies, which were disinclined to do so, and to the king, whose means of directly levying taxation had withered away since Tudor times.

The Colonies did, however, take in around 20 per cent of British exports (£1.1 million in 1767) and supplied 30 per cent of Britain's total imports (£1.9 million), and this gave the government significant leverage. A series of measures to increase the government's revenue from the Americas included the Stamp Act (which imposed a tax on all printed materials, including newspapers), the creation of a Customs board for North America to enforce the raising of tariffs, and the Indemnity Act of 1767, which forbade the importation of tea into New England in any other than British ships (and actually reduced taxes on tea imported by the East India Company in a bid to choke off smuggling via the Netherlands). The colonists' response was to pitch a consignment of tea into Boston Harbour on 16 December 1773, a protest which sparked a new round of repressive measures. The 'Intolerable Acts' closed Boston's port, effectively brought the Massachusetts colony under direct government control by abrogating its charter and allowed for the billeting of troops on the colonists.

The government's belief that it could simply smother the growing opposition in America was misplaced. Agitation grew, and in April 1775 a skirmish at Lexington marked the start of outright war. The colonists' rapid establishment of a political organization, through the Second Continental Congress which met at Philadelphia in May 1775 and the able leadership of George Washington, who took command of the Continental Army in June, aided their cause. The somewhat wayward strategizing of the British generals, such as Lord Howe, who wavered between blockades and forcing pitched battles, and a division of effort between the Canadian frontier, the securing of New York and the southern colonies (where Loyalist support for Britain was stronger) undermined their ability to crush the colonial armies. It was the intervention of the French, however, which proved decisive. The Treaty of Alliance between France and Britain's rebellious American subjects, signed in 1778, ultimately led to the positioning of two French fleets, under Admirals de Grasse and de Barras, in Chesapeake Bay, preventing reinforcements from reaching the main British field army under Lord Cornwallis, which was trapped in Yorktown. Cornwallis' surrender on 19 October 1781 was Britain's greatest military disaster since the Hundred Years' War, and it was said that his troops marched out of the town to the sound of the military band playing 'The World Turned Upside Down'.

Britain's world was indeed turned upside down, and the mental state of George III, who had suffered his first breakdown in 1765, was not helped by the news that his government had recognized the independence of the new United States of America in 1783. The war had divided Britain into pro- and anti-war camps, each of which conducted its own petitions regarding its conduct, and the need to engage in warfare against the predominantly Protestant colonists meant that patriotism could no longer be automatically equated to anti-Catholicism. Even so, attempts to repeal the penal laws against Catholics in 1778 led two years later to the Gordon Riots, a violent anti-Catholic demonstration in which a mob of 50,000 marched on parliament, suggesting that old sentiment died hard and that radical agitation could pose a severe threat to Britain's emerging constitutional monarchy.

A shrunken Britain faced its gravest threat to that monarchy when revolution broke out across the Channel in 1789. Initially the danger did not seem so serious, and some politicians such as Charles

James Fox welcomed the revolution (as did the poet William Wordsworth, who declared in 'The Prelude' that 'Bliss was it in that dawn to be alive'). The increasingly radical turn of the revolutionary authorities and the growing influence of radical tracts such as Tom Paine's *The Rights of Man*, which called for wholesale democratic reform, fed fears that the revolutionary infection might spread across the Channel. The execution of Louis XVI on 21 January 1793 using the newly devised guillotine shook the British out of the remains of their complacency – notwithstanding the fact that they themselves had judicially murdered a king little more than a century beforehand – and within just over a week Britain and France were at war.

The Revolutionary (and subsequently the Napoleonic) Wars would involve Britain in a series of military coalitions against France for the next twenty-two years, and for a while (in 1803–5) it looked as though the French might invade southern England. A more tangible threat appeared in February 1797, when a rag-tag force of 1,400 troops – many of them released convicts – led by the Irish-American soldier of fortune Colonel William Tate, landed at Fishguard in Wales. Unfortunately, Tate's ill-disciplined troops got riotously drunk on a looted store of wine and when the local militia arrived the next day the French rapidly surrendered. Such was the inglorious end of the last-ever invasion of mainland Britain.

A more serious landing took place in Ireland, where anti-English sentiment led the French to believe they would be well received. Indeed, the French Revolution had found many sympathizers in Ireland, where Wolfe Tone's United Irishmen had fed on the chronic grievances caused by the continued political marginalization of the Catholic population. An attempt by Tone to land with 15,000 French troops in December 1796 was thwarted by a violent storm in Bantry Bay, which dispersed the fleet. Tired of waiting for a new French expedition, the Irish then rose up in May 1798, but the insurrection was hampered by the pre-emptive arrest of radical agitators, and by the time General Humbert arrived with a French force at Killala in County Mayo in August the revolt was all but over. Humbert did manage to inflict a defeat on the British at Castlebar and established an ephemeral 'Irish Republic' on the style of similar pro-French states which Napoleon's generals grafted onto Italy, Germany and the Netherlands, but within two weeks the British authorities had recovered their equilibrium, and the French surrendered.

Ireland, though, remained a problem. Awkwardly attached to England since the establishment of the Kingdom of Ireland in 1541, its constitutional position satisfied neither the increasing body of Irish who, inspired by events in France, sought greater autonomy and rights for Catholics, nor the British government, which feared it might break away under revolutionary influence. The solution was to bind Ireland more closely into the British embrace. Proponents of the Union argued that Ireland would benefit economically, and, as Lord Castlereagh, then chief secretary for Ireland, put it, moving capital between the two would become 'as little inconvenient as the removal from one English county to another'. The close connection between political union and free trade areas was one which would return to vex his successors in the twenty-first century. The real motive, though, was security and the dilution of Catholic influence in Ireland. In a process that bore strong resemblances to the Union with Scotland two centuries before, an Act of Union was passed on 2 July 1800 that extinguished Ireland's separate political existence, in exchange for the installation of 100 Irish MPs in the Commons, and thirty-two Irish peers and bishops in the Lords.

The nation entered the nineteenth century, then, as the United Kingdom of Britain and Ireland, its penultimate incarnation, incorporating all of the islands of Britain into one political whole. The three kingdoms which had fought, supported rival dynastic claims and experienced very unequal economic and political development finally sat within one undifferentiated border. Joining them was an assortment of overseas possessions, in Canada, the Caribbean, West Africa and India, a strange patchwork that gave little sense of the extraordinary expansion to come. For, having passed through the trials of the Stuart and Hanoverian age, which, by almost breaking England (and then Britain) apart, helped forge a sense of British identity in opposition to those foreign forces who were perceived as seeking to dominate, absorb or dismember her, Britain was about to embark on its Imperial Age.

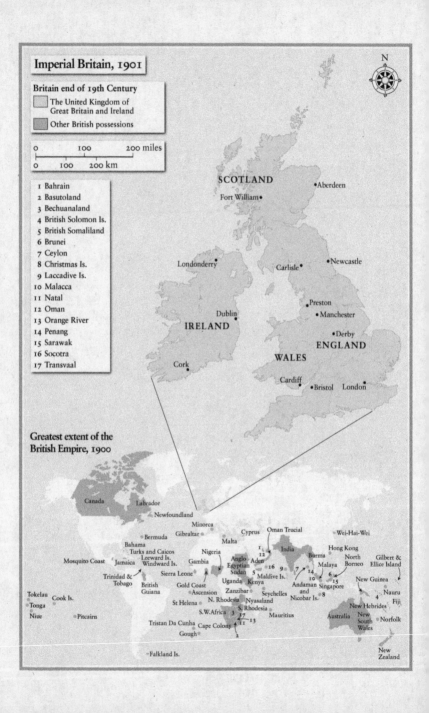

Imperial Britain, 1901

Britain end of 19th Century

The United Kingdom of Great Britain and Ireland

Other British possessions

0   100   200 miles
0   100   200 km

1 Bahrain
2 Basutoland
3 Bechuanaland
4 British Solomon Is.
5 British Somaliland
6 Brunei
7 Ceylon
8 Christmas Is.
9 Laccadive Is.
10 Malacca
11 Natal
12 Oman
13 Orange River
14 Penang
15 Sarawak
16 Socotra
17 Transvaal

N

SCOTLAND
Aberdeen
Fort William

Londonderry
Carlisle
Newcastle
Preston
Manchester
Derby
Dublin
IRELAND
ENGLAND
WALES
Cork
Cardiff
Bristol
London

Greatest extent of the British Empire, 1900

Canada
Labrador
Newfoundland
Minorca
Bermuda
Gibraltar
Malta
Cyprus
Oman Trucial
Wei-Hai-Wei
Bahama
Turks and Caicos
Leeward Is.
Nigeria
India
Hong Kong
Mosquito Coast
Jamaica
Windward Is.
Gambia
Anglo
Egyptian
Aden
Burma
North
Borneo
Gilbert &
Ellice Island
Trinidad &
Tobago
Sierra Leone
Sudan
Malaya
Singapore
New Guinea
British
Guiana
Gold Coast
Uganda
Kenya
Maldive Is.
Andaman
and
Nicobar Is.
Nauru
Ascension
Zanzibar
Seychelles
Fiji
Tokelau
St Helena
Nyasaland
New Hebrides
Cook Is.
N. Rhodesia
Tonga
S. Rhodesia
Australia
New
South
Wales
Norfolk
Niue
Pitcairn
S.W.Africa
Mauritius
Tristan Da Cunha
Cape Colony
Gough
Falkland Is.
New
Zealand

9 Imperial Britain

At the start of the nineteenth century, Britain was but an apprentice imperial power and one which had just lost the bulk of its empire to one revolutionary movement (in North America) and looked likely to fall victim to invasion by another (from France). The transformation in its position within just a few decades was startling, and the position of global hegemony it reached within a century yet more astonishing. How, then, did Britain achieve this act of historical reinvention and reach a position in which half the map was said to be painted red and anyone who dared challenge it might run the risk of a corrective invasion or admonitory naval bombardment (the original form of 'gunboat diplomacy')?

The first task was to survive. The 1802 Peace of Amiens proved to be a false hope, pausing the war for just two years and acting as a mere prelude to a new phase in the conflict with France, now led by Napoleon (as first consul from 1799, and then, from 1804, as emperor). Once again, Britain found itself caught in the quicksands of assembling coalition after coalition against the French (reaching the seventh by the time the emperor was finally defeated in 1815). The expenditure involved was enormous (by 1814 it had ballooned to £40 million for the army and £10 million for the navy), and the government found itself in dire financial straits. Having first tinkered with the problem by introducing taxes on hair powder and a levy on dogs (with a special exemption for sheepdogs), in 1799 the prime minister, William Pitt, pushed through the introduction of an income tax. The measure, supposed to be strictly temporary, was rescinded only briefly during the Peace of Amiens, and was reintroduced after fourteen months' pause when war loomed once more, never again to be repealed.

Despite an invasion scare in 1804, which led to the belated

establishment of a string of defensive Martello towers along England's south coast (far too late, as the invasion project had been abandoned by the time the first of them was substantially complete in 1806), the fighting did not touch the British mainland (save for the abortive invasion of Wales in 1797). Instead Napoleon tried to throttle Britain by a trade blockade instituted through his Continental system, which from late 1806 to 1812 forbade ports under French control or in countries allied to France to trade with Britain. Although Napoleon's version of a militarized trade war had some impact, it was undermined by the power of the British navy, by then the strongest in the world, to prevent its French counterpart from enforcing the blockade and by the unwillingness of other European powers (notably Russia from 1811) to damage their own commercial interests to appease the French emperor's lust for power.

The British learned the hard lesson that naval power was not enough – it could keep the French away from Britain's shores, cause them endless mischief in the West Indies and even gain signal victories such as Admiral Horatio Nelson's triumph at Trafalgar in 1805, but it could not win the war. The commitment of a large British army in Spain from 1808 marked the start of the Peninsular War, in which step by step Arthur Wellesley, a veteran of Britain's wars of expansion in southern India in the 1790s, pushed the French back towards their borders. The resources Napoleon had to devote to fending off the expeditionary force – with over 200,000 troops committed to controlling Spanish guerrilla activity and facing the invading British – sapped his strength elsewhere, and Wellesley (who was created Viscount Wellington in 1809, and Duke of Wellington in 1814) won a string of victories, culminating at Vitoria in 1813 and Toulouse in 1814. Napoleon's armies collapsed after a disastrous invasion of Russia in 1812 and a series of reverses in Germany, and in April 1814 he abdicated and was sent into exile on the Italian island of Elba. The Duke of Wellington's military skill was still needed to deliver the final defeat of Napoleon, after the emperor slipped away from his lightly guarded imprisonment and raised a new army of loyalists. The attempted imperial renaissance was snuffed out by an Anglo-Prussian army (led by Wellington and Marshal Blücher) at Waterloo, just south of Brussels, on 18 June 1815, and the emperor's renewed new place of exile, this time on St Helena in the Indian Ocean, was sufficiently remote that there was no hope of a second escape.

Wellington became a hero and has remained at the heart of Britain's military pantheon ever since, but the end of the war marked the start of a partial British disengagement from Europe that would last almost a century. Although Viscount Castlereagh, the British foreign secretary, participated in the Congress of Vienna in 1814–15, which tried to return Europe to the pre-Napoleonic status quo, and Britain took part in subsequent congresses. British governments avoided active participation in the increasingly conservative system of alliances which developed. On the whole Britain only intervened if its essential interests were being threatened, as when an expeditionary force was sent to Lisbon in 1827 to prop up a Portuguese government faced with a Spanish-supported insurrection. Even so, there was a touch of romantic regard for Classical Greece in the sending of a fleet the same year to the Aegean which blew apart the Ottoman sultan's navy at Navarino, immeasurably aiding the cause of Greek independence.

Britain instead turned its eyes outwards towards trade and empire. Its growing industrial might gave it products aplenty to trade – by 1880 pig-iron production would reach 7.9 million tons annually, as opposed to 400,000 tons sixty years earlier, and new inventions such as the Bessemer converter for producing steel (patented in 1856) helped generate new manufactures to fuel the seemingly inexhaustible international appetite for British goods. The empire played a key part in this, sucking in some 30 per cent of all British exports by the mid 1850s (which amounted to £32.5 million annually) and ensuring a captive market which provided a safety net for Britain's factories. The self-confidence, almost arrogance, that this inspired was given tangible form in the Great Exhibition of 1851, a showcase for Britain's manufacturing (with representation permitted from rival industrial powers, as though to show off their relative inferiority).

Over six million visitors came to Joseph Paxton's great Crystal Palace of glass and steel, paying as little as a shilling to gawp at exhibits as diverse as power looms, the Koh-i-Noor diamond and an alarm-clock bed that tipped the hapless owner onto the floor at waking-up time, and consuming around a million Bath buns.

There was a darker side to the Victorian industrial expansion. The population of England, Scotland and Wales rose from 16.3 million, according to the decennial census of 1831 (the fourth to be carried out since its inception in 1801), to 23.1 million in 1861 and then reached 37 million in 1901. Much of the increase was concentrated in towns – the urban population exceeded 50 per cent for the first time in the 1851 census – where a growing underclass lived in appalling conditions that pricked the consciences alike of philanthropists such as Lord Shaftesbury (who campaigned for improvements in the conditions of the legion of children working in factories) and novelists such as Charles Dickens. Overcrowding (London already had 2.3 million people by 1851, a figure which had almost doubled just thirty years later), lack of clean water, little or no access to formal education and epidemics of water-borne diseases such as cholera were troubling stains on a nation which counted itself at the very forefront of human progress.

Rural poverty worried British governments too. In 1815 they bowed to landed interests in the countryside and passed the Corn Law, a measure which forbade the importation of foreign grain until the price of British-grown corn had reached 80 shillings a quarter. Although intended to protect the income of farmers, the Corn Law in fact artificially inflated the price of bread, leading to an increase in rural distress, rioting and a large increase in the amount which had to be spent on local poor relief.

The influx of 300,000 demobilized soldiers into the labour market at the end of the Napoleonic Wars also aggravated economic tensions, which were already inflamed by increasing mechanization. Attacks by Luddites, skilled workers who broke up new industrial machinery in the textile industry which they saw as depriving them of jobs, reached their peak in 1811–12, and agitation for the right to form trade unions to protect the wages and working conditions of workers grew steadily in the first decades of the century. Although the 1799 Act which had forbidden such 'Combinations' was repealed in 1824, and more and more workers joined unions (such as the Grand General Union of Cotton Spinners, formed in 1829), governments did not sit back and let what they perceived as a threat to social order grow unchecked. In 1819 Lord Liverpool's administration passed the Six Acts, which levied a punitive duty on cheap newspapers, in an attempt to stifle the spread of seditious ideas and which virtually banned public meetings. Sterner measures were taken against organizations which were considered particularly subversive. In 1834 a group of agricultural labourers from Tolpuddle in Dorset fell foul of legislation against the taking of oaths in secret, and six of them were sentenced to transportation to Australia. A short-lived attempt the same year to form a national trade union organization – the General National Consolidated Trades Union – and to mount a general strike for a shorter working day foundered (the body gathered just 16,000 members), and only after the formation of the Trades Union Congress in 1868 did the unions establish themselves as a permanent part of the industrial landscape.

Such radicalism frightened governments, whether Tory or Whig, but they were also all too aware that failure to act to resolve some of the grievances might lead to uncontrollable revolutionary pressures. The response was a steady drip of concessions, none of them intended to be transformative, but which added up nonetheless to a significant liberalization of political life. Growing calls for the abolition of the Corn Laws were led by vocal exponents of free trade (an easy position to adopt when Britain's dominant political and economic position meant it was best placed to take advantage of this and could impose free trade agreements on terms which were disadvantageous to politically vulnerable countries, such as Ottoman Turkey in 1838 and Persia in 1841). The establishment of the Anti-Corn Law League by Richard Cobden and John Bright in 1839 increased pressure on the government and finally bore fruit in 1846 with the abolition of the Corn Laws (although the bitter parliamentary debates over the issue split apart the Tory Party and led to Peel's resignation, in an early example of the tension between free trade and protectionism which would trouble British conservatives well into the twenty-first century).

Religious change came to Britain, too. In 1828 the Test and Corporation Acts, which had prevented non-conformist Protestants from taking up public office since the late seventeenth century, were finally repealed, but restrictions on Catholics continued. Discontent at their second-class status was particularly rife in Ireland, where Daniel O'Connell's Catholic Association lobbied for changes (including his own standing for election in County Clare in 1828, knowing that even when he succeeded in being elected as an MP the law forbade his taking his seat in the House of Commons). Finally, in 1829, the Duke of Wellington, by then prime minister, gave way, and the Roman Catholic Relief Act enfranchised Catholics.

It did not, however, enfranchise the poor, or even the middle classes (and, as though to dissipate the goodwill it had raised, the 1829 Act increased the property qualification for voting in Ireland from 40 shillings to £10). By the 1820s the rules as to who was allowed to vote in elections had become varied and complex, ranging from boroughs which had property qualifications, to those which only allowed the town corporation to vote, or who granted the vote to all freeholders, to those paying municipal taxes or, in a few fortunate cases, to all male householders. The result was a variation in the size of the electorate from around 12,000 (in the case of Westminster) to 'rotten boroughs' such as Dunwich in Suffolk, a once-prosperous town which had largely fallen into the sea by the seventeenth century, but whose diminutive electorate of thirty-two still had the right to return an MP. Other 'pocket boroughs' had very few electors whose votes were bought and sold by local landowners, while large parts of the country, particularly towns which had grown significantly in recent decades, such as Croydon, had none at all.

The cause of parliamentary reform already had its martyrs. In 1819 a meeting of around 60,000 people at St Peter's Field in Manchester calling for the extension of the franchise was charged by a detachment of yeomanry on the orders of local magistrates. The 'Peterloo Massacre' claimed the lives of eleven of the demonstrators and set many conservatives firmly against any kind of voting reform. By 1831, the mood had softened somewhat, but even then, a first attempt at passing a Reform Bill was rejected in October 1831, before parliament finally agreed a watered-down version of electoral reform in June 1832. Fifty-six 'rotten boroughs', the worst examples of diminutive electorates, had their 111 seats removed, and these and thirty others were redistributed to industrial towns and under-represented counties. The total electorate was increased by around 40 per cent (to around 750,000 people), but this still left only one in five of the adult population in England and Wales eligible to vote, and less than an eighth in Scotland. Women, of course, were still entirely excluded from the franchise, and working-class radicals, whose vocal agitation had played such a vital role in pressuring the government to concede reform, received nothing for their efforts.

If politicians hoped the anger at this betrayal would dissipate and that the system could carry on much as before, they were mistaken. Instead it found an outlet in one of the first genuinely mass movements in British history. In 1838 petitions were circulated nationally, calling for genuinely universal suffrage, annual parliaments, the proper payment of MPs, voting by secret ballot and equally sized constituencies. It was a radical and surprisingly modern agenda (the last measure had still not been implemented by 2022, despite periodic calls for its adoption). The Chartist movement garnered 1.3 million signatures for the first petition in 1839 and 3.3 million for the second in 1842, including 200,000 from London alone (a third grand petition in 1848 was alleged to have 5.7 million appended, but was found on inspection to have only 2 million including the unlikely support of the Duke of Wellington – the problems of fakery in online polling clearly have their Victorian antecedents). Delegates assembled at national conventions in 1840 and 1842 under the leadership of Fergus O'Connor, an Irish former MP (who had been expelled for failing to meet the necessary property qualifications) whose newspaper the *Northern Star* helped spread Chartist ideas. A series of strikes in south Wales, the threat of a national strike and rioting in Glasgow and Birmingham alarmed the authorities, and leading Chartists were arrested. After a final attempt at a mass rally on Kennington Common in 1848 flopped, the movement fizzled out. Further electoral reform, when it came, was slow. Even after the Electoral Reform Act of 1884, only around three in five of the adult male population of England and Wales could vote, and genuinely universal male suffrage had to await the partial concession of the vote to women over thirty in 1918.

By the end of Victoria's reign in 1901, a large proportion of the population of the United Kingdom had, for the first time, some say in shaping the nation's future. Yet by then the queen had acquired a huge number of additional subjects who had no voice in parliament and little influence in determining their own destiny. The massive expansion of the British empire which took place in the nineteenth century gave Britain a dominant role as a global power which no other country had achieved before and modified its self-image in the direction of particularism and chauvinism. Late Victorian children, as well as being better educated than their grandparents, were brought up on a diet of imperial propaganda, the staples of which were works by authors such as George Alfred Henty (1832–1902), who penned stirring tales of past glories such as *St George for England: A Tale of Cressy and Poitiers* (1885) and *With Clive in India: or the Beginnings of an Empire* (1884). As a self-confident maritime imperialist power which could not (and should not) be challenged, Britain also pushed away from engagement with continental Europe, a legacy which bequeathed later twentieth-century governments significant policy headaches in their efforts to live up to and simultaneously to dismantle this heritage. While Britain ruled over a great empire it was relatively straightforward to be both internationalist, in championing the nation's right to a pre-eminent global role, and particularist, in dismissing alternative points of view. Once the empire was lost, this balancing act would become far more difficult to perform.

The British empire happened more by accident and piecemeal

decision-making than according to any centralized design or long-term plan. Some colonies, such as Canada and Australia, saw large-scale emigration from Europe, but the government had little notion when it established a penal colony around Sydney Harbour in 1788 that by 1861 there would be over a million white settlers in the Australian colonies, or that Canada would have a population of 7.3 million by 1911, overwhelmingly of European descent.

Elsewhere, it was trading interest that first drew British engagement, and the establishment of trading posts led to positions which needed to be defended and an ever-deeper military and political involvement in regions which finally led to an outright conquest which had not initially been desired or even contemplated. In India, the process began with the Battle of Plassey in 1757, after which the East India Company came to dominate Bengal, and proceeded, by dint of the over-enthusiasm of colonial administrators such as Charles James Napier, whose conquest of Sindh in 1843, against express order, led him to pen the mischievous (and unrepentant) Latin pun 'Peccavi' (meaning 'I have sinned'), to its culmination after the Indian Mutiny of 1857. Large numbers of sepoys (native Indian soldiers in British service) rose up against new conditions of service including, it was alleged, the issue of rifle cartridges coated in pork and beef fat, which made them impure to both Muslim and Hindu troopers. They briefly took control of large swathes of north and central India, before the British regrouped and drove them out. In the aftermath of the rebellion, a vengeful British government, shocked by massacres of British civilians at Lucknow and elsewhere, exiled the last Mughal ruler, Bahadur Shah II, from the remnants of his empire (by then little more than the environs of Delhi's Red Fort). They then took direct control of India from the East India Company, whose careless stewardship was seen as having provoked the crisis.

India was now British – barring a patchwork of client princely states – but the need to defend it drew Britain in an ever-more complex web of imperial entanglements. The 'jewel in the crown' was too important to let slip (never mind the imperial title which Queen

Victoria had awarded herself, as empress of India, in 1876). Already Britain had become involved in the Crimean War against Russia from 1854 to 1856, as part of an effort to prevent the collapse of the Ottoman empire and Russian control of the Balkans and the land routes to India. The conflict gave Britain another two building blocks in its national mythology: the Victoria Cross, the nation's ultimate medal for military gallantry, and Florence Nightingale, whose insistence on basic hygienic practices at a British military hospital at Scutari near Istanbul saved thousands of soldiers from death by infection and laid the foundations for modern nursing practice.

The Crimean War failed to save the Ottoman empire, and efforts to shore up Egypt, which had broken away from Ottoman control in 1805, resulted merely in its rulers falling deeper and deeper into debt, and further into dependence on British and French goodwill for the khedive's survival. A nationalist reaction erupted, led by Colonel Ahmed Urabi, which threatened to overturn the European duopoly. Amid fevered talk of anarchy and threats to British nationals, in 1882 Gladstone ordered an invasion, which defeated the nationalists, reduced the khedive's freedom of action and began a British presence which lasted until 1922. The occupation also gave Britain control of the Suez Canal (completed in 1869) and an imperial headache further south, as it inherited Egypt's protectorate over the Sudan and so had to face a rebellion by Islamic purists, led initially by the Mahdi, in the 1880s and 1890s. The last-ditch defence of Khartoum, by General Charles George Gordon, who died fighting on the steps of the British governor's palace just two days before the arrival of an expedition sent to relieve him in January 1885, gave Britain yet another imperial hero and was a sign of the country's inexorable advance in the Mediterranean and East Africa.

Elsewhere in Africa, British imperialism built on the slave stations which the country had established on the coast of west Africa since the seventeenth century. In the 1870s, explorers and missionaries such as David Livingstone acted as the vanguard of a British push into south-central Africa around the Great Lakes, while the British also acquired Cape Town from the Dutch in 1814, as part of the settlements at the end of the Napoleonic Wars. Once ensconced, British control pushed inexorably inland in the face of bitter resistance from the Boers, Dutch-speaking settlers, until a war in 1899–1902 smashed their resistance and led to the establishment of a British-controlled Union of South Africa in 1910. The disorderly acquisition of a string of additional colonies followed the Berlin Conference in 1884, called by the German chancellor Otto von Bismarck to resolve the increasing problems caused by rival European powers' claims in Africa. The conference, by establishing that nations should not lay claim to territory in Africa without notifying other European powers, in fact had the contrary effect – to prevent their own ambitions being pre-empted, France and Britain in particular sent out expeditions to stake claims far beyond the areas they currently occupied, leading to an uncontrolled 'Scramble for Africa' which left only Ethiopia and Liberia free of European colonial control by 1900.

By the time Victoria finally died in 1901, her empire had also grown to encompass much of the Caribbean, British Honduras (Belize) in Central America, Guyana in South America, Cyprus, the Malay Peninsula, New Zealand and a scattering of possessions in the South Pacific. There had been some loosening of the colonial apron-strings, with a measure of self-government achieved by Quebec and Ontario in 1846, New Zealand in 1852, and New South Wales, Victoria, Tasmania and South Australia in 1855. In 1867 the Canadian colonies were united into a single Dominion, with enhanced autonomy, as a kind of halfway house between a colony and an independent state (a status that was eventually extended to New Zealand and Australia, colonies with a significant population of European origin).

Britain was at its apogee. Trade lay at the heart of the empire, and this led to conflict, even where Britain did not have any direct territorial interests. In China, centuries of withdrawal from maritime exploration had left the country's rulers ill-equipped to deal with aggressive foreign powers. The shock of contact with Portuguese traders in the sixteenth century was unsettling, but that of direct confrontation with fully industrialized European powers in the mid nineteenth was profound. By the 1830s, the British East India Company had taken to selling Indian opium into China in exchange for the silver with which it would in turn then buy Chinese tea to help assuage the almost limitless demand for the beverage back home in Britain (which by Victorian times had become a truly democratic drink, consumed by all classes to the extent that per capita consumption tripled from 1.5 pounds in 1836 to 5 pounds in 1885). The side-effect of this was the creation of millions of addicts in China, and when the authorities there seized large stocks of opium in Canton in 1839, it sparked a war with Britain. The humiliating defeat of the Chinese forced them to cede possession of Hong Kong to the British (and permit the continuation of the opium trade) and a further Opium War in 1856–60 led to the forced opening of ten more 'Treaty Ports' to European trade in which Chinese jurisdiction did not run and the Europeans were in effect in full control.

Britain by the 1840s was a nation prepared to go to war in the cause of free trade, and the notion that tariff barriers should, as far as possible, be removed became a central tenet of political orthodoxy for many politicians, and in particular Conservative ones. That other European powers did not reciprocate (with Germany levying protectionist tariffs in 1879 and the French, Swiss and Austro-Hungarians following in the 1880s, followed by the punitive McKinley tariff, imposed by the Americans in 1890) rankled. There was a predictable reaction and calls for moves against what was seen as unfair competition. Some measures were comparatively minor, such as the Merchandise Marks Act of 1887, which required German imports to be labelled as 'Made in Germany' as a means to allow patriotic shoppers to avoid them.

Sterner action was called for by the Fair Trade League, founded in 1881, and its much more effective successor, the Tariff Reform League, established in 1903 by Joseph Chamberlain, which lobbied for 'Imperial Preference', a system under which British colonies could trade tariff-free with the mother country, but other nations would face restrictive barriers. Chamberlain saw tariff reform as the panacea for all Britain's imperial ills, claiming it would lead to the 'the realization of the greatest ideal which has ever inspired statesmen in any country or age'. His vision was of the creation of something new, a tight-knit imperial organization in which the resources of the empire would be used to support Britain's industries. Everyone would benefit. It was a mirage which became firmly lodged in the political mythology of the British Conservative Party, and the idea that the empire (or more latterly the Commonwealth) would ride to the rescue of the British economy was still being evoked in the early twenty-first century.

Free trade, though, did not mean unlimited tolerance for foreigners. This had always been in short supply in the growing cities of Victorian London, and in the country more generally, where fears over French intrusion and the loss of insular status had led plans for a Channel Tunnel to be shelved in 1882. By the 1890s, amid rising unemployment and fears over the influx of east European Jews fleeing pogroms in Tsarist Russia, pressure increased for a limit on the number of foreign workers allowed to enter Britain, and in 1905 Arthur Balfour's Conservative government passed the Aliens Act, the first legislative attempt to impose immigration controls. Just as it would a century later, a Britain that felt overwhelmed by the consequences of its engagement with the outside world turned inwards and attempted to build barriers.

The Britain that the protectionists sought to defend was one that had changed radically since the accession of Queen Victoria. The country was now bound together by the spread of a new form of transportation, the railways, which made the transport of freight and the carriage of passengers across long distances overland far simpler and cheaper than along the network of canals or roads of distinctly uncertain quality. The opening of the Liverpool and Manchester Railway in 1830 – although marred by the death of William Huskisson, the local MP, in a freak accident – marked the real start of the railway age and a speculative frenzy in the 1840s led to the installation of over 6,000 miles of track by 1850, in a network that spanned the nation from Aberdeen to Plymouth. Fifty years later, the system had almost doubled in size and carried over a billion passengers each year.

The rapid growth in Britain's urban population had created appalling problems, as overcrowded slum dwellings mushroomed, and the mid-Victorian era saw the beginning of measures to improve conditions for the urban poor. Local health boards were created, and the passing of a Sewers Act in 1848 sought to bring clean water to the cities. It was only a start, however, and there was still a major outbreak of cholera in 1854, while a particular hot summer in 1858 caused London's sewage to reek so badly that it was dubbed the 'Great Stink' and finally caused appalled MPs to legislate for a proper mains sewage system. Slums were cleared, and the upper-middle-class professions such as architects and civil engineers found ample employment in rebuilding them and in throwing up temples to the cult of philanthropy which shaped Victorian civic sensibility: even a town of modest size such as Blackburn acquired a grand town hall, with Corinthian columns, which cost the princely sum of £30,000, and public libraries spread after the passing of a Public Libraries Act in 1850, opening up sources of knowledge which had previously been difficult, if not impossible, for the working classes to access.

Education, too, became accessible to wider social groups. Previously only those rich enough to attend public schools such as Eton or Westminster, or fortunate enough to attend one of the small numbers of grammar schools had received adequate schooling (although one in large part confined to studies of the Classics). The Newcastle Commission (1858) looked at ways of providing education to the children of the working classes but did not envisage this continuing beyond the age of eleven. Steadily, state funding of elementary education grew, to supplement the patchy provision by Church and other private bodies, and by 1858 around 2.5 million children were attending such grant-aided schools.

University education also became more widespread, with the establishment of University College London in 1826, Durham University in 1832 and the institutions which would develop into

Manchester University in 1851. Victorian Britain became more open to intellectual experiment, contributing to a thirst for innovation which yielded the radical social and economic ideas of Karl Marx's *Communist Manifesto* (1848) and, most shocking of all, the publication of Charles Darwin's *On the Origin of Species* in 1859, containing the theory of evolution. Its successor volume, *The Descent of Man* (1871), offended conservative churchmen even more profoundly by suggesting that species had evolved over time and not been fixed at the time of the creation and outraged public sensibility by proposing mankind and apes shared a common ancestor.

In an age of such political, social and intellectual ferment, people clung to what had gone before, or at least to a comfortingly reimagined version of it. Thomas Hardy's Wessex novels, such as *Tess of the D'Urbervilles* (published in 1891) celebrated a rural past which, though harsh, had a timeless reassurance about it. As he observed, the economic changes of the past century had 'led to a break of continuity in local history, more fatal than any other thing to the preservation of legend, folk-lore, close intersocial relations and eccentric individualities'. The many manifestations of this nostalgia included the travels of the folklore historian Cecil Sharp in search of dying traditions and the mania of Victorian artists for pre-Classical forms of art, which yielded a rash of neo-Gothic buildings such as St Pancras station (completed in 1876), the medievalizing paintings of the pre-Raphaelite brotherhood and a flight from conservative literary traditions in the Romantic poetry of Wordsworth, Coleridge and Byron.

The late Victorian era was tinged with uncertainty, a sense of hesitancy at the very apogee of the country's power. The rash of reforms implemented by Conservative governments which promoted public health, strengthened controls on the sale of food and alcohol and on the quality of the new buildings being thrown up in the country's growing suburbs, were in part motivated by concern to avoid social unrest and to try to capture a part of the new urban working-class electorate. The Conservatives and Liberals, the heirs of the old Tory and Whig parties, found themselves facing genuine political competition for the first time as the trade unions gave birth to new organisations to provide the working class with proper political representation. In 1884, the Fabian Society was established, with George Bernard Shaw among its first members, to push for a gradual change in the direction of a centrally-planned economy which would redistribute the nation's resources more equitably. A more mass movement emerged in the 1890s with the foundation of the Independent Labour Party by Keir Hardie in 1893 and the Labour Representation Committee (the forerunner of the Labour party) in 1900, which by January 1910 held forty seats in the House of Commons and came close to holding the balance of power.

That it did not was thanks to developments in Ireland. Unlike Scotland, where opposition to the Union had quietened after 1745, Ireland had suffered the political marginalisation of its preponderantly Catholic population and little in the way of the investment which had sparked the Industrial Revolution in England. By the 1840s, much of Ireland's farming community had become unhealthily dependent on the potato, which could thrive in relatively poor soils and which provided a high calorie crop. In 1845, Ireland was struck by Phytophthora infestans, a mould accidentally imported from North America. The blight which followed caused the potatoes to rot in the ground, leaving almost nothing left to harvest and little seed to plant the next crop. The next three years were no better, leading to widespread distress and starvation. Although the government funded some soup kitchens and there were private attempts at relief, as well as imports of corn from India, exports of grain, badly needed to fill the nutritional deficit, were not stopped. Huge numbers of tenant farmers, unable to pay their rent, were evicted from their land. Hundreds of thousands simply starved to death. Disease, starvation and the emigration of those still strong enough to leave, wrought a devastating demographic toll on Ireland. The population fell from 8.2 million in 1841 to 6.6 million in 1851, at a time that of England and Wales rose from 15.9 million to 17.9 million.

The Great Famine stoked tensions in Ireland and helped give birth to the Fenian movement which agitated for Ireland's independence from British rule and carried out a number of high-profile attacks, including at Clerkenwell Prison in 1867 in which twelve people were killed. Attempts at reform by the Liberal party under William Gladstone, whose four stints as prime minister between 1868 and 1894 made him one of the Victorian era's most ubiquitous politicians, only nibbled at the problem. An Irish Land Act in 1870 improved conditions for tenants, limiting landlords' ability to raise rents or evict them without due cause and also providing for tenants to purchase their land if the landlord put it up for sale. The Anglican church in Ireland was disestablished in 1869, removing its privileges which had symbolised the inferior position of Ireland's Catholic majority. These tentative moves were nowhere near enough to satisfy Ireland's swelling nationalist feeling; in 1870 Isaac Butt, a Protestant lawyer – discontent with the constitutional arrangements was by no means confined to Catholics – established the Home Government Association, which soon evolved into the Irish Home League that won sixty seats at the 1874 general election Under the leadership of Charles Stewart Parnell from 1880, the League gained eighty-five Irish seats in the 1885 elections, winning nearly 70 per cent of the vote in Ireland and putting itself in the enviable position of holding the balance of power in a hung parliament (though it split after Parnell was involved in a scandalous divorce case in 1890). As the Irish nationalists ably exploited divisions in the Liberal Party – whose passing of a further Land Act in 1881 did little to quell dissent – the question of Irish Home Rule seemed intractable. In the end Gladstone introduced a Home Rule bill in 1886, which would have established a separate two-chamber Irish parliament without conceding full independence. It was too much for his own party, which fell apart, and ninety-three anti-Home Rule Liberals helped the Conservatives bring down the bill by 341 votes to 311. Gladstone's government collapsed and at the General Election which followed it the Marquess of Salisbury's Conservatives were elected with a thumping majority. Irish Home Rule was for the moment put on ice.

As the century waned, Britain was curiously weary. The queen had enjoyed an unprecedented diamond jubilee in 1897, but there was a distinct fin de siècle feeling. Britain found itself enmired in yet another imperial war, this time in South Africa, where an effective campaign on the part of the Boers stretched British resources and led to long sieges of Mafeking and Ladysmith and a gruelling guerrilla campaign even after the main Boer forces were defeated. Britain's scorched earth policy to root out pockets of resistance included extreme measures such as the eviction of thousands of Boer civilians into internment camps, in a foreshadowing of the tactics of total war which would blight the twentieth century. Victory, when it was finally wrung out in 1902, had cost Britain £217 million, more even than the Napoleonic Wars.

In 1898 Lord Salisbury, Queen Victoria's last prime minister, gave a speech outlining his view of foreign affairs and Britain's position in the world. In it he declared that 'You may roughly divide the nations of the world as the living and the dying,' with Britain unmistakably in danger of being placed into the second category. Although he spoke in confident terms that Britain was able to defend 'against all-comers that which we possess and we know, in spite of the jargon about isolation, that we are amply competent to do so', he warned of the growth of 'great countries of enormous power, growing in power every year, growing in wealth, growing in dominion, growing in the perfection of their organisation' and counselled 'international cooperation rather than a network of exclusive alliances [that] would . . . avert the armed conflict certain to attend the "cutting up" of the weak by the strong.'

It was a very sage warning, for Britain's transformation over the preceding 150 years from a predominantly agricultural society with limited reach abroad into an industrial leviathan with seemingly limitless military power concealed an inconvenient reality: others were catching up. Germany and the United States in particular had industrialized rapidly in the second half of the nineteenth century, with sectors such as petroleum, chemicals and telecommunications proving industries in which Britain failed to establish the dominance it had earlier enjoyed in coal, iron and cotton. Britain's very success created a particularism which, despite Chamberlain's warnings, led to a complacent assumption that the British navy would more than make up for any deficiencies in a land force which was a shadow of its Napoleonic strength, and which was more fitted to fighting colonial wars against ill-armed, if highly motivated, indigenous forces than the type of fully industrialized war which the artillery barrages of the Franco-Prussian War of 1870–71 suggested would be the future face of conflict.

With the Irish question unresolved, politics in ferment, increasing calls for further social, economic and electoral reforms and the British empire posing its administrators increasing headaches by virtue of its enormous size and diversity (from tiny Pacific islands to mature societies such as Australia, which demanded and received effective independence in 1901) – Britain was both at the height of its strength and appallingly vulnerable when Edward VII ascended the throne in 1901. The next century would see those challenges work themselves out with devastating consequences.

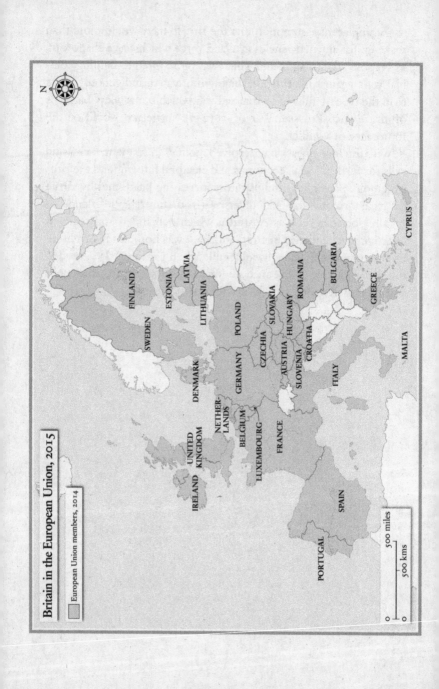

Britain in the European Union, 2015

European Union members, 2014

N

PORTUGAL

SPAIN

IRELAND

UNITED KINGDOM

FRANCE

LUXEMBOURG

BELGIUM

NETHER-
LANDS

DENMARK

GERMANY

SWEDEN

FINLAND

ESTONIA

LATVIA

LITHUANIA

POLAND

CZECHIA

SLOVAKIA

AUSTRIA

HUNGARY

SLOVENIA

CROATIA

ITALY

ROMANIA

BULGARIA

GREECE

MALTA

CYPRUS

500 miles

500 kms

0

0

10 Modern Britain

It has been a roller-coaster century for Britain. The unravelling of the empire was a long, and at times traumatic process. The self-confident imperialism and economic primacy which had sustained Britain in Victorian times was battered by the shocks of two World Wars, the Great Depression, the inevitable falling behind of a mature power as other, more nimble competitors, caught it, and the final, bewildering realization that the country was now a bit player in the struggles between new superpowers. The search for a new equilibrium was hampered by the pains of deindustriali-zation, the restructuring of the economy to face global competition and spasms of political yearning for the imperial past. The dis-content of those who felt marginalized by these processes and a brightly burning nostalgia for Britain's former glories led many to believe that a diminished role in Europe was an inadequate substi-tute. As a result, the British were always awkward and not entirely enthusiastic Europeans, even after the country's accession to the European Economic Community in 1973.

All this was far from the minds of Britain's ruling class in 1911. The death of Victoria in 1901 had caused trepidation – the removal of a long-fixed certainty was always unsettling – but also inspired a liberating sense of a new era in which Britain could con-solidate its imperial successes and enjoy even greater economic prosperity. On 12–13 December in a series of lavish ceremonies to commemorate his accession, George V received a succession of Indian princes on a dais in central Delhi, then appeared before a crowd of half a million at a window of the Red Fort, followed by the inspection of a parade of 50,000 troops in a potent display of Britain's military might in south Asia. The Delhi Durbar was the third of its kind: the previous ones had been held in 1877 and then in 1903 in celebration of the accession of George's father, Edward VII (although the new king did not attend, instead sending his brother the Duke of Connaught to represent him, who witnessed an extravagant parade, including several elephants with gold candelabras attached to their tusks).

For all the pomp and circumstance of the durbars, back home a new wave of social reforms was getting underway. In 1906 a new Liberal government came to power, and from 1908 under the energetic leadership of Herbert Asquith and David Lloyd George, his chancellor of the exchequer, it began to answer growing demands for social reform. Lloyd George's 1909 'People's Budget' marked a bold attempt to redistribute wealth by raising death duties, income taxes and land taxes, but it raised a storm in the Conservative-dominated House of Lords. The passing of the Parliament Bill in 1911 against the threat of the creation of scores of new Liberal peers removed the ability of the Lords to vote down money-raising bills, depriving the aristocracy of the rights they had won centuries before to curb the taxation-raising powers of the executive. Wars had been fought and kings executed over the matter, but now it was seen as a democratizing measure.

The Liberal government had already passed the Old Age Pensions Act in 1908, the first foundation stone in the future welfare state, which allowed for a very basic state pension of 5 shillings a week to the over-seventies. It went on to pass a National Insurance Bill in 1911, which made provision for workers to pay contributions to designated agencies (which included trade unions), in return for which they could receive sick pay and obtain treatment from approved doctors, and it liberalized trade union legislation, allowing unions to establish a political fund into which members could opt to contribute to help support the Labour Party (which after the December 1910 general election had forty-two MPs).

These moves did not, though, stem the rising tide of social discontent which manifested itself in rioting during a nine-month-long miners' strike in south Wales, and a wave of stoppages the following summer which hit the country's docks, mines and railways. Two striking railwaymen were shot dead in Wales, an event which escalated the feeling that radical socialists and anarchists were gaining undue traction in key industries.

As trade union activity increased (and membership of the TUC reached 2.2 million by 1913), the government faced pressure on another front. The late Victorian era had seen a rising number of women in the workforce and with it a demand for the political representation which they had been denied by successive Electoral Reform Acts (most recently in 1884). The National Union of Women's Suffrage Societies, established under the leadership of Millicent Fawcett in 1897, advocated genteel lobbying and a gradualist approach. Needless to say, this got them nowhere. The alternative, direct confrontation and militant activism, was espoused by the suffragettes of the rival Women's Social and Political Union. Founded in 1903 by Emmeline Pankhurst and her daughter Christabel, its members carried out attempts to break into the House of Commons, the disruption of public meetings where ministers were speaking, the bombing of Lloyd George's house and, most dramatically, the death of Emily Davison when she threw herself in front of the king's horse at the 1913 Derby. The authorities responded forcefully, arresting and jailing many suffragettes, and when they went on hunger strike in 1909, the government ordered that they be force-fed. Despite some talk of providing limited votes for women on the back of an extension of universal suffrage, in practice such measures were always blocked in the House of Commons.

A more alarming situation was developing in Ireland. The Irish Parliamentary Party (IPP) – which had replaced the Home Rule League – had continued to prosper electorally, reaching a tally of seventy-three seats in 1910. The foundation of Sinn Féin by Arthur Griffith in 1905 provided a more radical wing for Irish nationalism, which argued for Irish political and economic self-reliance and the re-establishment of Ireland's independence. An increasingly vocal Protestant opposition also emerged, led by Edward Carson's Irish Unionist Alliance, which was bitterly opposed to the idea of Irish Home Rule and alarmed by the prospect that the balance of power which the IPP held in the House of Commons might make this a real prospect. Unionist volunteers in Ulster, where the proportion of Protestants was at its highest, drilled publicly and demanded the preservation of the Union.

Sentiment among the Liberals was in fact quite favourably disposed not only towards Irish Home Rule, but to some measure of Home Rule for Scotland too (and possibly Wales). There was talk of creating a federal state, each with its own parliament, leaving an 'imperial parliament' in Westminster to handle the elevated subjects of defence, foreign policy and the economy. The 'Home-Rule-All-Round' proposal, which foreshadowed discussions a century later about the rebalancing of political power within the United Kingdom, was an idea too far ahead of its time. Although several Scottish Home Rule bills were introduced before 1914, they all failed.

Ireland, however, could not be ignored, and in April 1912 Asquith introduced an Irish Home Rule Bill, by which a two-chamber Irish parliament was to be established in Ireland (although a limited number of Irish MPs would continue to sit in Westminster). Simple demographics determined that the majority of these would be Catholic and frantic lobbying by the Ulster Protestants helped secure its temporary blocking in the House of Lords. Meanwhile the Protestants began to organize. By September 1912 over half a million Protestants had signed an Ulster Covenant – modelled on that by which the Scots had resisted Charles I – and in January 1913 a paramilitary Ulster Volunteer Force was set up, pledged to resist Home Rule by force. The Catholic side responded in November by establishing the Irish Volunteers to ensure its implementation. With little sign of a compromise solution, smuggled arms began to flood into Ireland, and a number of British officers resigned rather than take action against the Ulster Volunteers, raising the spectre of a widespread mutiny. In a desperate bid to prevent Ireland sliding into civil war, the government proposed an Amending Bill to the Home Rule Bill, under which any county in Ireland where a majority opposed Home Rule could be excluded from its provisions for six years (which would mean that at least part of Ulster might remain under direct control from Westminster).

An emergency conference in July 1914 to raise support for this compromise achieved nothing, and it looked like violent confrontation was inevitable. It was events on the other side of Europe that temporarily staved off the dissolution of the union with Ireland. The assassination of the Austrian Archduke Franz Ferdinand in the Bosnian capital Sarajevo on 28 June 1914 set off a round of ultimatums between the competing European alliances which had grown up since 1900. The Russians lined up behind the Serbs, the Germans behind the Austrians, while the French gave their support to the Russians. Mass mobilizations began, as the military doctrine of the time determined that if a country did not begin to do so, it would be critically disadvantaged by its neighbours who had been more decisive in setting their armies on the march (or on railway wagons).

On 4 August 1914 Britain joined the war on the side of France, Russia and Serbia. A wave of patriotic fervour swept the country as young men queued at army recruitment stations, keen not to be left out of the fighting, which, popular opinion had it, 'would be over by Christmas'. Domestic political issues were set aside; the Government of Ireland Act, which finally conceded Home Rule, became law on 18 September 1914 but was accompanied by a measure suspending its implementation until the war was over. The government rushed to cobble together a British Expeditionary Force – in large part made up of 'Pals Battalions', men from industrial towns who had all enlisted together – which helped head off a German advance that had sliced through Belgium into northern France, almost reaching the outskirts of Paris, and prevented the occupation of the Channel ports.

The war degenerated into a grinding slog of attrition as the fronts became frozen along fixed lines of trenches which snaked all the way from Switzerland to the Channel coast. Before long the horrific rate of casualties meant there was little left of the original BEF, and in January 1916 conscription had to be introduced, at first only for unmarried men, but eventually almost universally, so that by 1918 over 2 million had been called up. Nothing seemed to work to break

German resistance. Large-scale offensives served largely to cause mass casualties to the attacker: on 1 July 1916, the first day of the Battle of the Somme, almost 20,000 British soldiers died to gain scarcely 3 square miles of territory from the Germans. For years, the opposing armies languished in damp and unhygienic trenches, occasionally going over the top to charge through mud-churned no-man's lands and perish in their thousands against barbed-wire barricades and fusillades of machine-gun fire. An attempt in 1915 to land on the Gallipoli Peninsula and strike northwards to Istanbul, knocking out the Ottoman empire, a key German ally, became similarly bogged down. The campaign almost put a premature end to the career of Winston Churchill, the First Lord of the Admiralty, and helped launch that of Kemal Atatürk, the founder of modern Turkey, whose resoluteness and quick tactical thinking on the first day of the landings helped prevent a rapid Allied victory.

Poison gas, tanks and combat aeroplanes all made their first appearances in the middle years of the war, before the fronts were loosened up in spring 1918 by a massive German offensive. This failed to knock out the French, and then a series of counter-punches drove an exhausted Germany to sue for an armistice. When the war ended in November 1918, Britain had a death toll of around 900,000, and its colonies had suffered heavily too – including around 60,000 deaths in each of the Australian, Canadian and Indian armies. The war had taught the British contradictory messages. Britain's navy had for the first time since the sixteenth century not been a major participant in conflict, with only one major sea battle, at Jutland in June 1916, after which the German High Seas Fleet had remained largely bottled up in port. As a result, Britain's army had played the key role, inflating a sense that the nation was once more a major European land power. And although Britain had emerged victorious and Prime Minister Lloyd George was one of the 'Big Four' who drove the peace negotiations at Versailles in 1919, this masked the appearance of a new military and diplomatic power, the United States, without whose entry into the war in 1917 and its provision of divisions of fresh troops on the Western Front, the final Allied offensives might not have been won, or even possible. Britain was still a great power, but others were visibly snapping at its heels.

Although it had been won at enormous human and economic cost, the war also gifted the British an unexpected imperial expansion. Germany's empire was dismembered and many of its colonies in Africa (Tanganyika, Togo and Cameroon) were handed to Britain as League of Nations mandates, while a section of the Ottoman empire was sliced away and received similar treatment as the new mandates of Palestine, Jordan and Iraq. Britain, though, was already struggling to keep what it already had, and its Middle Eastern possessions were to prove especially troublesome. A revolt in Iraq in 1920 was only quelled by the Anglo-Iraqi Treaty (1922), which gave the country partial independence, while a wave of nationalist agitation in Egypt led to Britain's unilateral declaration of Egyptian independence the same year. At the moment of its seeming triumph, the British empire was already dissolving at the edges.

In the aftermath of the war, the contours of British politics shifted visibly. In 1918 women (or at least those over thirty) were finally granted the vote, in part as a reward for their participation in the war economy, working in factories while the men were at the front. Together with the extension of the franchise to all men over twenty-one, which brought in a large constituency of male working-class voters, this undermined the claims of the Liberal Party to be the authentic voice of progressive Britain. The party's vote and representation in parliament collapsed, until in 1924 it retained a rump of just forty MPs. Their place as principal opposition to the Conservatives was taken by Labour, which under Ramsay Macdonald formed its first government – albeit a minority one – in 1923. The growing power of the labour movement, too, was shown by its ability to mount a nine-day General Strike in March 1926, though the resolute response of Stanley Baldwin, the Conservative prime minister, meant that it ultimately failed.

By then, the constitutional order of the United Kingdom had suffered a severe shock and the first change in its territorial extent since the sixteenth century. Although the outbreak of the First World War had temporarily frozen the move towards Home Rule, many in Sinn Féin saw London's preoccupation with the European conflict as the perfect opportunity to assert Irish independence. On 24 April 1916, Easter Monday, around 1,600 Irish nationalist volunteers rose up, seized the General Post Office in Dublin and declared an Irish Republic. Their actions were not matched outside the Irish capital, and after six bitter days of fighting, the British authorities managed to wrest back control.

The repression which followed, which included the execution of the rebellion's leaders Pádraic Pearse and James Connolly, made heroes of the rebels, and the Irish nationalists established a break-away parliament, the Dáil, in opposition to the British-run assembly in Dublin Castle. The Irish Republican Army, formed in 1919, began a campaign of guerrilla attacks against the British Army and the Royal Irish Constabulary, and the struggle became even more bitter when Prime Minister Lloyd George sanctioned the recruitment of the 'Black and Tans', a British irregular force, to counter the IRA's tactics.

To prevent a wholesale breakdown of order, Lloyd George finally conceded the Government of Ireland Act in 1920. Under this, separate parliaments were to be set up in Belfast (where Protestants were in the majority) and in Dublin (where Catholics would dominate), while Westminster would retain notional overall control. The compromise failed, as the Irish nationalists, led by Eamon de Valera, refused to have anything to do with it, and the fighting continued. By summer 1921, however, both sides had grown weary of the bloodshed, and a ceasefire was brokered. On 6 December 1921 the moderate nationalists Michael Collins and Arthur Griffith agreed an Anglo-Irish Treaty, under which an Irish Free State was established, with full control over its economy, police and armed forces, but which assumed the status of a Dominion (like Canada or Australia) and was still technically a monarchy. Six of the nine historic counties of Ulster, where there was either a Protestant majority or a narrow Catholic one, were given the right to opt out and remain under British rule, which they did within a week of the Treaty coming into effect in December 1922.

As a result, the United Kingdom of Great Britain and Ireland became the United Kingdom of Great Britain and Northern Ireland, the form in which the British state exists today. The newborn state is still a comparative infant in international terms, being less than a century old. While the Irish Free State descended into civil war – the Dáil had only narrowly passed the Anglo-Irish Treaty (by sixty-four votes to fifty-seven) – Britain entered a period of disillusionment. The hopes raised that the Versailles peace settlement in 1919 would bring an end to conflict in Europe were dashed by the complexities of dealing with the break-up of the Austro-Hungarian empire, the bitter feeling in conservative circles in Germany that the nation's army had been betrayed by its politicians and the aftermath of Russia's 1918 Bolshevik Revolution, which brought an entirely new form of government to power, and one engaged in a traumatic reordering of its economy on communist lines.

The aftershocks of the 1914–18 conflict, which almost brought Britain into a war with Turkey in October 1922, were exacerbated by the Great Depression, which gripped most of the world's economies from 1929 and led to unemployment in Britain spiralling up to 2.7 million (or around 22 per cent of the workforce) by 1932. Chronic underinvestment, increased foreign competition in coal, steel and textiles, industries where Britain had traditionally been pre-eminent, and the drying-up of investment funds led to a spectacular economic contraction, widespread social distress and 'hunger marches', which snaked from the most badly affected north-eastern towns, such as Jarrow, down to Westminster in a futile bid to shame MPs into action.

Gradually the economy did recover (and unemployment fell to 8 per cent by 1936). Much of the south and south-east had been less severely affected by the depression, while newer industries, such as car manufacturing, had continued to thrive in the Midlands. Britain's foreign policy became less activist, too, as the government averted its gaze from the danger signs in Europe, where pluralist democracy had been weakened by the economic turmoil and populist parties had gained ground. In Germany, in particular, Adolf Hitler's

NSDAP (Nazi Party) had been able to exploit dissatisfaction at the traditional parties' running of the economy – hyperinflation caused prices to spiral, to the extent that a single egg cost 80 million marks and a pound of butter 6 billion marks, while unemployment spiked to over 30 per cent in 1932. Resentment at the reparations Germany was forced to pay under the Versailles settlement increased support for the Nazis still further.

In July 1932, they had become the largest party in the Reichstag, and within six months Hitler had secured his appointment as chancellor. He began stealthily to rearm Germany just as the British were running down their defences, cutting the Royal Navy's battle fleet and almost abolishing the Royal Air Force. By 1936, when Hitler's armies marched into the Rhineland, Britain was in no shape for war (a report from the chiefs of staff in December 1937 warned with untimely optimism, 'We cannot foresee the time when our defence forces will be strong enough to safeguard our trade, territory and vital interests against Germany, Italy and Japan simultaneously,' precisely at the time this was becoming a real possibility). Prime Minister Neville Chamberlain engaged in frantic rounds of diplomacy to contain Germany's ambitions, while at the same time triggering a programme of British rearmament. As a result, Britain stood passively by as a series of crises culminated in the German occupation of Sudetenland in western Czechoslovakia (home to a large German-speaking population), and at an emergency meeting with Hitler at Munich in September 1938 Chamberlain obtained a series of guarantees which proved as worthless as the piece of a paper containing them which he brandished at Heston Aerodrome on his return home.

By September 1939 Britain was at war, after Chamberlain's patience finally snapped when Hitler ordered his army into Poland, which the British had pledged to protect. The six years that followed tested Britain to the limit and added new entries to the catalogue of its national mythology: Winston Churchill, who replaced Neville Chamberlain as prime minister in May 1940 and whose reassuringly solid figure and dogged determination guided Britain through the darkest days of the war; the evacuation of 300,000 British and Allied troops from Dunkirk in June 1940, after the Germans invaded France and threatened to cut them off; the Battle of Britain from July to October 1940 in which the skill of Britain's fighter pilots and the new technology of radar helped the RAF to prevent the Luftwaffe gaining control of Britain's skies and enabling a German invasion across the Channel; the Blitz, in which Hitler turned the Luftwaffe to a bombing campaign against major cities, and in particular London, hoping to shatter British morale and killing around 40,000 civilians; and the D-Day landings, in which over 150,000 American, British and Commonwealth troops stormed ashore in Normandy in the biggest seaborne invasion in history, so beginning the final phase of the war, which ended with Hitler's suicide in April 1945 and Germany's unconditional surrender on 7 May.

The cost to Britain had been enormous. Apart from the more than 400,000 service personnel who had died, British prestige had suffered damaging blows, as the Japanese had been able to occupy Malaysia and Singapore with surprising ease in 1941 (and had then conquered much of Burma and pressed against the borders of India). It was also quite clear that Britain – although it stood defiantly alone against Germany in 1940 – could not have won the war without the assistance of the United States, which overcame its isolationist qualms after the Japanese attack on its naval base at Pearl Harbor in December 1941. When the Allied powers organized a conference at Yalta (in the Crimea) in February 1945 to determine the shape of the post-war settlement, it was clear that President Franklin Roosevelt and the Soviet leader Joseph Stalin, not Winston Churchill, were the dominant partners.

The economic toll was enormous, too. Britain had only been able to continue the prosecution of the war through American aid via the Lend-Lease system, which provided over $31 billion of oil and war materiel to the British empire free of charge, but the war effort left it heavily in debt and struggling to finance the necessary reconstruction at home at the same time as maintaining the empire. The Americans demanded a heavy price for their aid, insisting at the end of the war that the United Kingdom sign up to the new international architecture it was constructing by joining the new International Monetary Fund, eliminating the system of Imperial Preference, which favoured trade with Commonwealth countries, and by agreeing to make sterling convertible. The demands of millions of demobilizing soldiers, most of them working-class, for a more equal distribution of national resources led to the resounding defeat of Winston Churchill in the 1945 election and the return of the first majority Labour government under Clement Attlee. This implemented the wartime recommendations of the 1942 Beveridge Report for the institution of a universal healthcare service backed by a national insurance levy on wages.

By 1948 the Labour government had established the National Health Service and nationalized key industries including coal and electricity (1947), railways and gas (1948) and steel (1949). Although the economy expanded rapidly in the post-war years, the slow grind of reconstruction and the continuing of rationing until 1954 (when restrictions on the sale of bacon and other meat were lifted) led to a sense of austerity, a feeling that, while the war had been won, the rewards had not yet been reaped. The government tried to lift the gloom through the Festival of Britain, intended to commemorate the centenary of the Great Exhibition by showcasing British products, culture and architecture (most notably by the rejuvenation of the South Bank of the Thames), but it fell to a Conservative resurgence in 1951, which brought Winston Churchill back to Downing Street. The accession of a new young monarch in 1952 really did lift the national mood, inspiring a rash of predictions that this new 'Elizabethan age' would be just as glorious for Britain as the first one had been (at least in the collective historical imagination).

Domestically, the 1950s broadly saw a period of national economic consensus, with a commitment to low unemployment, partial state ownership in a mixed economy and the welfare state. The convergence of the policies of the two main parties gave the prevailing policy climate the nickname of 'Butskellism' (for Rab Butler, Conservative chancellor of the exchequer from 1951 to 1955, and Hugh Gaitskell, Labour leader from 1955 to 1963).

This comparative political tranquillity at home masked very real political challenges for Britain abroad. The country had ended the Second World War still in control of its global empire, but facing a rising tide of nationalist sentiment, which was particularly developed in India, where Mahatma Gandhi and the Indian National Congress had led an able campaign of opposition to British rule in the 1920s and 1930s. Weariness with the difficulties of maintaining control while conceding just enough to the nationalist movement to keep it quiet was compounded by a shift back towards free trade and tariff reduction as the world economy recovered in the 1950s, which made the case for retaining Britain's colonies less compelling. Empire no longer paid.

In India, the government recognized that it could not retain power in the face of concerted opposition from both Hindu and Muslim nationalists and in August 1947 it granted full independence, although at the cost of partitioning the subcontinent into Hindu-majority India and predominantly Muslim Pakistan, a division which set off a mass migration by those who found themselves on the wrong side of the religious divide, and the deaths of as many as 2 million people. In Palestine, the League of Nations mandate to govern the areas which the British had acquired after the First World War was a poisoned chalice, as it proved impossible to find a compromise between the interests of Palestinian Arabs and Jewish settlers who had migrated to the area in increasing numbers since the 1890s and who saw the historic lands of Israel as a safe haven for a state in the aftermath of the Holocaust which had decimated European Jewry. Faced with a campaign by Jewish guerrilla units – who blew up the King David Hotel in Jerusalem in 1946, causing ninety-one deaths – the British gave up, acceded to a United Nations partition and hurriedly withdrew before the proclamation of the Jewish State of Israel in May 1948.

In Africa, Britain faced new generations of pro-independence leaders who lobbied for the end of British rule. In Kenya the Mau Mau revolt, which erupted among the Kikuyu people in 1952, was only put down at the cost of at least 11,000 lives, a clear indication that if Britain wished to keep control of its colonies against the

eople, the cost would be unacceptably high. On 3
ile on a visit to Cape Town in South Africa, Prime
d Macmillan gave a speech acknowledging this fact,
red 'The wind of change is blowing through this contin-
nether we like it or not, this growth of national consciousness
a political fact.'

Already Britain had granted independence to the Gold Coast
(which became Ghana) under the leadership of Kwame Nkrumah,
and one by one the other African colonies followed (notably Nigeria
in 1960 and Kenya in 1963). Only Rhodesia remained unfinished
business (because its large white settler community had declared
independence unilaterally in 1965 in a bid to stave off rule by the
black majority population, a knot which was only finally unravelled
in 1980 with the former colony's definitive grant of independence as
Zimbabwe).

The conceit among Britain's ruling elite that, despite the dissolution of its empire, it remained a first-rank power had already taken
a knock with the country's inability to act against a communist insurrection during the Greek Civil War in 1947, prompting the British
handing of the mantle of protector of the Balkans to the United
States. The reliance on American power in the final phases of the
Second World War and the establishment of a Soviet hegemony
over much of eastern Europe by 1948 led the British to participate
enthusiastically in the formation of the North Atlantic Treaty
Organization (NATO) in 1949, which acted as a security umbrella
for its members in the face of possible Soviet aggression. The global
leviathan of 1900 was now a middle-ranking power which needed to
act deftly in order to 'punch above its weight'.

Britain still sought to act autonomously, however, and when the
Egyptian revolutionary leader Gamal Abdel Nasser nationalized
the Suez Canal in 1956 (threatening British supply routes to Asia),
the British, with French assistance and the connivance of Israel,
sent troops to Suez to seize it back. The expedition was a fiasco:
President Eisenhower, enraged that Britain had acted without con-
sulting the Americans and fearful of Arab reaction, ordered the

French and British to pull out. Humiliated, Prime Minister Anthony Eden was forced to agree and, in the full glare of international disapproval, Britain's claims to be an imperial power with a fully independent foreign policy were proven to be hollow

In a speech in 1962 at the US Military Academy at Westpoint, former US Secretary of State Dean Acheson pointedly remarked that Britain had 'lost an empire and not yet found a role. The attempt to play a separate power role – that is a role apart from Europe, a role based on a "special relationship" with the United States, a role based on being the head of a "commonwealth" which has no political structure, or unity or strength ... this role is about played out.' The comment caused a certain level of irritation in Britain among commentators who did not take kindly to being told some home truths (although the great economist John Maynard Keynes had as long ago as 1944 declared that 'we cannot police half the world at our own expense when we have already gone into pawn to the other half').

Britain had already tacitly acknowledged its political dependence on the United States by participating in the formation of NATO. This did not resolve the country's increasingly evident economic frailty – Britain's share of global trade in manufactured goods, which had been nearly 30 per cent in 1913, had shrunk to 13.9 per cent in 1965, while growth sagged and inflation nudged higher (to 5 per cent in 1956) and wages outpaced productivity. Other European countries had recovered far more quickly after 1945, with massive spending on infrastructure to repair war damage and investment in modernization, particularly in housing and education. In 1951 six European countries established the European Coal and Steel Community. The Schuman Declaration which announced the formation of the new organization explicitly stated that it aimed to create a common market across its area (beginning with coal and steel) and to promote economic integration with the aim of making war between members impossible.

Britain, under Harold Macmillan, haughtily stood aside from the ECSC, although wishing it well. The nation still viewed its economic future as a globalist one, heading the Commonwealth of its former colonies as a substantial British-aligned and sterling-trading group. In strategic terms, the British government clung to the alliance with the United States, claiming the 'special relationship' as the bedrock of international security. Yet by the time the 1957 Treaty of Rome transformed the ECSC into the European Economic Community, many politicians in Britain came to see that the failure to join the EEC had been a historic mistake. In 1960 Britain established the European Free Trade Association (EFTA), together with Austria, Denmark, Norway, Portugal, Sweden and Switzerland, to promote closer economic cooperation in Europe, without participating in the EEC's common market. The club for all those not in the EEC club was typical of an ambivalence towards Europe which would bedevil British politics for the next sixty years.

In July 1961, encouraged by younger Conservative cabinet members such as Edward Heath, and pushed by several sterling crises, in which runs against the pound threatened to undermine the government's ability to control the economy, Macmillan announced Britain's application to join the EEC. Unfortunately, the French president Charles de Gaulle was as acutely aware of the ambiguities of Britain's position as Macmillan himself and, citing the country's close links with the United States and the Commonwealth which he considered would dilute the EEC down into an amorphous transatlantic free trade agreement, he vetoed British membership.

Macmillan's successor, Harold Wilson, received the same stern 'Non!' when he put in a second British application for EEC membership in 1967. Instead British governments were forced to concentrate on domestic reforms and investment. Wilson's vision was of 'a new Britain' that would prosper in the 'white heat of the technological revolution', with significant investments in new industries such as computing and an expansion of universities to offer a higher education to previously excluded social groups.

The 1960s were an age of modernization in other ways, too. The emergence of mass youth cultures such as the mods and rockers in the late 1950s overflowed in the next decade into a profusion of counter-cultures whose one uniting feature was their rejection of the old and espousal of a less restrictive, more liberal society. For long the epitome of Victorian stuffiness, Britain found itself at the vanguard of this transformation, with designers such as Mary Quant and musicians such as the Beatles finding a global market.

Disappointing economic performances at the end of the 1960s led to the defeat of the Wilson government in the 1970 general election and the return of a Conservative administration under Edward Heath. His enthusiastic advocacy of British EEC membership – and the disappearance of de Gaulle from the French political stage, replaced by Georges Pompidou in 1969 – meant that a renewed British application was received more favourably, and on 1 January 1973 the United Kingdom joined the European Economic Community (together with Ireland and Denmark). Although the negotiations had been hard, and a large body of the Conservative Party was concerned about the impact of the EEC's Common Agricultural Policy on food prices, while left-wingers fretted about obstacles to the government's ability to subsidize ailing industries, sentiment was generally positive: George Thomson, one of Britain's new European commissioners, joined a large crowd in Brussels in a torchlit procession to celebrate the EEC's latest member, a demonstration of European amity that would be distinctly lacking in the coming decades.

For the past four centuries (since the loss of Calais), Britain's engagement with Europe had been at the level of diplomacy or outright warfare. Apart from the anomalies of William of Orange's joint rule as British king and Stadtholder of Holland and George I's position as Elector of Hanover, Britain was now in a closer relationship with Europe than it had been since Plantagenet times. The country, though, did not quickly reap the kind of economic rewards which Macmillan, Wilson and Heath had hoped for. A crisis associated with the Yom Kippur war in 1973 between Israel and a coalition of Arab states led to the quadrupling of the price of oil by 1974. Although its abundant supply of coal and the beginnings of oil and natural gas extraction in the North Sea partially shielded Britain from the worst of this dramatic increase, the oil price rises triggered a spiralling inflation rate, which reached 16 per cent in 1974 and touched 26 per cent in June 1975. Trade unions responded with increased wage demands to protect the incomes of their members – pay rises spiked as high as 35 per cent.

The efforts of James Callaghan, Wilson's successor as Labour prime minister, to cap wage settlements and prevent Britain becoming stuck in a state of 'stagflation' (simultaneously high inflation and high unemployment) led to a rash of strikes, culminating in the 'Winter of Discontent' in 1978–9, after which an impatient electorate turned to the Conservatives under Margaret Thatcher, who promised radical reform and a reduction in the power of the unions.

Although the British electorate had endorsed the country's EEC membership in a referendum in June 1975 (by a margin of 67 to 33 per cent), confirming for the moment Britain's destiny as a Europe-facing power, the United Kingdom was facing strains which threatened to tear it apart. In Northern Ireland, the Catholic population had never been reconciled to the 1922 settlement which left them as a minority in the predominantly Protestant province. Discontent at widespread discrimination in education and employment, where Catholics complained they received lower-quality schooling and were denied jobs, led to a growing civil rights movements and marches in Londonderry in 1968 and 1969 which degenerated into confrontations and violence between marchers and the British security forces.

The Irish Republican Army, which had long been largely dormant, split in December 1969, and one faction, the Provisional IRA, began a campaign of attacks on British security force and Protestant targets. The first British soldier was killed in February 1971, and the government responded with the despatch of more troops, the internment of republican suspects and a clampdown which went badly wrong when British troops shot thirteen republican demonstrators in Londonderry on 30 January 1972 ('Bloody Sunday'). The 'Troubles' which blighted Northern Ireland throughout the 1970s and 1980s pitted the IRA (and the leading republican party, Sinn

Féin), who demanded an end to the British security presence in the province and the establishment of a united Ireland, against Protestant groups, which established their own militias to defend the Union, including the Ulster Defence Association and the Ulster Volunteer Force. In March 1972, the Heath government suspended the Stormont assembly (the Northern Ireland parliament), gambling that rule from Westminster would prove more calming than the prevailing Catholic–Protestant confrontation.

It proved a vain hope. The death toll, which had reached nearly 1,230 by 1974, continued to rise over the next twenty years. The IRA remained capable of high-profile attacks, such as the attempted assassination of Margaret Thatcher by bombing the Grand Hotel in Brighton in 1984, and Protestant paramilitaries were also active. Finally, weariness with the seemingly intractable conflict brought elements of Sinn Féin to open back-door negotiations with the British government, and, after ceasefires in 1994 and 1997, the Good Friday Agreement, signed in Belfast on 10 April 1998, brought an end to the conflict. A referendum in Northern Ireland agreed the establishment of a new assembly which, though it was periodically suspended (including a three-year hiatus between January 2017 and January 2020), allowed parties such as the Protestant Democratic Unionist Party and Catholic Sinn Féin, previously bitter rivals, to cooperate in the governing of the province.

Nationalist sentiment, although of a much less violent kind, was also on the rise in Wales and Scotland. Plaid Cymru ('the Party of Wales'), founded in 1925 to fight for the preservation of the Welsh language, added the aspiration of self-government to its manifesto by the 1930s, but languished electorally, failing to win its first seat at Westminster until 1966. It succeeded in getting the Welsh Language Act passed in 1967, which gave Welsh (which around 21 per cent of the population then spoke) equal status with English. Even so, a referendum on whether Wales should be granted its own assembly was heavily defeated (by 79 to 21 per cent) in March 1979, and a Welsh assembly – the first legislative body there since the parliament held by Owain Glyndwr at Machynlleth in Powys in 1404 – was only con-firmed by a further referendum in 1997. With its own legislature in Cardiff, Wales began gently to tug away at its centuries-old ties to England.

The Scottish succeeded in obtaining a far higher level of auton-omy, in the main through the highly effective campaigning of the Scottish National Party (SNP), founded in 1934 by the merger of two previous nationalist parties. The SNP made its electoral break-through in 1967 with a startling by-election victory at Hamilton and succeeded in lobbying for the establishment of the Kilbrandon Com-mission, which in 1973 recommended the setting-up of devolved legislatures for Scotland and Wales. The second half of the 1970s brought disillusionment to the nationalist cause; although a referen-dum in 1974 decided narrowly in favour of a Scottish assembly, it failed to pass a turn-out hurdle that required 40 per cent of the total electorate to vote for it. Although the SNP received 30 per cent of the Scottish vote in the October 1974 general election, after that, as Labour reasserted itself in Scotland, the nationalists went into retreat.

Continued anger at the perceived neglect of Scottish interests by successive Westminster governments, and in particular the feeling that the revenues from taxation of oil extraction in the North Sea were being diverted from Scotland, kept the SNP's cause alive. When Scotland finally voted for the establishment of a parliament in 1997 (with the first elections to it held in 1999), Scottish national-ism underwent a renaissance. Taking a turn to the left, it argued for a specifically Scottish social democracy, with higher levels of gov-ernment spending and, ultimately, for the complete independence of Scotland within the European Union. It was a potent message for Labour's traditional working-class supporters, and in 2007 the SNP overhauled Labour for the first time in the Scottish assembly elections (with forty-seven seats to Labour's forty-six) and formed a majority administration in 2011. In elections to Westminster the SNP made steady gains until it won a landslide in 2015 under the leadership of Nicola Sturgeon, gaining fifty-six out of fifty-nine Scottish seats (with 50 per cent of the vote), leaving just a solitary

Scottish MP from each of Labour, the Conservatives and the Liberal Democrats.

With such a powerful mandate, the SNP was in a strong position to lobby for a referendum on Scottish independence, which Conservative Prime Minister David Cameron finally conceded in October 2012. The SNP published *Scotland's Future* in November 2013, setting out the case for the restoration of the independence which had been lost in 1707 (and arguably in 1603). The campaign was a hard-fought one, with debate focusing on how Scotland's relations with the European Union might work, its relationship with NATO, whether it could continue to use Britain's currency and on whether revenues from taxing oil (which then stood at around $100 a barrel) would be enough to keep an independent Scottish economy solvent. The result was uncomfortably close – David Cameron's advisers had assumed that Scots would opt for safety and the status quo in the face of dire warnings about the extreme fiscal distress Scotland would suffer as an independent nation.

After a brief scare in early September, when opinion polls indicated that the 'Yes' vote for independence might reach 51 per cent, the 'No' camp won in the final vote on 18 September by a margin of ten points (55 per cent to 45 per cent). The independence cause was discomfited, with suggestions that another vote should not be held for a generation. It seemed that, after coming perilously close to break-up, the United Kingdom had for the moment been preserved. Soon, however, David Cameron faced worse storm clouds which threatened to undermine the role Britain had seemed – decades after Acheson's warning – finally to be finding for itself in the world.

The issue was Europe. Large sections of the Conservative Party had never been reconciled to Britain's membership of the EEC, a sentiment particularly strong in Conservative-leaning rural areas, where issues such as the imposition of metric measures for goods (made compulsory in 2000) rankled with traditionalists who preferred Britain's imperial measures (such as pounds and gallons). The steady enlargement of the community, starting with Greece in 1981 and extending into eastern Europe after the collapse of the Soviet hegemony there in 1989, until it reached twenty-eight members in 2013, provoked nervousness about a dilution of British influence. The deepening of economic and political ties made British Conservatives even more uneasy. By 1992 the EEC had virtually completed the work necessary to construct a European Single Market, in which tariff barriers between member states had been abolished, giving Britain access to the largest free trade area in the world. However, the Maastricht Treaty (1993), which transformed the EEC into a European Union committed to greater political and economic integration, and in particular to the establishment of a single European currency, the Euro, caused considerable trouble for John Major's Conservative government. He faced resistance from around a dozen anti-Maastricht MPs from his own party, whose numbers, given the government's slim majority, threatened to bring it down at any moment.

Major survived (at least until 1997, when Labour's Tony Blair was elected by a landslide), and he was able to score a victory for British particularism by winning an opt-out for Britain from membership of the Euro. Britain also won exemption from the Schengen Agreement (which allowed visa-free travel between those EU member states which were a party to it). He was thus able to add to the budget rebate which Margaret Thatcher – a great champion of the EU's single market – had negotiated for Britain in the 1980s.

Britain opposed further moves for deeper integration in fields such as taxation and defence and when it did not get its way, as when the Lisbon Treaty (2007) introduced majority (rather than unanimous) voting in the Council of Ministers (the executive body of the EU made up of ministers from member states), many on the right-wing of the Conservative Party were furious. A rising tide of Euroscepticism had pushed the anti-European wing of the party from a relatively marginal faction in the 1980s to an influential caucus by the time the Conservative Party was re-elected in 2010 after thirteen years in opposition. It faced competition on the political right from the United Kingdom Independence Party (UKIP), established in 1993 by a group which had fought against the Maastricht Treaty. The new party was able to exploit uncertainty about Britain's future, a feeling that somehow British 'values' were being watered down by the need to conform to European standards, and it fed off a diet of often misleading stories put about by anti-EU journalists about measures the European Union was alleged to be about to foist upon Britain (such as the outlawing of 'bent' bananas). More seriously, many areas of the United Kingdom had been left behind, as industry was hollowed out in the 1980s and 1990s in areas such as Wales, the Midlands, the north and Scotland, where iron, coal, steel and shipbuilding had provided steady jobs for generations of men. These regions found themselves devoid of employment and felt excluded from the economy of the south-east and London, where finance generated significant wealth and pulled in large numbers of well-educated European Union citizens who, under the terms of the EU treaties, could live and work freely in the United Kingdom (and in the other twenty-seven member states).

Against this background and under a banner of protecting Britain from the alleged betrayal of its interests by the two main political parties, UKIP prospered. From achieving a vote of only 0.3 per cent at the 1997 General Election, it rose to 3.1 per cent in 2010 and then to 12.6 per cent in 2015 (when it achieved its first elected MP). Much of that rise in votes had been at the expense of the Conservative Party, and a panicked David Cameron, fearful that UKIP might make further inroads, promised that a referendum on Britain's membership of the European Union should be held in the lifetime of the parliament (which was a key demand of the anti-EU right wing in general). Having seen off the threat of a nationalist victory in Scotland, Cameron thought that he could pull off a similar triumph and defuse the Eurosceptic threat for the foreseeable future.

It was a terrible political miscalculation. In a bad-tempered campaign, the 'Remain' side never really sparked the enthusiasm of its natural supporters for continued membership, while the 'Leave' camp deployed a series of highly emotive images and messages to insinuate that, if people thought the European Union was bad, it was about to get a whole lot worse, including the imminent membership – so it was claimed – of Turkey and the establishment of an EU army.

Promises were made that leaving the EU would deliver an enormous bonus – commonly put at £350 million a week – which could be spent on the National Health Service. It mattered little that many of the claims were dubious, patently false or even disowned later by those who made them, because they tapped into a genuine fearfulness about the direction in which Britain was travelling.

When the votes of the referendum, held on 23 June 2016, were counted, it was clear that there had been a political earthquake. Over 17 million people had opted for 'Brexit', as Britain's exit from the EU was dubbed, amounting to some 52 per cent of voters, against 16 million who had voted to remain. The shock was tremendous, as Britain, which had been a member of the EU for over forty years (if not always an enthusiastic or even a constructive one), and which had made wholesale changes to its legislation, economic structure and diplomatic stance to accommodate itself to Europe, now found itself facing the daunting task of extricating itself from this European web.

More than this, new questions were raised about Britain's international role. The United Kingdom had begun the twentieth century still at the head of a great empire. Its self-image as an imperial power had persisted long after the reality had disappeared, hampering the nation's efforts to recreate itself and to engage more fully with its European neighbours. By the 1960s there was a general acknowledgement that to survive, economically and politically, Britain needed to turn its face once more to Europe, to resurrect the kind of close engagement with its neighbours which had seemed perfectly natural in pre-Tudor times. Yet knitting itself into the fabric of the European Union had been accompanied by neglect of the fabric of the United Kingdom itself. The result was the referendum vote, which meant that Britain in 2016, having long lost its empire, was further than ever from having any clear notion of its role in the world.

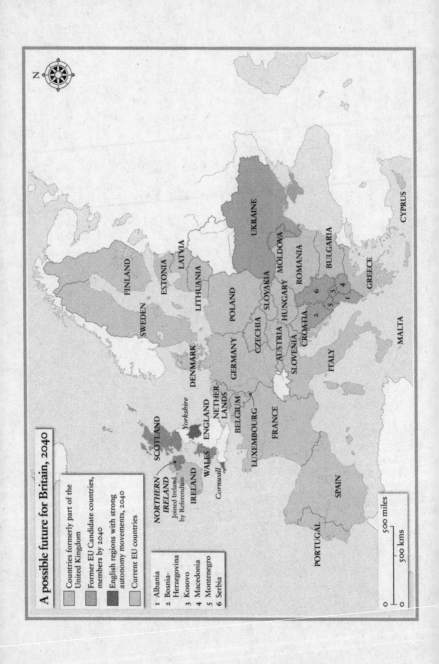

A possible future for Britain, 2040

Countries formerly part of the United Kingdom

Former EU Candidate countries, members by 2040

English regions with strong autonomy movements, 2040

Current EU countries

1 Albania
2 Bosnia-Herzegovina
3 Kosovo
4 Macedonia
5 Montenegro
6 Serbia

N

PORTUGAL

SPAIN

FRANCE

LUXEMBOURG

BELGIUM

NETHER-LANDS

IRELAND

WALES

Cornwall

ENGLAND

Yorkshire

SCOTLAND

NORTHERN IRELAND
Joined Ireland by Referendum

DENMARK

GERMANY

CZECHIA

AUSTRIA

SLOVENIA

CROATIA

ITALY

MALTA

SWEDEN

FINLAND

ESTONIA

LATVIA

LITHUANIA

POLAND

SLOVAKIA

HUNGARY

UKRAINE

MOLDOVA

ROMANIA

BULGARIA

GREECE

CYPRUS

500 miles

500 kms

11 The Future of Britain

When the United Kingdom awoke on 24 June 2016, everything had changed. Against the expectations of most (and above all of Prime Minister David Cameron), the electorate had voted to leave the European Union. That vote had been large – some 17.4 million people had cast their ballots in favour of Brexit – but also close, as the margin of victory – 51.9 per cent to 48.1 per cent – did not show a nation united in its determination to effect a radical change in its relationship with Europe.

The referendum result unleashed political chaos, as no one seemed to have a well-articulated plan as to what to do next. What was clear to all, however, was that this was a moment which represented another turning point on the journey of Britain's national identity and might even lead to another significant change to her shape on that map.

Leaving the European Union means withdrawing from a unique project for the pooling of economic and political sovereignty and taking a step back from cooperation with Britain's European neighbours. Whatever the exact nature of our diplomatic and trading relationship with them – and this will take some years to fully emerge – it will be a changed one. It will mean seeking alliances and trading arrangements across the globe with countries which have their own diplomatic and economic agendas. In the nineteenth century, at the height of Britain's imperial might, there were few with the power to do other than accede to British demands. In the twenty-first century, the bargaining is proving much harder.

Change may also come within the United Kingdom itself. Scotland voted by a decisive margin (62 to 38 per cent) to remain within the European Union, while in Northern Ireland the majority against leaving was also considerable (56 per cent to 44 per cent). In

Scotland, in particular, voices were soon heard protesting that the country should not be forced to leave the EU against the will of the majority of Scots. The matter of a new referendum on Scottish independence soon re-entered the political arena; its proponents argued that it would give the chance for an independent Scotland to opt to remain within the EU. In Northern Ireland, difficulties over how to regulate the border with the Republic of Ireland after Brexit raised the prospect of the reappearance of a hard border between the two, policed by customs officers and the security services, something which breached the terms of the Good Friday Agreement, which had ended the Troubles. Although the British government twisted and turned in the months following the referendum vote to find a solution to the Irish border question, the Protocol that it finally negotiated proved so disagreeable to many of its supporters, that it threatened to abrogate its own agreements. Many in Northern Ireland warned of a return to violence if a hard border was imposed on the province, while support in opinion polls for a united Ireland was rising.

The debate which broke out about how to implement the result was in many ways more bitter, and certainly more prolonged, than the referendum campaign itself. The most contentious points both before and after the vote regarded immigration and national sovereignty. There were over 3.4 million people born in the other twenty-seven European countries who were resident in the United Kingdom in 2016, and the Leave campaign successfully exploited a feeling – particularly in areas of low income and where traditional heavy industries had disappeared in the 1980s – that this was too many and claimed that countries such as Turkey would soon enter the EU, increasing the number still further. Pro-Leave organizations also played on a widespread sentiment that the United Kingdom had given up too much sovereignty to the European Union, arguing that in order to prosper a state needed to be free to make its own trade deals, police its own borders and determine the direction of its own diplomatic policy.

Much of this was a mirage. Turkey was unlikely ever to join the

EU against Britain's wishes, as the United Kingdom, in common with the other twenty-seven EU members, had the power to veto it, while EU-born residents play a vital role in many industries, such as healthcare, restaurants, retail and agriculture. In any case, absolute sovereignty is an unattainable goal for Britain. In a globalized world, trade agreements need the cooperation of others, and – as Britain had discovered after Suez in 1957 – complete freedom of action diplomatically is a luxury the United Kingdom lost long ago.

Further sobering reminders that Brexit had not frozen Britain's political destiny in place came with the outbreak of the COVID-19 pandemic in 2019 and the Russian invasion of Ukraine in 2022. In both cases, Britain could not possibly act alone to face the huge challenges posed by these unexpected external shocks. In reacting to the most serious geopolitical crisis in Europe since the Second World War, alliance-building and co-operation with European and American defence partners was a far more effective approach than pulling up the drawbridge and retreating into insularity.

Illusion, will o' the wisp or glorious opportunity, the electorate did vote for Brexit. The defining feature of all the arguments which won its passage was a nostalgia for the past, for a historical era in which Britain was perceived to have been truly great and in which other nations did not dare to boss it around. This yearning for the past also extended to a mental reconstruction of Britain's imperial age, in which its borders (within the United Kingdom) were solid and in which its reach projected far beyond Europe to all corners of the globe. The nation's progress from Britannia, to the British Isles, to the British empire appeared to have stalled there in the popular imagination. The conflict between this self-image and the harsh reality of a middle-ranking economic power with overstretched armed forces and an introspective political class will be a key challenge for Britain in the coming years.

If history has one principal lesson, it is that the past is a place we can argue about, analyse, lament and partially reconstruct, but to which we can never return. Although many architects of the Leave campaign sketched out a vision of Britain reaching out to the world outside the European Union, they tapped into a desire to return to a kaleidoscope past that evoked the uncomplicated prosperity of the 1950s, the Dunkirk spirit, Queen Victoria's Diamond Jubilee, the Battle of Waterloo, the Spanish Armada and Alfred the Great's victories against the Vikings.

The long story of Britain's history and the many modifications its physical shape and national identity have undergone in that time suggest that it is foolish to think that we can return to a fixed point in the past (or concoct a mélange of past glories to paste onto our present). It is similarly unwise to maintain that the challenges we now face are utterly unique. Britain's sovereignty has been expanded, absorbed and pooled into that of neighbouring nations and its people have been built through a long series of migrations, whose participants have merged into the pre-existing population over time. Where the migrations have not been large-scale (as may be the case with the advent of the 'Celts' into Britain, and certainly with the Vikings), they have still been transformative in terms of the ideas, technologies and political structures they have brought with them.

Britain was for four centuries a military colony of the Roman empire (a European 'project' if ever there was one) and prospered mightily as a consequence. Its subsequent history, with invasions by Anglo-Saxons, Vikings and Normans all transmuting the nation in turn, makes clear that whatever Britain has become, the building blocks which made it up are very varied. By the Middle Ages, England was part of a cross-Channel empire in which its destiny might have been as one half of an Anglo-French realm, and when it emerged from the medieval period it was ruled successively by Welsh, Scottish, Dutch and German dynasties.

A certain ambiguity about sovereignty and a blurring of borders is almost an essential part of the political DNA of Britain. It is one of the means by which the nation has, over time, looked outwards, acquired new rulers (by force of negotiation) and magnified the reach of its power. The acceptance of incomers has always been a more problematic affair. The idea of the 'other' – whether it be the Danes whom King Aethelred ordered slaughtered in 1002, the Jews who were executed in 1255 on the entirely fabricated charges of murdering a small Christian child, or the foreigners who were attacked after the Great Fire of London in 1666 – has always provided a convenient scapegoat for other ills, but incomers' labour, skills and roles as merchants, warriors or marriage partners have made them an essential part of society throughout British history.

Britain has always had a strong level of engagement with the outside world, from the first mammoth hunter who crossed the glacial landscape northwards from Europe, to the modern City of London, which engages in trillions of pounds of transactions each year across the globe. Over time, it has done so in the form of small Celtic kingdoms which supervised the operation of the tin trade, the Roman empire, which stretched from the Tyne to the Tigris, the Angevin empire straddling the English Channel, the unions with Wales, Scotland and Ireland, the British empire and, most latterly, through the European Union. Throughout all these avatars, Britain has been most successful when it has been outward-looking and not sought to enclose itself within these islands. When consumed by bouts of internal strife (such as the civil wars of Stephen in the twelfth century, the English Civil War in the seventeenth century or the bitter debates over Brexit) it has made itself vulnerable to other, more determined powers.

Periodically, Britain has become obsessed with an external enemy, often as a means to secure a power structure at home by conjuring loyalty to it out of fear of subjugation to the will of others. The aftermath of the Reformation is the prime example: initially sparked almost by accident through Henry VIII's desire to ensure an heir, it resulted, through mishandled diplomacy in his break with Rome, in the creation of an English Church and the identification of anyone, internally or externally, who still supported the Catholic Church, as an enemy. This anti-Catholicism shaped Britain's foreign policies and domestic politics for centuries – Charles I's less-than-wholehearted adherence to the Protestant cause sapped his popularity, while his son James II was deposed for his Catholicism, and the German Hanoverian George I was made king in 1714 principally because he was a

Protestant. The Spanish Armada in 1588, by which Philip II of Spain sought to depose the Protestant Elizabeth I, the Jacobite uprisings in 1715 and 1745, the anti-Catholic Gordon riots in 1780, the long resistance of Ireland to integration in the United Kingdom and the Northern Irish Troubles of the 1970s are all examples of the surprisingly persistent labelling of adherents of a minority religion as a potential enemy to the mainstream.

In the twenty-first century, Europe has in some ways replaced Catholicism as the enemy of choice for those in British politics in search of an external threat to our national identity. Just as Catholics could be accused of answering to a foreign power (in Rome), so could enthusiasts for greater European integration be painted as being in the thrall of another (in Brussels). In a way, the Treaty of Rome has replaced the Pope in Rome as a convenient scapegoat for a range of domestic economic and political ills.

There is a very select group of national myths which have lodged themselves in our collective consciousness – from Boudicca's revolt against the Romans, which came tantalizingly close to success, to Alfred's unlikely victory against the Danes, Harold's death at the Battle of Hastings, Henry V's victory at Agincourt, the Spanish Armada, Wellington's triumph at Waterloo, and the Battle of Britain, fought by the 'few' of the RAF against the 'many' of the Luftwaffe. All these share in common a sense of Britain standing alone, without allies (although in reality it often did have them: Wellington depended on the Prussians for his victory and Henry V needed his Welsh archers). The break with the European Union is in danger of becoming another one of these myths – with Britain, as its advocates of Brexit portray it, pushed into a corner, and emerging, isolated but unbowed, to recapture its position on the podium of global power.

Whatever the United Kingdom chooses to do now, standing still or stepping backwards is not an option. History is not an anchor to which we can cling, but a river that carries us forwards. Britain came about through an accumulation of many changes, their pace accelerating over recent centuries and decades. To try to arrest this change is an impossible task, and to consume the nation's energies in doing so would be a quixotic gesture. The map of Britain has changed many times, and it will do so again. Those living at any of the eras which the maps in this book illustrate may – if they thought about it at all – have considered that the age in which they lived would stretch on unchanged and that the version of Britain in which they lived was immutable. In each case it was not so. The Britain in which we now live is less than a hundred years old and if history is any guide, in a century more it will look rather different in terms of its constitutional make-up, demographics and politics to our 'Britain' today, irrespective of current political decisions regarding Europe.

Britain's vote to leave the European Union was less a vote for change than an attempt to halt it, a cry for a sense of permanence and stability. It sought to arrest the evolution of the relationship between Britain and Europe within the European Union which might, some decades down the line, have transformed it into something like a nation-state (or equally, have diverted into an entirely different direction). The choices, and consequences of those choices, may be painful: Britain is like a Siamese twin insisting on separation regardless of the dangers. Those who wanted no more change may well be surprised – Britain cannot remain adrift and alone for long, and whatever decisions its government makes, for closer ties to the United States, for some form of rejuvenated Commonwealth, an entente with China or Russia or even renewed membership of the European Union, they will all involve change and evolution.

As the great Italian novelist Giuseppe de Lampedusa has a character say in his novel *The Leopard*, 'Everything must change so that everything can remain the same.' Change is a constant. How we manage that change, and whether we accept that it cannot be avoided, will shape the next map of Britain.

Acknowledgements

I have worked on historical mapping for nearly three decades now, and so many of the conversations I have had which have informed this book took place some time ago, long before I knew that I would be writing it. I would, though, like to thank Barry Winkelmann and Thomas Cussans for introducing me to the joys of historical cartography and to the many ways it can illuminate our past and present.

For the present title, I am grateful to Dan Bunyard at Michael Joseph for commissioning the book, and to Jillian Taylor for shepherding me through the long editorial process, for the many stimulating and enjoyable discussions I have had with her over the course of its writing and for the many suggestions which have hugely improved my original manuscript. Trevor Horwood and Beatrix McIntyre were able and diplomatic copy-editors, suggesting many sharpenings to the text. I would also like to thank Lauren Wakefield for a wonderful cover design which really encapsulates the spirit of the book, Fran Monteneiro for the text design and Jeff Edwards for the maps, which are the visual stars of the book in charting Britain's progress from the Stone Age to Brexit.

As ever, Cara Jones has proved a wonderful and supportive agent, helping keep the book on track from contract to completion. My particular gratitude is due to the London Library and its staff. Virtually every word of this book was written there and its vast resources have provided the answer to many an obscure question.

Finally, I would like to thank my partner, Tania, and our daughter, Livia, who have been subjected to many months of long working hours, obsession with the meaning of Britain's borders and authorial grumpiness. Their tolerance shows one way forward to the question of how we can all deal with the changing times in which we live.